M & E HANDBOOKS

M & E Handbooks are recommended reading for examination syllabuses all over the world. Because each Handbook covers its subject clearly and concisely books in the series form a vital part of many college, university, school and home study courses.

Handbooks contain detailed information stripped of unnecessary padding, making each title a comprehensive self-tuition course. They are amplified with numerous self-testing questions in the form of Progress Tests at the end of each chapter, each text-referenced for easy checking. Every Handbook closes with an appendix which advises on examination technique. For all these reasons, Handbooks are ideal for pre-examination revision.

The handy pocket-book size and competitive price make Handbooks the perfect choice for everyone who wants to grasp the essentials of a subject quickly and easily.

The M & E HANDBOOK SERIES

Sales and Sales Management

P. Allen
BSc. (Econ.), AMBIM, AMISM, MBIMA.

*Senior Lecturer in Marketing at
the Polytechnic of Wales*

SECOND EDITION

MACDONALD AND EVANS

Macdonald & Evans Ltd.
Estover, Plymouth PL6 7PZ

First published 1973
Reprinted 1975
Reprinted 1976
Second edition 1979

© Macdonald & Evans Ltd. 1979
7121 1962 0

Printed in Great Britain by
Richard Clay (The Chaucer Press), Ltd.,
Bungay, Suffolk

Preface to the Second Edition

Selling is a little understood and much maligned aspect of business. It is perhaps characteristic of the British to have slight respect for an activity in which there is no room for amateurism; an attitude not shared by our competitors for world trade. The Japanese, in particular, have placed great importance on selling ability, and their selling teams, complete with engineers or designers, are to be found in the world's markets. Selling is an activity which attracts publicity, too much of which is sensational, and the day-to-day transactions of thousands of salesmen, which in aggregate keep industry working, are forgotten. The role of export salesmen is vitally important to our national welfare and is conducted by highly trained, technically expert men and women. In the highly competitive conditions of a world recession and a desperate struggle for a share in the world markets it is imperative the role of selling in the total marketing function is not overlooked.

The HANDBOOK of *Sales and Sales Management* is intended to bring together the theory of management as applied to the selling activity, and the practical aspects which can be acquired only from experience and training.

Expert salesmanship and sales management can be obtained only by careful application of sound principles. It is necessary for the salesman and essential for the sales manager to have a thorough knowledge of all aspects of the marketing function in its application to selling.

This HANDBOOK looks at the total marketing function from the viewpoint of the salesman and the sales manager. It will be a valuable source of information to younger students studying for the Ordinary National Certificate and Higher National Certificate and Diploma in Business Studies, the Diploma in Management Studies, B.A. in Business Studies, the BEC National Award option module on Principles and Practice of Salesmanship and the G.C.E. "A" Level in Business Studies, for it has been written with as many practical examples as are necessary to make a point clear. The HANDBOOK is also intended as a source of information for those taking examinations for the Institute of Marketing, Institute of Exporting, Communication, Advertising and Marketing Education Foundation, as well as Diploma

Courses in Marketing offered by various Polytechnics and Technical Colleges. Many institutions offer courses in which emphasis is laid upon management theory or business history and invariably these include marketing aspects. Courses for examinations of the Institution of Works Managers, Institute of Work Study Practitioners, and the courses in Supervisory Studies for N.E.B.S.S. are covered.

Apart from its use to those taking examinations the HAND-BOOK is intended to be a guide to all those engaged in the highly competitive world of selling, whether industrial, retail or exporting, both as salesmen and sales managers.

I would like to acknowledge and thank those who have allowed me to quote examples from business and examination questions, including:

> *Strads International Limited*
> *Institute of Marketing*
> *Communication, Advertising and Marketing*
>   *Education Foundation*
> *Cambridge Examining Board*
> *Cornwall Technical College*
> *Falmouth Technical College*
> *Institute of Work Study Practitioners*

Figure 17 is reproduced from *Principles of Management* by Henry L. Sisk, by permission of South Western Publishing Co. Inc.

Contents

Contents

Contents

List of Illustrations

CHAPTER I

The marketing function

INTRODUCTION

1. Rise of marketing. Until some twenty years ago, the term "marketing" was not widely used outside the United States, where it described the function concerned with creating customers and distributing the company's products to them. A description of the primary functions of a business organisation would have identified production, sales and finance.

The term "marketing" has since come into wide use and is accepted as a replacement for the term "sales". It is not unusual for sales to be relegated to a sub-activity of the marketing function. The reasons behind this change in terminology seem to derive from a belief that to "sell" to the customer is a secondary consideration to the aim of "marketing" the company's goods or services.

2. Economic origins of marketing. This century, especially since the First World War, a fundamental change has come over the economic system of supply and demand. Before the advent of mass production there was a greater demand than could be met by industrial output. This meant that companies had no great difficulty in selling their products and in consequence there was little incentive to improve products or to find better ways of selling them. The industrial countries were also, in the main, the most important colonial powers, and with great empires, largely undeveloped, there was no shortage of customers. The poor communications systems at home, in spite of the railways, produced a reliance on local markets through established wholesalers who were the principal selling organisations. Abroad, the colonial system gave advantages to the manufacturing industries of the colonial power, and reduced the effects of competition from other industrial countries. On the whole competition was not a dominant feature of the supply system.

Following the First World War, developments in manufacturing on a mass scale, scientific management, and the great increase in the number of industrialised countries led to an enormous expansion of supply that would eventually exceed effective demand. But this was not all. The advent of the large-scale use of motor transport and better communications both nationally and internationally led to greatly increased competition. The increased bargaining power of labour through their unions led to more realistic wage structures and to a consequent increase in production costs.

Since the Second World War, the factors which began to be felt between the wars rose to be dominating factors in the economic system. Ever-increasing production, better and more widespread credit facilities, better informed population, ease of communication, more leisure time and the ever-rising costs through inflation have brought about a need for more specialised forms of customer creation and service.

Marketing has arisen as a concept in response to these conditions and also as a cause of the situation. Successful companies now have to seek advantages over competitors by whatever means they can identify. This can be through:

(a) better research and development;
(b) well conceived product innovation;
(c) more effective distribution;
(d) creating a wider market for their products by advertising; and
(e) better selling techniques.

APPLYING MARKETING TECHNIQUES

3. The marketing concept. When a company reaches the point in its development at which it sees the need for a re-orientation of its policies to give the maximum consideration to the desires of the customer, it is undergoing a fundamental change in outlook. It will recognise the necessity of involving the company at all levels in the process of satisfying the customer. The marketing concept will involve all the activities and resources of the company being combined to take advantage of opportunities offered by the market for its products. Beyond this, the firm will no longer be committed to a narrow spectrum of the market, but will perceive that its future is bound up with satisfying consumer needs in whatever way its skills, experience, techniques and resources, both capital and human, allow it to do.

4. Adopting a marketing concept. The adoption of a marketing concept is not difficult, although its implementation may be. In many companies the change is brought about by replacing nameplates on doors, i.e. "sales manager" becomes "marketing manager", "export sales" becomes "export marketing" and so on. All this derives from the basic difficulty of changing long-entrenched attitudes and replacing them with the new and dynamic approach that is vital to the adoption of a marketing concept. This change in attitude is accomplished only by a process of:

(a) adaptation;
(b) re-education;
(c) explanation; and
(d) co-operation.

5. Customer–company orientation. In the conditions of a changing environment, brought about by increased competition, wider knowledge of suppliers, higher standards of living, and greater technological innovation, only companies with sound marketing concepts and an efficient and developed sales organisation will be able to operate effectively.

There are several factors in the business environment as it exists which determine how successful a company's operations will be.

(a) In virtually all industrialised Western markets, the standards of living are rising appreciably and this leads to an increase in consumers' spending power.

(b) Companies are often obliged to operate with considerable capital expenditure which may be on:

(i) automated plant;
(ii) extended development programmes;
(iii) high cost of research;
(iv) expensive product innovation; and
(v) high costs of developing new designs and packaging to meet consumers' demand.

(c) Many companies have high initial costs of launching a product including testing, advertising and promotional activities generally.

6. The need for marketing growth. If a company recognises the three concepts put forward above can it safely assume that it will increase its sales volume by relying upon the increased population and spending power to promote growth? To this the answer must be no. Against the increased spending power and larger market, a company must put the rise in competition and costs, both of which make its share of a growing market more uncertain.

Any company that wishes to make sure of its increased growth must have an active marketing function that will influence the company to:

(*a*) develop an active marketing research activity, upon the results of which it will base its production, selling and distribution policies:

(*b*) enable itself to:

(*i*) manufacture products to standards that will harmonise with consumer and user demands;

(*ii*) sell, promote and distribute its products in ways that will be sure to reach developing markets.

EXAMPLE: The British menswear producer, Strads, eager to expand its international selling, particularly in Europe, was faced with the possibility of having to make virtually a different style for each European country. The need to make what the market wanted would have put too much strain on productive capacity, in view of the small orders that would initially be placed. Strads was instrumental in forming an international organisation, known as Euro-Guild. Euro-Guild comprised a major manufacturer of menswear from each of Norway, Sweden, Finland, Denmark, West Germany, Austria, France, Belgium, Italy and Spain. The group as a whole did not set out to make identical products, as the very physiological differences between Europeans made this virtually impossible. Instead they sought to establish an internationally acceptable standard of menswear. Members of the group met frequently to explore developments in manufacturing techniques and to exchange new ideas. The only recognisable identity agreed was the "Euro-Guild" sew-on label which was put into each garment. The exchange of information obviated the need for extensive market research and the joint promotion throughout Europe of the "Euro-Guild" label gave each manufacturer an identification that helped to sell its own name in countries where it was not so well known.

The example illustrates two essential marketing principles:

(*a*) the company was guided in the exporting programme by an appreciation of marketing factors;

(*b*) they promoted and distributed their menswear in a manner likely to reach a growing market.

7. Marketing and capital expenditure. The ever-increasing commitment to high capital expenditure can only be recovered by increased volume of sales. It is necessary for the company to devise a way of ensuring this increased sales volume is accomplished. This can be done by:

(a) persuading customers to buy more often, i.e. improving refrigerators and television sets, so that people buy every three years instead of waiting for the old one to wear out;

(b) selling to new customers, i.e. developing an export programme.

A company that can accomplish the increased volume of sales needed to cover its accelerating developing costs by a consideration and understanding of customer needs is moving towards a marketing orientation.

8. Changing distribution patterns. A company must always be able to innovate on the pattern of distribution to ensure a lower cost of distribution and reach more customers, thereby gaining an advantage over competitors.

EXAMPLE: A manufacturer of raincoats wished to break into the German market. Market research showed that it was the practice of the market for wholesalers to buy in bulk and resell to retail shops. The high cost of importing British raincoats and the promotional problems made wholesalers reluctant to take on the British company's offer of an agency. The export consultant manager of the firm visited Germany and spent some time investigating the market, including the alternative ways of distribution.

To sell direct to a sufficient number of smaller stores that used existing wholesale channels was impossible due to the high cost of freight, etc. The problem was eventually resolved by selling to only three of the biggest department stores, each of which had branches in the main German cities. The problem of packing raincoats which became easily soiled and misshapen was overcome by selling in large quantities to the stores and shipping in containers. This reduced the unit cost and enabled a competitive price to be quoted, permitting bulk buying. The garments needed no packing, being simply hung on rails in the containers and the unit cost of freight was almost negligible, due to the numbers in each container.

9. Marketing in the modern business environment. The highly competitive conditions of the modern business environment, whether considered at a national level or in terms of international trade, are growing. The need for an active marketing commitment working with a strong and creative selling function is emphasised by:

(a) growth in consumer spending power;

(b) derived from the growth in consumer spending power, the increased levels of investment in industrial production;

(c) the higher levels of capital expenditure with which companies now have to operate.

(d) rapidly changing distribution channels and better communication generally;

(e) the necessity for companies to establish themselves in international markets;

(f) the growth of world trade and the emergence of powerful economic markets; and

(g) the growth of companies with modern management using modern marketing techniques to full advantage.

THE FUNCTIONAL OBJECTIVE

10. The functional title. In Chapter III, the problem of creating logical and dynamic organisations will be examined in more detail and the relationships between production, sales and marketing examined. It is fair to say that the relationship between sales and marketing is still in a state of flux and subject to different interpretations. There appear to be three basic alternatives, which are to:

(a) make "*marketing*" *the functional title* and place "sales" within it as an activity responsible for the narrow areas of selling and the sales office, as shown in Fig. 1;

(b) make "*sales*" *the functional title* and under it group those activities directly involved in the selling process, or ancillary to it, as shown in Fig. 2; or

(c) *distinguish between* "*sales*" *and* "*marketing*" *at the functional level*, sales containing those activities relating to the selling process and which might be termed tactical, and marketing responsible for all the activities relating to the over-all concept of customer creation and strategy, as shown in Fig. 3.

It is reasonable to say that the method adopted by any company will be a reflection of its attitude to the entire function of selling its goods or services to the customer. It will also reflect the size of the company, as an organisation structure such as (c) would obviously require a larger commitment to it than either (a) or (b). The degree of research, planning, product development and ad-

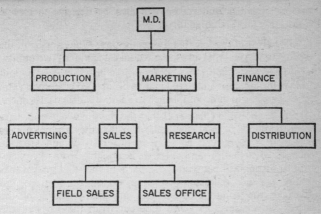

FIG. 1. *Organisation with "marketing" as the functional title.*

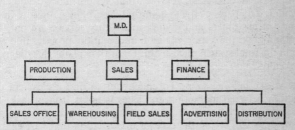

FIG. 2. *Organisation with "sales" as the functional title.*

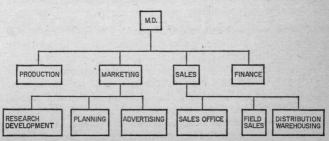

FIG. 3. *Sales and marketing as equal functions.*

vertising activities undertaken will also be decisive factors in determining the functional form.

11. Objectives of the functional organisation. Whatever form the eventual functional title takes, it must take account of two points.

(a) The most important consideration in a business organisation is the creation and maintenance of satisfied customers; and

(b) A sale has to be accomplished to achieve satisfied customers.

It will be shown in Chapter II that the ways in which goods are put in the hands of final customers, whether they are consumers or industrial users, can be seen as two distinct and separate processes, distribution and sales. It is possible from this viewpoint to distinguish between those parts of the total system that identify product opportunities, innovate on production, and undertake the communication and informative parts of the process; advertising, as being different from the parts of the system concerned with persuading customers to buy; organising; distribution, and servicing customers. But it is an ambiguous distinction nevertheless, for the total system has no end, it is circular. The parts of the system that ensure the goods are in the hands of customers and giving satisfactory service are only the beginning of the reporting and information process that will begin the total system once again. Figure 4 explains this diagrammatically.

12. Marketing and sales. To endeavour to find a clear-cut distinction between marketing and sales is not a fruitful task; the creation and satisfaction of customers is the main task and companies will create the type of organisation that best enables them to accomplish their objectives. In spite of this generality, the over-all commitment to "marketing" does produce difficulties, especially if in the process management neglects the vitally important aspects of selling.

13. Consumer goods and industrial goods. The entire marketing/selling process is always easier to see in relation to consumer goods than industrial goods. For this reason, many of the innovations in marketing have arisen from consumer-oriented companies where the selling process may be all but obviated by the system of merchandising, the creation of demand among consumers by advertising and promotion leading to shops being obliged to stock goods by demand from consumers. In this form of marketing the purely selling activity has become far less evident than it was twenty years ago. That it has been successful cannot be

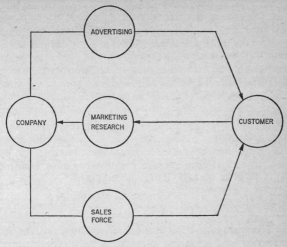

FIG. 4. *The total functional system.*

denied and it is to the advantage of consumers generally that it should be so.

Problems arise when companies making industrial goods, especially, adopt and try to emulate the successful manufacturer of consumers' goods, pushing their products into markets by advertising and neglecting the pulling element that can come only from effective salesmanship.

Perhaps it is not too drastic to say that some of the failures of Britain to export successfully are derived from a lack of understanding of the different problems of *merchandising goods at home* and *selling goods abroad*.

The traditional attitude of British industry towards exports has been: "... plan for the home market and hope overseas customers will like them. ..." It may well be satisfactory to rely upon the marketing process at home to create customers, but the creation of customers in export markets invariably means personal selling to accomplish the task.

14. Effective sales function. Any organisation which exists to create customers must have an underlying characteristic of effective sales management. It is sales management that will provide a creation centre from which many of the company's policies will derive. A product will remain as design and productive skill until sales management can translate its basic idea into a concept that accords with customers' needs. If marketing management has derived the idea from feedback originating with the sales force and used it to call into production some new product it then relies upon the creativity of sales management to produce some original selling idea. It will rely upon sales management to impart the enthusiasm and will to succeed that can motivate the sales force to sell the product to consumers or users. In the creation of a successful sales organisation the company must consider:

(*a*) the qualities of leadership and direction that the sales manager can give to those working under his control;

(*b*) the size and form the sales organisation takes, and whether it is adequate for the tasks it must accomplish.

PROGRESS TEST 1

1. The changes in economic conditions following the Second World War have given rise to marketing as a concept. In which five ways may companies seek marketing advantages over their competitors? (2)

2. "In the conditions of a changing environment, only companies with a sound marketing concept and an efficient and developed sales organisation will be able to operate effectively." Discuss. (5)

3. How can the marketing function ensure that increased sales volume is accomplished? (7)

4. What are the objectives of the functional organisation? (11)

5. What are the two points which must be considered in creating a successful sales organisation? (14)

CHAPTER II

The Tools of Marketing

MARKETING INVESTMENT ALTERNATIVES

1. Introduction. All industries and professions have developed their own methods, tools, systems, customs or implements which will be pertinent to the practice and will be deeply involved in its success.

Marketing is no exception to this rule; its own system of tools being:

(*a*) channels of distribution;
(*b*) marketing research;
(*c*) sales force;
(*d*) advertising;
(*e*) sales promotion; and
(*f*) pricing.

The choice of scale upon each marketing tool used can be considered as a measure of *investment*.

Figure 5 is a simple example of two alternative investment

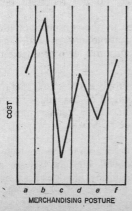
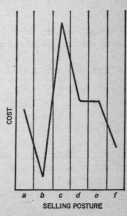

FIG. 5. *Two alternative investment postures.*

11

postures. The merchandising posture "invests" in market research, distribution, advertising and competitive pricing; the selling posture lays little emphasis on exploring the market and instead "invests" in the sales force—high-calibre salesman, high commission and incentives, and looks to the salesman's ability to overcome price disadvantages.

Like all investment decisions, the choice of marketing tools will be subject to:

(a) understanding of the proposition;
(b) realistic forecasting of results; and
(c) evaluation of alternative solutions.

CHANNELS OF DISTRIBUTION

2. Reaching the consumer. The channel of distribution is a tool of marketing used to explain and understand the methods by which products are able to reach the final consumer. The final consumer is all important to the manufacturer as it is only by accomplishing a sale that the business purpose is fulfilled.

Business Purpose = Profit.
Profit achieved by making a sale.
Making a sale implies a customer.
This must be a satisfied customer.

The sale of goods by a manufacturer to a wholesaler, factor, contractor or retailer, or from a wholesaler to a retailer, are only steps in the distribution chain. They do not represent final consumption.

If it is true that demand is satisfied by the consumer or user only, then it is reasonable to assume that the services of all those involved up to the point where the consumer or user is able to obtain them are the process of supply.

3. Flow of supplies. The equalising of supply and demand is at the root of marketing and the accomplishment of this balance is the purpose of the channels of distribution. These channels must be so conceived as to maintain an efficient flow of supply at all times.

Channels of distribution will vary according to the needs and circumstances of the market. So too will vary the pattern of concentration and dispersion. Surmounting all considerations will be the need to meet the demand in terms of time and place. The concepts of *time utility* and *place utility* will be the most important purpose of distribution at all times.

4. Concentration of supplies. This is the collecting of the output of diverse suppliers and its concentration by wholesalers or manufacturers, with the objective of sorting, grading, assembly, further processing and ultimately of sale.

Concentration is important both when the product is to be consumed in its original form or when it is to be further processed. The process for marketing complex manufactured goods involves considerable concentrations of parts, both from within the company and from other manufacturers. Televisions, cars and aircraft all result from assembling enormous numbers of component parts made by various suppliers.

Equilibrium is primarily accomplished at the point of centralisation. Supply is generally undertaken in anticipation of demand for most goods, while supply undertaken against specific orders is comparatively rare.

Farmers produce for markets which will deal in larger quantities than individual consumers will wish to purchase, but in less than wholesalers will require to satisfy their total consumer needs. The equilibrium of supply and demand is undertaken by wholesalers who buy in bulk from many farmers and growers and break the bulk into convenient sizes for dispersal to retailers and final consumers.

The process of concentration fulfils an essential aspect of marketing that adds value to the product in terms of *time*, *place* and *form*. As an aspect of the marketing process it provides for:

(*a*) storage of current supplies against future demand;

(*b*) storage of supplies at a place where demand is anticipated to occur; and

(*c*) transforming of the product by sorting, grading or processing.

Those products subject to wide fluctuations in supply and demand benefit from the services of middlemen who dampen the extremes of fluctuation.

5. Dispersion. The process of marketing necessitates the concentration of production at certain stages to provide the form and quantity required by subsequent stages. From each concentration there follows a dispersion, leading to the final distribution to the final consumer or user. Dispersion occurs in several forms, for example:

(*a*) to *retailers* and then to final consumers;

(*b*) to *manufacturers* for further processing;

(*c*) to *wholesalers* for distribution to retailers; or

(*d*) in *exporting*, where it may be through importers who will behave like wholesalers or retailers, according to local practice.

The pattern of concentration, equating and dispersion differs considerably between commodities. The distributive pattern for industrial goods or producers' goods differs generally from that of consumers' goods in that the user of such goods is himself a producer. Since the goods are often of high individual value, they are frequently sold direct to the user.

6. Choice of distributive channels. There are several channels of distribution available to the manufacturer.

(*a*) Direct to the ultimate customer;

(*i*) *through "tied" outlets*, e.g. flour millers who own bakery shops or bread rounds, breweries selling through their own hotels or pubs; or

(*ii*) *direct to the user*, or to the door, e.g. industrial cleaning materials, brush sales.

(*b*) To the retailer via the wholesaler.

(*c*) Direct to the retailer.

7. The transvection concept. Individual sales are termed transactions, and the entire chain of stages in a channel of distribution is termed a transvection. (*See* Fig. 6.)

For the sales manager the transvection concept is an important way of understanding how his production reaches eventual customers. Decisions have to be taken on the evaluation of each stage in the process and on whether greater efficiency would result from modifying the distribution channel.

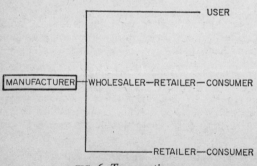

FIG. 6. *Transvections.*

8. Cost and efficiency. The concentration of industry into larger production units has put greater emphasis upon the need to influence mass consumer markets, which in turn increases marketing costs. The greater demand from consumers with a higher disposable income has led to an increase in the costs of advertising, packaging and promotion. Mass production has done much to offset the additional costs.

Careful analysis of the existing distribution channels, and creative innovation in streamlining or otherwise modifying the transvection are increasingly important tasks of sales management.

MARKETING RESEARCH

Marketing research can be defined as the application of scientific methods to the solution of marketing problems. It endeavours to provide information such as:

  (a) whether a market exists;
  (b) the possibilities of creating a market;
  (c) comparison of quality and price with competitive products;
  (d) extent to which demand is satisfied by existing suppliers;
  (e) the opportunities for advantage over competitors;
  (f) examination of competitors' sales techniques; and
  (g) evaluation of alternative methods of distribution.

Marketing research must be a continuous process, as economic and political changes both at home and abroad keep situations fluid, and market conditions may change rapidly. Competitors may break into the field and gain an advantage with an unsuspected product innovation. Amendments to marketing plans may be necessary at short notice.

9. Effective marketing research. To be effective, marketing research recommendations must be incorporated quickly with skill, and management must allocate the full time necessary for their accurate implementation.

Effective marketing research tends to be expensive and, as it usually brings its results only in the long term, it is difficult to relate its costs with results. This frequently leads to a reluctance to provide adequate funds for the necessary research.

10. Research as an aid to decision-making. Management's job is to take decisions on:

(*a*) what must be done;
(*b*) specifying the personnel to do the work;
(*c*) seeing that the work is done; and
(*d*) evaluating how well the work was done.

Management's effectiveness in carrying out its task will depend upon the sensible use of information. This in turn creates the need for information of the correct quantity, quality and relevance to enable management to undertake its basic elements of planning, co-ordinating and controlling work.

Managers are receivers of information which they will use to take decisions and which will determine their ability to take better decisions. Such decisions must be based on facts and ways have to be found of lowering the degree of uncertainty and risk. Improvement will originate in the systematic:

(*a*) selection;
(*b*) collection;
(*c*) processing;
(*d*) analysis; and
(*e*) communication

of relevant information, and in the capacity to make sound assumptions for accurate forecasting and planning decisions.

11. The process of market research. Market research arranges its task in two ways. It:

(*a*) collects information about the market and its customers; and

(*b*) analyses its findings.

Information may be collected in three ways.

(*a*) *Simple:* by personal observation of consumers' buying habits and trends.

(*b*) *Desk research:* by the use of official publications and statistics.

(*c*) *Original research:* by undertaking sample surveys, designed to reveal new information in answer to specific decision needs.

The cost and the technical nature of the research increases from (*a*) which is the cheapest and can be undertaken by any sensible businessman, to (*c*) which can incur high costs and is usually undertaken by specialist firms.

12. Sources of information. Information needs will depend upon the nature of the problem; the following are some usual sources.

(*a*) Internal sales data (i.e. invoices, records).

(*b*) Published information (government statistics, economic data, market surveys).

(*c*) Data available on request but not generally published (e.g. information frŏm government sources or trade organisations).

(*d*) New data collected by sample survey methods.

MAIN TYPES OF MARKETING RESEARCH

13. Economic research. Economic conditions within the world in general react on the individual countries and on the businesses carried on there. Economic research provides guidance for forecasting economic trends which is essential for:

(*a*) export marketing;

(*b*) product innovation; and

(*c*) investment appraisal.

Economic research summarises its findings under two main headings:

(*a*) the general state of the economy; and

(*b*) the condition of particular sections of the economy.

It aims to review both the short- and long-term trends in the economy, especially those sectors likely to affect the market in which the organisation is concerned, or intends to operate.

14. Marketing research. In this study the term is used to embrace all those research activities which are intended to aid marketing management. It can be considered in three aspects which are:

(*a*) *consumer* research;

(*b*) *market* research; and

(*c*) *advertising* research.

15. Consumer research. In undertaking consumer research the object is to detect prevailing attitudes of consumers or users of the product. It is a simple approach to begin the enquiry in terms of "what do consumers require?" or "how will they regard the product?"

In reality the situation is rarely easily answered. Few people can express a positive yes or no in response to a particular question. We could indeed make up a typical list of questions that we could ask.

(*a*) Who buys the product? (According to sex, age, social group, occupation, married/single, location, etc.).

(b) Where is the product purchased? (Local shop, grocer, engineers' store, builders' merchants, and so on.)

(c) When will the product be used? (Breakfast, dinner, or during industrial shut-down periods, winter or summer.)

The responses to our questions will aid in building a picture of the likely conditions under which we will be selling to consumers. However, we must also question whether the basic market concept is right.

16. Market research. An investigation for a particular product leads to an appraisal of the market. As an example we can take a product that will fit into both the consumer and the industrial market—a litre of paint. A number of pertinent questions will help to reveal the market.

(a) When do you use the paint?

(b) In what quantities?

(c) What colours do you like?

(d) What special problems must it overcome?

(e) What price range must it fit into?

The replies will reveal much about the paint we should be producing. We could then take the investigation a stage further and consider the competition we are likely to encounter. The following question then becomes relevant.

(f) How does the product compare with competitive products? (For colour, quality, price, etc.)

In reality any marketing plan constructed from this type of information is failing to take account of all the forces that will play against the product. It may be understood and accepted that our product will compete with other similar products, but it is also necessary to appreciate that a pot of paint has also to compete with other protective measures, including:

(a) liquid plastics;

(b) timber preservatives;

(c) fungicidal treatments;

(d) plastic laminates;

(e) formica;

(f) galvanising; and

(g) new methods of construction.

This brings into question whether we are working in the "paint market". We are really working in the market for which paint is intended. Thus a *paint for treating domestic window frames* is connected with the building and timber markets while *paint for coating steelwork* may be in the corrosion market, or the structural market, or the chemical market, or the fabrication market.

Whatever markets the products are really concerned with, they will all operate within the complexities of that market. We will be competing not only with other paints that will do the job equally well, but also with other forms of treatment, and all these may be competing with other choices that may be wholly unconnected with our particular concern.

> EXAMPLE: A company manufacturing liquid plastic paints wishes to exploit the growing market for slaughterhouse treatments. The work requires materials with special qualities of nontoxicity, hygiene, durability and ease of cleaning. It competes not with other paints, which cannot really stand up to the aggressive conditions of slaughterhouses, but with tiling, terrazzo, laminates and chemically hardened rendering; further investigation may reveal that the firm will be competing with another alternative to coatings, chemical cleaners.

If the analysis of competitors' products is correct, then the company has to make out a case for its product which must be concerned with far more than a statement of quality, colour, durability, etc. It must give evidence that its product is superior to those of its competitors, that it can, for example, save the buyer money which could then be allocated to other requirements.

17. Advertising research. Advertising research is a specialised aspect of consumer research and is concerned with understanding consumer motivations and predicting results of advertising messages.

Its role in developing a "brand image" has long been one of its most important aspects but in recent years it has sought to identify underlying reasons for consumers' loyalty to, or dislike of, particular propositions. Advertising research has turned to psychology in an endeavour to understand the deep-rooted feelings consumers may have towards certain products. This application of "depth-research" into such apparently straightforward propositions as instant coffee, cigarette smoking and cosmetics have thrown new light on consumer buying behaviour. When this knowledge is accurately and sensibly applied it becomes a powerful tool of marketing.

THE SALES FORCE

In this section we will be concerned with the sales force as an investment alternative to other tools of marketing.

18. Role of the sales force. The role of the sales force has been influenced in recent years by developments such as:

(*a*) a widespread use of advertising by means of:

(*i*) television;

(*ii*) newspapers, magazines and journals;

(*iii*) poster advertising; and

(*iv*) mailed "special offer" promotions;

(*b*) a higher investment in "brand" names and the resultant high promotional activity;

(*c*) the development of better communications, leading to greater ease of travel and distribution which has reduced the number of salesmen; and

(*d*) a combination of all the foregoing developed as merchandising.

The trends have become evident in retailing, and many writers pay little attention to trends in other sectors of trade, i.e. export selling and industrial selling.

19. Need for improved sales force. In the sectors of trade other than retailing, developments in the use of the sales force have certainly occurred, but unlike the retail sector in which personal salesmanship both in the store and in "commercial travelling" has declined, in exporting and industrial selling it has led to a need for *better* salesmanship, such as:

(*a*) greater technical proficiency;

(*b*) greater personal skill; and

(*c*) an ability to identify product opportunities.

This means the sales force is still a key factor in modern marketing, but marketing now calls for greater efforts from both sales management and salesmen. Management must realise that the skills of the sales force are as important as all other functional personnel in the organisation. In some highly competitive sectors, such as exporting, they are vital to the company's success.

20. Management's task. To obtain the right calibre of salesmen, management must pay attention to:

(*a*) remuneration—a higher basic salary and less "incentive" in the form of commission;

(*b*) a greater realisation of and respect for the salesman's skill—less of the "carrot and stick" approach;

(*c*) greater leadership from management which will motivate the sales force to higher aspirations; and

(*d*) by delegation of responsibility creating more job satisfaction and more job prospects.

The important aspect of leadership from management will be dealt with fully in Chapter XII. The other vital areas of management of the sales force will also be explained in subsequent chapters.

ADVERTISING

21. Informing customers. The marketing process is concerned with understanding consumers' needs, motivating the sale of a product or service, and distributing it to consumers—advertising is that part of the process which is concerned with informing consumers of the existence of the product or service.

Promotion of a manufacturer's products can be of three main types.

(*a*) *Non-personal:* advertising.

(*b*) *Semi-personal:* sales promotion.

(*c*) *Personal:* salesmanship.

Whatever kind of promotion is employed at a particular time, it will have as its objective several aims.

(*d*) To build goodwill for the company.

(*e*) To maintain continuing customer satisfaction.

(*f*) To keep sales volume at a profitable level.

Advertising and sales promotion are identified as two distinctive tools of marketing, fulfilling different purposes. In this they offer the businessman a choice for investment. It is not an absolute choice between one or the other but rather a decision on *how much* to invest in each.

22. Objectives of advertising. Advertising has been defined by the Definitions Committee of the American Marketing Association as ". . . any paid form of non-personal presentation and promotion of ideas, goods, or services by an identified sponsor."

It is an aspect of marketing that is both cause and effect of modern industrial productivity, enabling mass manufacture to produce for mass consumption as a result of mass demand.

Advertising's function is one that has become basic to the

modern economy in the capitalistic society; this results from its role in the communication system. The need for information about a vast range of ideas, products and concepts has arisen from the advertising process.

Manufacturers have been able to create the mass market by constantly seeking and achieving reduced costs, and this has been made possible to a large degree by efficient distribution aided by effective advertising.

The importance of advertising was recognised in the nineteenth century by Lord Macaulay who argued: "Advertising is to business what steam is to machinery—the great propelling power."

23. The role of advertising. Since advertising as a concept has become fundamental to the industrialised society its role in marketing has become an important aid to individual manufacturers and businesses of every kind. Its essential role is:

(*a*) to aid the creation and maintenance of sales;
(*b*) to persuade prospective consumers to become actual consumers;
(*c*) to inform consumers and create demand; and
(*d*) to increase demand for a product or service.

24. The communication gap. Consumers are faced with a wide range of choice in satisfying their needs—many products, although not identical, can be substitutes for one another. Advertising is a means of bridging a communications gap and accelerating the satisfaction of consumers' wants. It does this by communicating:

(*a*) that products or services exist;
(*b*) what they are like;
(*c*) their relationship with consumers' needs; and
(*d*) their price.

Once a shop or warehouse has been suitably equipped and a satisfactory range of merchandise assembled, it is the role of advertising to attract customers and induce them to buy. In doing this advertising has a role in serving the customer as well as the business, for rather than trying to sell unwanted goods, it must recognise that certain needs exist as a part of the human condition and that this is a measure of the progress that a society has made.

Brand names and advertising are closely linked: the role of

advertising is to quicken the process of acceptance of a brand image by consumers.

25. Limitations of advertising. It must be recognised that advertising is only *one* of many causes of consumer purchases, which also include:

(*a*) price;
(*b*) presentation and packaging;
(*c*) ability of the sales force; and
(*d*) quality of the product.

Advertising is a medium of communication and does not sell products, it only motivates needs.

(*a*) Advertising will not sell products unwanted by consumers.

(*b*) Advertising will not sell products by itself, it requires the co-operation of all the marketing processes.

(*c*) Advertising has to be used continuously to succeed in motivating customers.

(*d*) Advertising may motivate consumers to buy without establishing a brand loyalty.

(*e*) Advertising has a great influence on "impulse buying".

EXAMPLE: Mr. Jones sits watching television on a warm summer evening. An advertisement appears exhorting him to buy brand "X" beer. Unable to resist temptation any longer, Mr. Jones leaves his house intent on buying a glass of brand "X" beer. The first bar he comes to sells only brand "Y" beer—Mr. Jones, motivated to buy beer goes and buys a glass of brand "Y", thereby benefiting the advertiser's competitor.

26. Problems of advertising. Advertising as an investment tool of marketing is difficult to quantify both in terms of predicting and of measuring results.

£X,000 invested in a campaign results in sales of Y,000 articles. For the manager the question becomes one of determining the relationship between the amount invested in a campaign and the level of sales achieved. There is considerable difficulty in determining whether the level of sales owes anything to the advertising, or would have been more or less if no campaign had been mounted. The decision on advertising then can be reduced to a major question, "should we advertise at all?" If the answer is positive, then:

(*a*) *how much money* to invest?
(*b*) *where* to advertise?
(*c*) *how to organise* the advertising campaign?

27. General considerations. Among the general considerations affecting the amount to be invested in the advertising appropriation will be the following.

(a) Is the product, or service being advertised, new, established or declining?

(b) What is the nature of the product or service?

(c) A consideration of competitive activity.

Whenever a manufacturer has capacity to produce sufficient volume of goods to develop a mass market, some form of advertising will be essential to realise full potential.

28. How much to invest. For the manager responsible for determining marketing and sales strategy, decisions on advertising are primarily concerned with how much to invest in advertising. He may consider three alternative approaches. These are:

(a) advertising/sales ratio approach;

(b) economic approach; or

(c) relation to competition approach.

29. Advertising/sales ratio approach. Using this approach the manager is making a projection based on actual sales achieved in the previous year. To this figure a given percentage is added which will be the advertising appropriation for the current year.

EXAMPLE:
Advertising/Sales ratio:

Sales achieved in units	100,000
Value of net sales per unit	£1·25
Net value of sales	£125,000
Pre-advertising profit	25%
Actual profit pre-advert.	£31,250
Advert. budget (actual)	£6,250
Advert. budget/Sales ratio	5%
Unit expenditure	£0·0625
Estimated net profit	£25,000
Net profit as percentage of net revenue	20%

The disadvantage of advertising/sales ratio as a method of deciding investment level lies in the rigid expenditure based upon the previous year's results. The advertising/sales ratio does not permit a rapid, defensive campaign to be mounted in the event of changing circumstances, such as:

(a) new product innovation;

(b) new distribution area; or a

(c) major campaign by a competitor.

In other circumstances a fixed percentage may be a waste of resources; i.e. when demand equals or exceeds production. The fixed ratio should be a guide to expenditure, but should never be allowed to become a deciding factor, for it is too mechanistic and deprives the campaign of its essential flexibility.

30. Economic approach. The economic approach shown in Fig. 7 determines the level of expenditure from a consideration of cost and revenue. It determines that the investment in advertising is

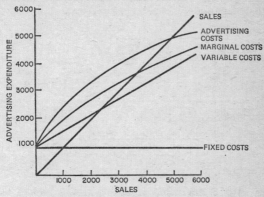

FIG. 7. *The economic approach to advertising.*

worth while so long as the resulting increase in sales exceeds the cost of advertising and the marginal cost of meeting the extra demand. When the marginal cost added to the cost of advertising exceeds marginal revenue then the expenditure is considered to be unreasonable.

The practical application of the economic approach creates problems.

(*a*) It is difficult to determine when the marginal revenue does, in fact, exceed marginal cost.

(*b*) Advertising is only one among several ways of increasing sales volume.

(*c*) The activity of competitors is ignored by this approach.

(*d*) Since the approach puts great emphasis upon the relationship between cost and revenue, it tends to ignore the long-term achievements.

31. Relation to competition approach. This approach leads the manufacturer to study the advertising activity of his competitors as a guide to his own level of expenditure. It has the basic fault that the company that adopts the approach must lag behind and react to competitors. It is most frequently applied by brand leaders whose expenditure on advertising is likely to be the largest among competing products. So long as the brand leader maintains his differential, he considers that his expenditure is correct. Companies who are not brand leaders adopt the approach in relation to the brand leader in the belief that if they do not maintain their expenditure in line with the brand leader, they will gradually lose their market position.

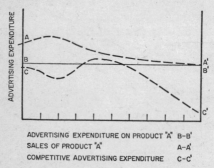

ADVERTISING EXPENDITURE ON PRODUCT "A" B–B'
SALES OF PRODUCT "A"   A–A'
COMPETITIVE ADVERTISING EXPENDITURE   C–C'

FIG. 8. *Advertising in relation to competition.*

The fundamental drawback to this approach is once again the assumption that advertising is the only way of accomplishing an advantageous position. It ignores the competitive advantages to be gained from using other tools of marketing, channels of distribution, pricing, sales force and sales promotion.

Its relation to competitors' activity is important also in terms of trying to maintain a product in the market when perhaps the general trend is to some other product. If expenditure is maintained at a given level when all the competitors are reducing theirs it will generally lead to an over-all decline in demand anyway, as shown in Fig. 8.

SALES PROMOTION

32. Promotional activities. Sales promotion can be defined as any activity which promotes sales; in this sense the concept can include:

    (*a*) advertising;

(*b*) sales force; and
(*c*) pricing.

33. Sales promotion. Here we are concerned with sales promotion as set out in **21**: a semi-personal short-term motivation. We can perhaps imagine advertising as a broad "scythe" of a weapon, and sales promotion then is the "rapier". It is a precise tool of marketing which can be used to stimulate sales for particular purposes such as:

(*a*) product innovation and launch;
(*b*) new territory exploitation;
(*c*) stimulating sales at particular periods; and
(*d*) encouraging sales personnel to sell certain products.

34. Methods of promotion. In the widest context marketing management will use promotions in a wide variety of circumstances and will employ many methods which could include:

(*a*) pricing;
(*b*) trade offers;
(*c*) consumer offers;
(*d*) sales aids;
(*e*) packaging and presentation;
(*f*) exhibitions;
(*g*) in-store promotions;
(*h*) special occasion promotions; and
(*i*) public relations.

35. Product innovation and launch. The purpose of sales promotion in relation to new products and their successful launch will have as its objective a general widening of distribution and an establishment and increase in the stock or use of the product.

In industrial selling, promotions may take the form of displays, demonstrations or even the practical application for a specific job or period of time. The intention is that users of the product will gain experience of the product and find a continuing use for it.

In the distributive field of wholesaling and retailing, promotions have two objectives which are:

(*a*) *to stimulate the public* to demand the product; and
(*b*) *to induce stockists to increase stocks* of the product in anticipation of consumer demand.

36. Trade promotions. Here the manufacturer offers an incentive to the trade to purchase his products.

(*a*) *A percentage discount*, or a cash allowance for a given quantity, a case, barrel etc., that he buys.

(*b*) *An extra product* is given with each order. This has an advantage to the manufacturer in that it ensures the distributor passes on the allowances to the retailer.

(*c*) *Gifts* may be given in return for certain quantity orders.

37. Consumer promotions. These are aimed at the consumer and have as their objective the stimulation to try, or to purchase more of a product.

(*a*) *Coupons*: these are vouchers of a specific value which are passed direct to the consumer who obtains a price reduction on presentation to his stockist. The manufacturer expects to gain certain benefits from coupons, including the fact that:

(*i*) it will act as an incentive to consumers to sample products;

(*ii*) the retailer will be encouraged to stock the product in expectation of demand; and

(*iii*) the salesman will have an opportunity to obtain additional display for the product.

(*b*) *Self-liquidating offers:* in this form of promotion the consumer is invited by the manufacturer to send a sum of money and a number of package tops for a particular product.

The article is normally offered at a bargain price which the manufacturer is able to do by bulk purchases. Very often the manufacturer utilises the offer to aid the salesman to obtain window or store display space. The method suffers in particular from a difficulty in assessing results as the number of applications received is not always a sound criterion.

(*c*) *Bargain packs:* the manufacturer offers a product for sale at a reduced price for a short period. Normally the reduction is clearly marked on the packaging, e.g. "3p off". It is really a temporary price cut.

(*d*) *Sampling:* the consumer is given a small free sample as an inducement to try the product in the hope it will persuade him to develop a brand loyalty.

Since the sample distribution must be large if it is to be effective, the method can incur considerable expense, such as:

(*i*) production of special size sample packs;

(*ii*) cost of distribution of samples; and

(*iii*) the cost of "lost sales", inasmuch as some consumers who receive the free sample might have bought the product anyway but will now defer purchase until they have finished the sample.

38. New territory exploitation. Sales promotion has a particularly important role in developing the company's products in new territories. This may be considered in two aspects.

(a) Home trade.
(b) Export trade.

In home sales, development of a territory will usually have some continuity with adjacent territories. It is unusual for a product already selling in a home territory to be completely unknown elsewhere in the home trade. Sales promotion would serve as an extension of the sales force in the role of a quick stimulus to develop trade in order to achieve a profitable level of sales as quickly as possible.

39. Home trade. The methods adopted will vary according to the nature of the business. In the retail sector it can be in-store promotions, shop-within-a-shop arrangements, or window displays linked with advertising, or it may be linked to methods suggested in 37, e.g. special offers, bargain packs, etc.

Industrial sales promotion differs essentially from retailing in that almost always it is a *derived demand*, that is, the products are not wanted for themselves but to accomplish some other objective, e.g. to produce more beer, to move earth faster, etc. This requires industrial promotional techniques to be much more positive in their appeals. Ideally they should communicate ideas such as:

(a) saving time;
(b) reducing labour costs;
(c) lowering handling costs;
(d) quicker movements;
(e) harder wearing; or
(f) less down-time, etc.

The ways of achieving results will necessarily vary according to the industry but the following are typical methods.

(a) *Demonstration.* Co-operation of an operator is sought to apply or use the product practically, which may vary from a bulldozer to a pot of paint. A demonstration is then staged to which other operators are invited.

(b) *Trade show.* Products are shown in a hotel, or similar premises including manufacturers' or stockists' showrooms, where practical. The buyers are invited to view and discuss their problems with the company's representatives who may be sales director, sales management or salesmen. It is usual to provide buffet and drinks as an added attraction.

(*c*) *Individual demonstrations.* A team of demonstrators will visit, by prior arrangement, individual firms and demonstrate the equipment to executives and operatives.

(*d*) *National exhibitions.* Manufacturer will take a stand at prominent National Exhibitions, i.e. Motor Show, International Men's and Boys' Exhibition, etc.

40. Export promotions. Development of new territories in exporting is generally a long-term operation requiring careful planning over a long period. The operation will have commenced with market research with the objective of determining:

(*a*) the market to go for, e.g. Germany, Brazil;

(*b*) the nature of demand in the selected market;

    (*i*) high or low cost,

    (*ii*) men or women,

    (*iii*) heavy industrial, consumer, etc., and

    (*iv*) methods of distribution, wholesaler, direct, users, etc.,

(*c*) the recognised buying periods and expected delivery times;

(*d*) any suitable promotional events, e.g. British Weeks, National events, etc.; and

(*e*) the most suitable selling arrangements, e.g. local representative, subsidiary office, agent.

Having established as much information as possible it is usual for a senior representative of the company to visit the territory to establish contact with prospective buyers, investigate the market and make a personal assessment, and meet the local representatives of the British Overseas Trade Board, the commercial councillors attached to embassies, etc.

From this point the promotions would then follow the pattern of the home trade for both industrial and consumer goods, except of course when local conditions require an entirely new approach which could only be determined after exhaustive investigation.

41. Stimulating sales at particular periods. A great number of products whether consumer or industrial tend to be seasonal to a greater or lesser degree. Sales promotion can be used to stimulate trade in anticipation of a likely decline at a given time. Promotions may also be employed at periods of intensive buying when it is realised that competition will be greatest. This may be at Christmas when manufacturers will want to direct consumers' purchasing power to their products; or in industry before the holiday periods when major maintenance work will be carried out.

It becomes vitally important for manufacturers, contractors, distributors and retailers to recognise that the additional sales accomplished as a result of increased promotion are only achieved at increased cost. Once again, if marginal cost exceeds marginal revenue, the operation will hardly have been worth while.

42. Encouraging salesmen to sell certain products. As an alternative to aiming the sales promotion at the customer a manufacturer may direct the promotion at his sales force. This is particularly effective in industrial selling.

EXAMPLE: A manufacturer of paints has a range of six products, from which he wishes to intensify sales of two, products A and F. The reasons for this decision may be: (1) the products have not been sold in sufficient quantity; (2) they are profitable products; (3) introducing new, or improved products; (4) seasonal demand; or (5) over-production.

A competition is organised among the company's twenty salesmen. Each product is awarded a number of points when they are sold within a given period of time. At the end of the promotional period the winning salesman receives a gift, e.g. a holiday for himself and his wife, a camera, a Christmas hamper. Those products which the company wishes to push are given additional weighting in points and since the salesman can improve his competitive position with these, he tries to sell more of them.

PRODUCT A	per 20 litres	10 points
,, B	,, ,, ,,	2 points
,, C	,, ,, ,,	3 points
,, D	,, ,, ,,	1 point
,, E	,, ,, ,,	4 points
,, F	,, ,, ,,	10 points

The concept has advantages in that it stimulates sales of the required products to users, some of whom may continue to repeat their orders. On the debit side it has a tendency to:

(a) lead to large numbers of small orders;

(b) the competitive spirit may lead to less co-operation among the sales force who may not pass on tips or information to one another;

(c) it is a short-term concept and ignores the importance of selling forward and of spending time in negotiating long-term and large-scale business; and

(d) the "opportunity costs" of (a), (b) and (c) may exceed the marginal revenue.

PRICING

If we take the view expressed earlier, that the tools of marketing may be regarded as alternative investments, then pricing becomes an obvious factor in adjusting the company's competitive posture.

43. Pricing problems. "I see no problem in pricing, I allow my competitors to guide me." This statement is one frequently offered as an answer to the question "How do you set the level of your prices?"

It is an answer that many serious and capable executives have given in the past and will no doubt continue to do so in the future. As an answer it falls short in many respects and certainly, if taken in the literal sense, it is not a statement of fact.

There are Trade Associations, professional organisations and some government bodies which do set prices at a generally agreed level to which members are expected to adhere.

It is true that manufacturers will wish to know at what levels their competitors have set their prices, and will certainly be influenced by them, but the decision on fixing his own prices is the manufacturer's alone.

For most manufacturers this decision of fixing his price level is an extremely difficult one. In many cases the manufacturer not only has to determine his selling price, but if the products are going to be distributed by a wholesaler or factor, and then through a retailer, he may have to determine the suggested level at which they will offer the products for sale.

44. Pricing is a policy decision. The levels at which prices are to be set will determine the broad strategy of the company, and vice versa. If the policy is to go for the mass market served by large volume production then the general price level will be low.

Henry Ford did not achieve low prices by making his cars in quantity, but achieved quantity production at low cost by a deliberate policy of creating a mass demand by a low-priced car.

In this respect the pricing decision will have to take into consideration:

(a) the nature of the product;

(b) the importance of the product;

(c) the market at which it is intended;

(d) the form of production needed to manufacture;

(e) economies of scale; and

(f) ease of distribution.

The level of prices is implicit in the policy of the company.

45. Competition pricing. Direct competition pricing generally is not a satisfactory way of differentiating a product and as a concept it is not usually favoured by manufacturers. There are several considerations to be taken into account.

(a) *Price cutting* is a simple operation and competitors may carry it out rapidly. Since one manufacturer's initiative in price cutting will certainly be followed by others, competitive positions will be re-established at a lower price level.

(b) There is a *psychological reluctance* among manufacturers to increase prices and it follows that once prices have been cut the customers would have resistance even to a return to a former price level.

(c) There is a tendency for manufacturers and re-sellers to favour competing from a "*high price*". Advantages will be sought by means of advertising, promotion, selling or distribution.

(d) Among smaller manufacturers there is often a realisation that price cutting cannot succeed against much larger competitors. They decide to "*upgrade*" *their product* and aim for a smaller but less competitive market.

46. Price revision. The manufacturer will have an objective for his product; in assessing this objective he will have been guided by marketing research. In deciding on the tactics to achieve the objective he will have considered the "tool" of pricing.

(a) He will know the *price structure of the market* which he considers the most advantageous for his products.

(b) His price will be *closely related with his brand image*, e.g. the high-class cosmetic manufacturer, oozing sentiment and sex appeal on his latest creations, will not offer it at "bargain price".

(c) The planned objectives must be flexible enough to react to a *constantly changing market*.

(d) There will be *fluctuations in commodity prices*, as there will be in other raw materials and packaging.

(e) *A periodical review* does not of course necessarily mean a change in price levels is called for.

PROGRESS TEST 2

1. What are the six tools of marketing? **(1)**

2. How do different investment postures affect the choice of marketing tools? **(1)**

3. How does the purpose of distribution add utility to goods, and in which ways? **(3)**

4. What is the process of market research and in which ways may information be collected? **(11)**

5. How would you determine the essential role of advertising? **(23)**

6. What considerations would you take into account in pricing policy? **(44)**

CHAPTER III

Sales Organisation Structures

FUNDAMENTALS OF ORGANISATION

1. Introduction. Effective organisation is fundamental to good management. In any business there must be some form of organisation structure which exists to carry out the company's policies. In sales organisations the structure will vary according to such elements as size of firm, type of product or service and according to the wishes and desires of the owners or directors.

Many firms have evolved methods of organisation peculiar to themselves over long periods of time and in such cases re-organisation is often necessary. A management consultant or a manager assigned the task of assessing the logic and capabilities of a firm's existing organisational structure is usually concerned with the reorganisation of that firm's current structures, not with the creation of entirely new ones. Thus there are limiting factors in drawing up so-called "ideal' organisation structures.

2. Organisation and the selling function. Firms exist because of their ability to satisfy the needs of their customers, and since these are continually changing as a result of other pressures, environmental, technological, cultural, educational or medical, then so the successful firm must adapt to accord with the latest consumer or user patterns of needs.

Marketing has in recent years laid great stress on the desirability of flexibility in production, yet the modern approaches which are leading to more flexibility in production and marketing frequently enforce a greater rigidity in the form of organisation developed to meet these same needs.

In understanding the importance of organisation to sales the aims must be threefold.

(*a*) To define what is meant by "organisation".

(*b*) To examine the structures that different kinds of sales organisations have developed to meet their specific needs.

(*c*) To note the major prevailing trends in sales organisations.

In any selling organisation the structure must be based upon the specific needs and objectives which form the strategy of the firm. Further than this, an organisation structure must be flexible enough to meet changes in conditions where and when they occur.

3. Nature of organisation. There are many definitions of organisation, all varying in degree of definition and scope. For example, Milward defines organisation as follows:

> "Organisation is a process of dividing work into convenient tasks or duties, of grouping such duties in the form of posts, of delegating authority to each post, and of appointing qualified staff to be responsible that the work is carried out as planned."

We may also state that in simpler terms, organisation structures define the responsibilities and formal relationships throughout the enterprise, and further, that these responsibilities have to be clearly and formally stated in the form of schedules of responsibilities.

The implication of defining schedules for sales personnel is that the emphasis on clarity and decisiveness in drawing up individual schedules of responsibility may well be a straitjacket which will work efficiently in some forms of organisation, such as the military, but which may be more of a stranglehold when applied to the dynamic business firm. In this respect one can quote MacGregor: "The personalities of the men who control enterprises have a profound effect upon the efficient operation of it."

It is reasonable to say that inflexible attitudes of mind can have disastrous effects if applied rigidly to a highly competitive environment such as that in which the modern business firm competes.

4. Limitations of organisation. If organisation theory is applied indiscriminately the result may be the very rigid disciplinary organisation which may have been acceptable in the early theorists' days, but which does not allow the dynamic initiative which is essential in today's changing world. It could, if applied rigorously, lead to widespread "management by committee"—indeed this has already occurred in some American Department Stores' organisation structure. C. S. Deverell, in his book *Business Administration and Management*, puts it succinctly: "An excessive specialisation planned on doctrinaire lines in a rigid functional structure can provide a disastrous case history of valid theory unintelligently applied."

Between similar enterprises, there may be some comparison in the pattern of delegation in certain appointments but there is no basic pattern. Neither is there a typical model for schedules of responsibility, and from this point of view each enterprise is unique. This appreciation of the unique nature of the enterprise is in itself a further problem area, particularly to the mind trained in the principles of organisation structure. If the manager recognises this degree of difference in firms he may well endeavour to solve his problems by bending the principles to fit the firm. Organisation problems may be overcome by compromise solutions, but any such modifications forced on top management to satisfy the existing personnel can only be regarded as transient. There can be no excuse for neglecting to plan a structure.

Since organisation structures have to be adapted to the individual needs of unique companies, it follows that each organisation structure must be developed to meet the requirements of the enterprise it serves. In this way the firm will construct a structure capable of adaption since it will create the one which fulfils its needs at a particular time and will then constantly review the operating conditions. P. F. Drucker says in *The Practice of Management*: "Good organisation structure does not by itself produce good performance . . . but a poor organisation structure makes good performance impossible, no matter how good the individual managers may be."

5. Common functions. There are certain functions which are common to all business enterprises, no matter what the size or purpose of the enterprise. All business enterprises will have some form of policy-making cell, and there will be an executive who will have over-all responsibility for translating the policy into action and be responsible for its effective operation throughout the enterprise.

The policy-making and policy-translation functions are innate. In a small one-man business, the owner will be responsible for both functions while in a large public company it is usual for a board of directors to formulate company policy and a managing director, or a general manager, to translate and ensure its effective implementation.

Certain functions are fundamental to all business, although they may be referred to in different terms. These are:

(*a*) sales (or marketing);
(*b*) finance, and
(*c*) production (or distribution, or operations).

In addition it is becoming normal practice to incorporate a fourth basic function:

(*d*) personnel.

Other functions may be incorporated in some firms but are not fundamental to the enterprise. In small companies one person may be responsible for some or even all the functions while in larger companies separate persons will be responsible for each.

6. Organisational development. As a business grows from a one-man firm to a more complex organisation the work-load related to each of the basic functions increases to the point where it exceeds the capability of one man to carry out the work efficiently. At this point functions will be physically separated. The responsibility for one, or more, functions will be allocated to a specific person. This person will become a specialist in the function and will be responsible to his superior for the efficient undertaking of the function. At this point we have the beginnings of delegation of responsibility.

Assuming the business continues to grow the organisation will develop along recognisable lines.

(*a*) Functions will be physically separated requiring people with specialist functional responsibility, e.g. advertising might be separated from sales promotion.

(*b*) Additional functions will be established creating a need for more specialists with functional responsibility, e.g. an export department is created and an export manager with the necessary experience is appointed.

(*c*) The tasks within the functions will become greater and eventually it will be necessary to separate activities making up the functions. The responsibility for separate activities will be delegated to individuals. The delegation will be by the functional head to whom the people responsible for the activities will report direct; e.g. a developing sales force may, by successfully exploiting all possibilities, eventually distinguish types of customers, or areas. This creates the need for additional salesmen, thus a specialist salesman may be appointed to sell only to local authorities.

Development is both vertical into levels of responsibility and laterally as more activities are added.

EXAMPLE: A firm selling cosmetics direct to consumers developed both vertically and laterally in order to allow for growth. The territory was initially divided into two areas, east and west, and two salesmen appointed. As business grew the territories were subdivided and more salesmen appointed. In due course, the first two salesmen were promoted to group leaders and vertical growth had begun. Figure 9 clarifies the development.

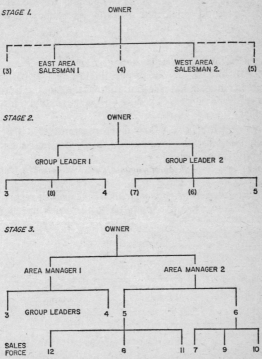

FIG. 9. *Stages in the development of a sales force.*

7. Delegation and responsibility. The provision for growth of an organisation structure is a planning activity and a basic management task. It should include:

(*a*) the delegation of responsibility and authority to cover the total activities of the enterprise, and

(*b*) the determination of formal relationships within the enterprise.

8. Types of organisation. Organisation structures must be created to fulfil the needs of the enterprise to be served.

(*a*) *Line organisation*—responsibility and authority are direct from superiors to subordinates and are reciprocal.

(*b*) *Functional organisation*—each specialist activity has a direct line of responsibility and authority to the point of application.

(*c*) *Line and staff organisation*—line and functional organisations employed together and having lines of direct executive responsibility and specialist services.

Types (*a*) and (*b*) are illustrated in Figs. 10 and 11.

9. Requirements of an organisation structure. Since an organisation structure defines the responsibilities and formal relationships in an enterprise, it is important that they should be formally stated in the form of a Schedule of Responsibility. This should provide:

(*a*) *a chief executive* who will be responsible to the policy-making body for the manner in which the entire enterprise accomplishes its objectives;

(*b*) *an adequate and logical delegation of responsibility* allowing a decentralisation of decisions;

(*c*) *clear channels of communication* and lines of responsibility linking the chief executive to all the operations of the enterprise; and

(*d*) *rational spans of control.*

FIG. 10. *Line organisation.*

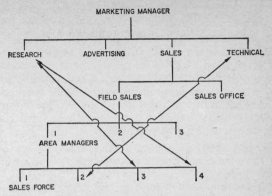

FIG. 11. *Functional organisation.*

10. Schedules of responsibility. The implications of defining schedules of responsibility for sales personnel needs further elaborating. Most teaching of organisation fails to distinguish between its different forms, and many examples are drawn from the military, education and medical organisations, as opposed to business enterprises.

Personnel in teaching, military or nursing join an institutionalised structure in which advancement is by fulfilling the needs of the organisation. A nurse has a particular schedule of responsibility limiting her horizon. Whatever advancement is attempted is by moving within the framework of that organisation, or a similar institutional organisation.

A businessman, or a salesman, within his chosen career may move from one organisation to another and is able to advance by his personality and his ability and willingness to shoulder additional responsibility. Nothing so encourages promotion as a person's willingness to take on extra work. The limitations to this "empire-building" will be:

(*a*) the diminishing effectiveness of the individual; and

(*b*) the ability of colleagues to influence or resist this "empire-building".

In the institutionalised organisation structure, the structure is designed to limit the movement of the individual to the precise requirements of the organisation. For the dynamic business organisation the rigidity may be a death-knell of profit. The dynamic organisation needs scope for individual flair which is a necessary stimulus for business. The institution, with its non-profit goals, has no need for the individual's flair, and personal ambition may be "harmful" to the organisational goals.

11. Organisation and goals. Organisation must be related to goals. If the purpose is profit the structure must allow individuals to develop ideas and abilities which will favour the firm. If the purpose is some non-profit objective the system may be mechanistic, in which case personal limits may lead to frustration if individual goals and ambitions cannot be realised. It is possible to determine two organisation structure types.

(*a*) *Profit-centred organisation.*

(*i*) The business organisation's survival is directly related to profitability.

(*ii*) The organisation must be adaptable to the changing needs of the environment and have no commitment to one purpose.

(*iii*) The people who form the organisation are motivated by job satisfaction and financial reward for which they are prepared to accept a degree of insecurity.

(*iv*) They will be adaptable people and will tend to enlarge their personal parameters of responsibility up to the point where they are limited by the ambitions of their colleagues.

(*b*) *Community-centred organisation.*

(*i*) Typified by the institutional organisation, it is totally related to the needs of the community, has no need of adaptability, and is wholly committed to one purpose.

(*ii*) The people who form the organisation are more motivated by job security for which they are prepared to accept a lower degree of job satisfaction and financial reward.

(*iii*) The people tend to be less adaptable and work within narrow, well determined parameters and schedules of responsibility.

We have become accustomed to job satisfaction and job evaluation in production units, and the sales manager must apply the same concept to sales forces and design the organisation to permit it.

CHARACTERISTICS OF ORGANISATION STRUCTURES

12. Organisation structures. As an organisation grows it will become more complex and managers of expanding sales organisations will be faced with both vertical and lateral growth. The characteristics of organisation structures are that:

(*a*) the work to be accomplished is divided; and,
(*b*) it is arranged into manageable portions.

Sales managers faced with the task of arranging the work into manageable portions will, by a process of analysing, dividing, and arranging, undertake a system of *departmentalisation*.

By creating such an organisation, the manager of each department will carry out his tasks in accord with a senior manager so that each department may be co-ordinated. The number of departments reporting to the senior manager is a structural characteristic depending upon the manner in which the work is organised. For the senior manager, who may be termed sales manager, divisional manager, etc., these will be the number of departments that must be co-ordinated. From this derives the term *span of management* (*see* Fig. 12).

FIG. 12. *Span of management.*

13. Bases of departmentalisation. The creation of manageable departments or work groups is not an end in itself but a means of achieving objectives. As we have noted above (*see* 1) few organisational structures are created anew, but are usually the result of the reorganisation of existing structures. It is essential therefore that an organisation structure should be dynamic. Since all businesses are different the selection of a basis for departmentalisation will be dependent upon particular needs and objectives. There are, however, several well-recognised and accepted bases which are:

(*a*) function;
(*b*) product;
(*c*) customer;
(*d*) geographical;
(*e*) process;
(*f*) sequence.

14. Function. Function signifies activities which can be related, because of the similarity of the skills required in their performance. All businesses will have the primary functions represented in some form. Production (or distribution or operations), finance and marketing.

In particular relation to the process of selling we are concerned with those activities grouped together under the general heading of marketing. The way in which different types of selling organisation developed will be examined later, here we are concerned with these activities which will be found in most marketing organisations. The organisation may be departmentalised by: advertising; public relations; distribution; research and development; marketing research; product planning; sales force; statistical records; sales office; credit control, etc. A simple example is shown in Fig. 13.

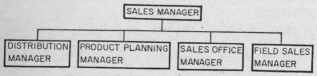

FIG. 13. *Simplified marketing organisation plan.*

15. Product. Organisation by product is a familiar system, when growth is accompanied by diversification of products. Initially all of a firm's product will probably go to the same type of customer but after growth different products may be produced for a wide range of customers. This will lead to organisation of the sales force under product managers and even into divisional vice-presidents for different products, as with the "3M" company.

In retailing, most stores organise departments under different product headings, e.g. hardware, food, furnishings, and the larger stores will have buyers for each type of product: *see* Fig. 14.

FIG. 14. *Organisation by production.*

16. Customer. Just as product diversification may be a basis for organisation, so growth of customers may produce a logical basis. Firms selling to both trade and retail, local authorities and heavy industry, motor trade and the oil industry will all distinguish the fundamentally different needs of each customer and employ specialist salesmen to deal with them, as shown in Fig. 15.

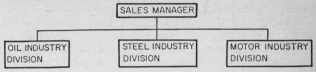

FIG. 15. *Customer oriented organisation.*

17. Geographical. Geographical organisation is logical where the area of sales coverage is too large for a single sales manager to be able to adequately administer, or where regional differences in the market dictate a more specialist organisation.

In large countries like the United States it is quite usual for a big company to be organised into geographical divisions for both the reasons given. In Britain it is more likely to be found in companies with a high density sales coverage, e.g. retail stores, supermarkets, breweries and some specialist direct selling companies.

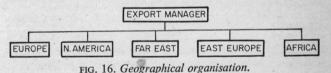

FIG. 16. *Geographical organisation.*

Organisation by geography, *see* Fig. 16, is frequently employed in exporting, where sales areas may be logically grouped together.

18. Process. The degree to which departmentalisation may be based upon a manufacturing process may depend upon its divisibility.

From the viewpoint of sales organisation it is rarely a practicable system although many of its customers may be organised in this way and the sales force should be made familiar with them, e.g. steel works organised into raw materials, smelting, rolling, tinplating, finished products, etc.

19. Sequence. Some departments may be organised on an alphanumerical basis of sequence. A section of a sales office may be organised to deal with customers in alphabetical or numerical order.

SPAN OF MANAGEMENT

20. How wide a span. Once the basis of departmentalisation has been determined, another problem arises—how many departments should be placed under the direction of one person?

The problem is often referred to as the span of control, but the term span of management is a more accurate description. The span of management is interconnected with the number of hierarchical levels in an organisation, and this, in turn, determines the length of the *lines of communication.*

It is a fundamental of organisation structures that if the span of management is increased, the lines of communication are shortened and vice versa.

21. Limitations of span of management. There are limits on the span of management which prevents unlimited development in the span. The hypotheses explaining a limited span are generally attributed to the work of three men, General Sir Ian Hamilton, A. V. Graicunas, and Lyndall F. Urwick.

22. Hamilton's recommendations. ". . . The average human brain finds its optimum work level when handling three to six other brains." The number of persons under one supervisor should be greater at the lower levels of the organisation than the number supervised at the top.

23. Graicunas' theory. Graicunas perceived that in establishing a satisfactory span of management a number of possible interactions might occur between a manager and his subordinates, *see* Fig. 17.

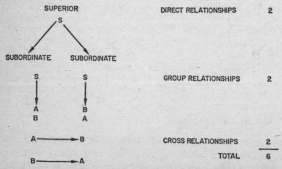

FIG. 17. *Graicunas' "Relationship in organisation".*

When a third subordinate, C, reports to S, one additional direct relationship is established between S and C; but seven additional group relationships are possible (AC, CA, BC, CB, ABC, CBA. BAC). Also four more cross relationships bring the total possible interactions to eighteen. (A→C, B→C, C→A, C→B).

Subordinate 4 possible interactions   44
,,   5   ,,   ,,   100
,,   8   ,,   ,,   1,080

The mathematical analysis of all possible relationships as propounded by Graicunas is significant for two reasons.

(a) *It underlines the intricate social interactions* between a superior and his subordinates.

(b) Understanding of the theory enables *the rate at which the interactions increase to be appreciated*.

Graicunas' theory did not envisage such complex interactions occurring on a daily basis, or even occurring at all. It rather suggested that at some time there would be one additional interaction too many—which would be "the straw that broke the camel's back". While it may be true that there will be a final addition which proves too much for the system, it ignores the idea that before that position is reached the manager's effectiveness will have deteriorated.

24. Urwick's principle. Lyndall F. Urwick offered as a reason for limiting spans of management the recognised psychological pattern that man has a limited span of attention. This concept limits the number of items that can be attended to by a person at any particular time. There will be other limiting factors, such as the amount of energy or the space of time available. Essentially, Lyndall F. Urwick recognised the variable complexity of the supervisor's job.

25. Diminishing marginal effectiveness. Economists have long recognised that the law of diminishing returns can and does apply to personnel. It is possible to adapt this concept of diminishing marginal returns to the span of management (*see* Fig. 18), for while it will be the extra unit in the span that will diminish the effectiveness, the marginal unit will be indistinguishable from all the other units. It is thus possible to suggest a rule for management's diminishing marginal effectiveness:

"Successive additions to a manager's span of control will, other things being equal, produce a diminished marginal effectiveness."

Diminishing marginal effectiveness is a limitation which must apply, otherwise "one man could control all". This phenomenon of a limited span of attention also explains the gradual limitations of effectiveness which Graicunas' hypothesis is unable to do.

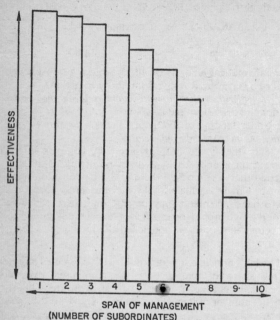

FIG. 18. *Diminishing marginal effectiveness.*

26. Importance to sales management. That sales management pays too little attention to rational spans of management is manifest in the many examples of firms with unwieldy spans. The existence of these organisations often arises from uncontrolled growth. The early successes of the company are naturally attributed to personalities in control at the beginning, but as the organisation grows these personalities aggregate subordinates until the span of management is unwieldy and frequently uncontrollable. Then rapid changes often occur resulting in salesmen being dismissed for poor results when perhaps the blame lies in management's lack of control, guidance and poor communication generally. The span of management should:

(a) enable sales management to enjoy face to face relationships with its immediate subordinates;

(b) allow adequate attention to training and guidance to individual salesmen; and

(c) permit optimum two-way communications to develop and be maintained.

EXAMPLE: A company founded in the late 1950s marketed paints, which were manufactured for it by a larger company. The firm grew essentially as a marketing organisation. In the early stages of growth the sales force was small enough to allow excellent relationships to develop between management and the sales force. Later the company sold its products nationally and the sales force grew rapidly. This led to the development of a pyramid structure with a sales manager, area sales managers, group leaders and salesmen. For some years the firm progressed reasonably well, until personalities began to exert themselves. The group leaders were abandoned and the entire country divided into two areas, each under a sales manager with approximately twenty-five salesmen each. The effectiveness of the sales force declined rapidly and with it grew insecurity. Training programmes were increased in frequency, more meetings were held and frequent dismissals and appointments became evident, leading to a general lowering in the standard of the sales force and a widespread frustration and dissatisfaction.

ORGANISATION STRUCTURES

27. Organisation charts. The purpose of an organisation chart is to illustrate how work is divided into manageable portions and allocated to the people in the enterprise. It can serve both as a blueprint of a proposed structure, or reorganisation structure, or a record of the way in which an enterprise grows. The organisation chart has five main uses.

(a) It is an aid to management in considering the way in which *duties are distributed* within the enterprise.

(b) During periods of changing conditions, it enables *rapid identification* of those jobs or personalities needing *modification*.

(c) It serves as a general guide to the way in which *duties are distributed* and assists the staff in their contacts with other parts of the organisation.

(d) At the induction of new staff it is a *valuable training document* to explain the organisation.

(*e*) It enables the *delegation of authority to be recorded* and responsibilities to be clarified and is a guide in any reappraisal of the existing structure.

An organisation chart is an important factor in planning the organisation structure.

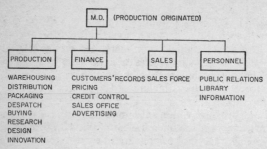

FIG. 19. *Marketing activities in a production oriented organisation.*

28. Production oriented structures. Before companies adopt an outlook which recognises the importance of the customer in the determination of its strategy, they tend to be production oriented.

In this form of organisation, selling and, in the wider context, marketing, are subordinate to the objective of optimising production. Product development will be related to the firm's experience and skill rather than to customers' needs. Technical research will be more important than market research and advantages will be derived from cost reduction more than by applying marketing ideas and innovations.

Personnel will tend to be oriented towards technical and production abilities, and marketing and selling skills are not held in high regard. Generally the senior managers will be drawn from production and promotion will favour technical people.

The structure will reveal the inherent policy. Selling as a function will be relatively unimportant, and salesmen regarded more as "order-takers" for production than the motivating force. Activities such as pricing, credit control, customer records, etc., will usually be under the financial function, and activities such as packaging, despatch, warehousing, under production. A typical production oriented structure is shown in Fig. 19.

29. Sales oriented structures. When the importance of the customer is appreciated in the context of maintaining full production,

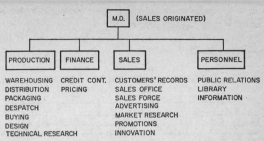

FIG. 20. *Marketing activities in a sales oriented organisation.*

the organisation tends towards a sales oriented structure, as in Fig. 20.

The abilities of the sales force receive wider appreciation and sales personnel will begin to have a stronger voice in the policy-making decisions of the company. Although engineering or other technical skills still dominate production and research, they are subject to consideration by sales management.

More activities will be controlled by the sales function, and greater emphasis on marketing research is evident. Advertising tends to be less information-biased and adopts a more dynamic note. The sales force grows in importance and frequently high-calibre salesmen are employed to "push" goods at customers.

30. Marketing oriented structures. The realisation that service to a customer is the central objective of the company will lead to a marketing oriented structure, as shown in Fig. 21. In this the entire policy of the company undergoes a change inasmuch as all strategy begins with consideration of customers and their needs.

Senior management will be drawn from marketing personnel and promotion will tend to favour marketing personnel. Practically all innovation will stem from marketing and consumer research and innovation will frequently be in anticipation of consumers' needs. Similarly distribution will be in accord with recognisable consumer needs and will be a dynamic instrument to create and maintain customers.

In adopting a marketing oriented structure a company is, by means of an influential marketing function, ensuring a consistent share, or even enlarging their share, of their market. The organisation structure will:

(*a*) enable production of products of a design and performance *in accord with customers' demand*;

(*b*) it will promote and distribute its production by *methods most suitable to dynamic markets*; and

(*c*) production, promotion and distribution will be based on *continuous marketing research*.

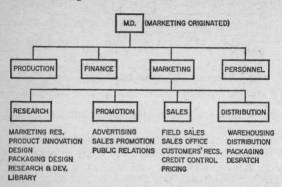

FIG. 21. *Marketing activities in a marketing oriented organisation.*

31. Product management. Many large corporations with extensive product lines prefer an organisation structure which allows a segregation of product lines, with separate executive responsibility for each line, *see* Fig. 22.

FIG. 22. *Product line organisation.*

Sales managers in this structure are often known as product managers, although where a number of related products are grouped together, e.g., soaps, cake mixes, he may be termed divisional managers. Du Pont uses the term "industry sales manager" for the post responsible for a specific product group.

In the product management structure, a staff of sales experts is organised for each line, providing the advantages of specialisation which produce these benefits.

(a) The customer develops greater respect for the company and its products due to the organisation's more intimate, specialised knowledge.

(b) The selling qualities of products are better understood due to concentration of effort.

(c) The sales approach can be specifically adapted to a particular type of product line and better training methods evolved.

(d) The sales costs are easier to budget resulting in better profits.

(e) Quotas may be determined more readily and results are easier to assess.

This type of structure produces a better balance of lines and assures adequate attention to each. Each customer receives equal attention while better field intelligence gives better research results.

32. Export organisation. The growth of exporting within a business will generally follow a similar pattern to that of other structures. A single person will, in all probability, begin by obtaining occasional export orders, which would be handled in the same way as home trade orders. Later when orders are more frequent responsibility will be delegated to persons within the organisation, although special problems of documentation and shipping may be left to banks and shipping agencies. Once orders grow in volume, an organisation will develop to administer them.

Initially an export manager will be appointed, although often it is only the delegation of responsibility for exports to a non-specialist. Once growth is achieved a more formal structure will be evolved. This usually goes through a basic stage—the basic export unit. This will consist of the following people.

(a) Export manager, who will be in over-all control. He may be responsible to the marketing manager, or to the managing director. His main concern will be for promotion of exports, including research, sales agents, selling and overseas travelling.

(b) Shipping manager, responsible for dealing with all export orders as they are received. He will arrange packaging, invoicing, documentation, shipping.

(c) Assistant to above who will undertake the routine office work, typing, records, progress chasing.

As the department grows it may evolve its activities apart from the home trade, and will undertake its own advertising, research, and product innovation. The development in organisation can be seen in Figs. 23 and 24.

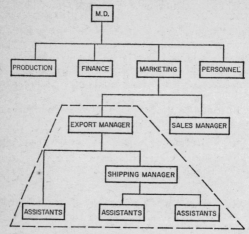

FIG. 23. *Basic export unit.*

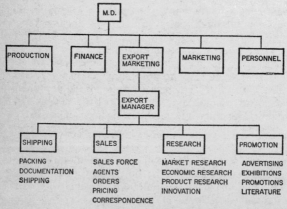

FIG. 24. *Advanced export organisation.*

ORGANISATION IN RETAILING

33. Flexible organisation. It is recognised that the oganisation structure of a store must be based firmly upon its specific needs in satisfying customers' requirements. Any retail organisation must be flexible enough to meet changes in environmental conditions. It is important to emphasise three points.

(*a*) Organisation tasks differ widely between small and large retailers.

(*b*) The organisation task is a continual task as conditions change and structures evolve to meet them.

(*c*) Good organisation in itself has a great value in store operations. It:

(*i*) defines function and authority of constituent units of the entire organisation;

(*ii*) determines and establishes responsibilities for the performance of objectives;

(*iii*) encourages a specialisation of effort and the advancement of skills in special aspects of the company's work;

(*iv*) expedites improved planning and obviates wastage of resources;

(*v*) accomplishes greater effectiveness of the total organisation; and

(*vi*) in a fast developing business, organisation charts become rapidly obsolete, frequent revision highlights all of the foregoing.

34. Organising the store. Departmentalisation is an important aspect of retail store structure. As small stores grow larger it becomes increasingly difficult for proprietors to maintain control over each line of merchandise, leading to:

(*a*) uneconomic use of resources, i.e. cash, capital and space.

(*b*) loss of actual, or potential customers through lack of merchandise, or the wrong merchandise.

Proprietors are less able to determine and correct weaknesses in merchandising activities as the store grows. The process of departmentalising begins with the division of various lines into a number of definite groups, each becoming a department with a person responsible for its operation within the corporate policy.

35. Organisation bases in retailing.

(*a*) *Smaller retail stores.* Typical organisation in a very small store is a two-functional system which separates merchandising operating activities.

(*b*) *Medium and large stores.* Most widely accepted is the four-functional plan, generally referred to as the Mazur plan (the system was set out in a report by Paul Mazur). The Mazur plan identifies four functions.

(*i*) Merchandising.

(*ii*) Publicity.

(*iii*) Operation (store management).

(*iv*) Accounting and control.

Figure 25 illustrates the plan diagrammatically.

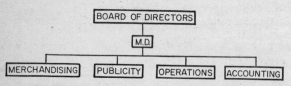

FIG. 25. *The Mazur plan for functional organisation of large stores.*

36. The Mazur plan.

(*a*) *Weaknesses.*

(*i*) The responsibility for profit performance remains with the managing director and cannot be logically delegated further.

(*ii*) The managing director is frequently overloaded and cannot devote sufficient time for planning strategy, and policy.

(*iii*) Responsibility for the selling function is broken down and spread over too many areas, including merchandising, promotion, operations and accounting. In this it resembles the production-oriented organisation, and lacks any one functional head.

(*iv*) There is often a tendency for buyers to become involved with aspects of the selling function in addition to their merchandising activities.

(*b*) *Sources of improvement.* Figure 26 illustrates ways in which some of the practical weaknesses of the four-functional system may be overcome. Essentially it divides responsibility for the planning and control functions. Planning and research are grouped together under an executive reporting direct to the managing director and aids in the determination of strategy. Control and co-ordination of the merchandising, promotion, financial control, selling, personnel and operations are the responsibilities to subordinate managers.

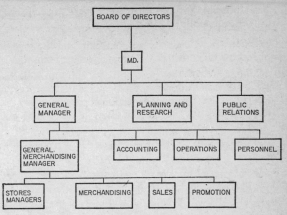

FIG. 26. *An improved four-functional system.*

37. Merchandising function. The merchandising function's responsibilities are based upon the buying and selling activities. These are to:

(*a*) interpret and accomplish the merchandising policies as determined by the board of directors and the managing director;

(*b*) co-ordinate the efforts of all departmental buyers and managers to ensure a unified image is presented to the consumers and public;

(*c*) ensure all relevant information on current trends, economic and market conditions is communicated to buyers;

(*d*) provide an objective for all buyers and ensure it is in line with company policy;

(*e*) establish and monitor a merchandise control system;

(*f*) plan sales promotions and ensure merchandise, publicity and selling efforts are co-ordinated; and

(*g*) provide maximum aid to buyers, by assisting in location of resources, and by planning and supervising comparison shopping.

38. Publicity function. It is the responsibility of the publicity function to:

(*a*) organise and be responsible for all forms of publicity, including advertising, promotion, window displays, excluding counter displays;

(*b*) plan and control sales promotion events, in co-operation with the merchandising function;

(c) be responsible for consumer and advertising research; and
(d) organise all public relations activities.

39. Operations function. The responsibility of the operations function, otherwise known as store management, includes:

(a) maintenance of the store, fittings and furnishings, and the purchase of store supplies, equipment and other property;

(b) security of the store and protection of merchandise;

(c) responsibility for personnel's safety, training and welfare; and

(d) responsibility for equipment and safety of workrooms and offices.

40. Financial control or accounting. With increased competition and difficult economic trends responsibility for the effective use of resources has expanded rapidly, and now covers:

(a) devising and maintaining satisfactory accounting records;

(b) merchandise budgeting and control;

(c) budgeting and control of expenses;

(d) development of systems to achieve control;

(e) planning, calculating and taking physical inventories;

(f) preparation of financial reports for general management;

(g) responsibility for abiding by and implementing all governmental regulations;

(h) insurance of property, personnel and merchandise; and

(i) safekeeping of all records.

PROGRESS TEST 3

1. What are the limitations of organisation? (4)
2. What are the common functions of business? (5)
3. What are the primary functions of a business? (5)
4. Describe the recognisable lines along which an organisation will grow. (6)
5. List some of the recognised bases of departmentalisation. (13)
6. What is the relevance of the span of management to sales management? (26)
7. What are the benefits of a product management structure? (31)
8. What activities comprise the basic export unit? (32)
9. What is the Mazur plan? (36)

CHAPTER IV

Sales Forecasting and Planning

PLANNING AND OBJECTIVES

1. Importance of planning. Planning is one of the basic elements of management and has a prime position inasmuch as it is the start of any sequence of management functions. Planning also has a profound effect upon other management and organisational activities.

Planning is unique among the elements of management as it may warrant no further action. A company may, as a result of investigation carried out to formulate plans, decide not to pursue the project further.

Implementing the results of planning is fundamental to the functions of organising, motivating and controlling. Planning activity is essential to effective sales management and may be directed in several ways, such as planning of:

(a) product mix;
(b) channels of distribution;
(c) sales force requirements;
(d) physical distribution, warehousing;
(e) promotional activities;
(f) control activities; and
(g) financial resources and allocations.

In addition to the responsibility for planning the operational needs as above, sales management will also determine objectives for the organisation, in accordance with the stated policy of the company.

(a) Corporate policy.
(b) Company objectives.
(c) Department objectives.
(d) Management objectives.
(e) Individual goals.

2. Objectives. Objectives may be defined as: "The recognisable and predetermined goals to which the efforts of the organisation are directed."

Any organisation must have clearly defined objectives to which it directs its efforts if it is to avoid meaningless progression of ideas. The statement of an objective is a recognition of a purpose and when applied to sales management it becomes the *raison d'être* of the function. Objectives must be clearly stated in writing and made known to those who will be involved in its accomplishment.

John F. Mee in his book "*Management Philosophy for Professional Executives*" writes "Before initiating any course of action, the objectives in view must be clearly determined, understood, and stated."

3. Characteristics of objectives.

(*a*) The essential characteristic of an objective is that it is *predetermined*, a fact which isolates it from the process of accomplishing the objective.

(*b*) An objective has to be *clearly stated*, generally in written form which assists in clarifying the objective and commits personnel to its accomplishment.

(*c*) Objectives should be *logical and attainable*, but they should serve to encourage the organisation to greater effort to ensure their accomplishment.

Objectives have four benefits to the organisation resulting from their statement.

(*a*) *Direction*: objectives by their definition provide a goal to which management and sales force will direct their efforts. They also serve to co-ordinate the efforts of the entire organisation towards common goals.

(*b*) *Motivation*: once an objective has been defined and clearly stated it serves to motivate sales personnel. Incentives in the form of extra commission, bonus, or promotion may be used in conjunction with functional and personal targets.

(*c*) Clearly defined and realistic objectives form a basis for the *control* process. Plans are made to achieve particular goals and the control element monitors the results to determine whether goals are achieved and if any modification to plans is needed.

(*d*) Objectives provide a basis for the *style of management*. Management by objectives avoids the alternatives of "management by reaction"—reaction to unforeseen problems. Applied to sales management, management by objectives provides the essential continuity and also flexibility which is both responsive to, and in anticipation of, consumer trends.

4. Control. Business organisations take many forms, single-man company, partnership, limited companies, corporations or nationalised concerns, but whatever form is taken, control will be vested in some authoritative person. The person in command will have the task of ensuring the accomplishment of the general business objective.

A manager's ability to effect the success of the business may be restricted by factors which will be outside the company's control in the short term. These are:

 (a) size and efficiency of the plant, or store;
 (b) amount of working capital;
 (c) efficiency and ability of management and staff;
 (d) reputation of the firm; and
 (e) quality and variety of its products or merchandise.

These are factors in the business environment which management may not be able to remedy in the short term; indeed, it may take a number of years for a business to change. Not only physical factors, such as plant size, or capital, but also psychological phenomena are involved. A department store wishing to upgrade its quality and attract consumers in higher income brackets may find considerable consumer resistance for a long period of time.

Management can however take swift remedial action if it has established the correct organisation structure to ensure that the element of control is effectively fulfilled. While control cannot ensure that profit will automatically and rapidly follow, it will contribute greatly to the accomplishment of this aim.

5. Determining objectives. The determination of objectives is a management planning task and like all management decisions must be based upon reliable information.

Sales management's task in determining its objectives is a particularly onerous one, for it is dealing with factors which are largely outside its control:

 (a) consumer trends;
 (b) economic trends;
 (c) general level of investment; and
 (d) social influence.

It is a field in which change may be brought about very swiftly, by exploitation of new resources, technological discoveries, technical innovation, and in the retail and distributive industries, trends in traffic control, out of town shopping, discount stores, etc. The increasing technical complexity of many products means that the development period is both long and costly, while the rapid increases in knowledge will, by advancing more rapidly, overtake the development time and cause early obsolescence. This is very clear in the development of military aircraft, but it is equally true, at the other end of the scale, in terms of ladies' fashion. Sales managers faced with these problems have to answer the questions, "what will consumers want in X years that they don't have now, can we profitably make and market it, and for how long will they want it?"

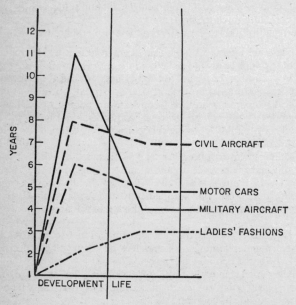

FIG. 27. *Sales prediction graph*.

Before a company commits itself to producing a product involving prolonged research, high development costs and perhaps a limited life it has to attempt to predict the level of sales and the length of time in which the product might be sold. Figure 27 shows a possible pattern.

A new and automated plant, necessary if ever-increasing labour costs are to be contained, is usually very expensive and generally it is not very adaptable. A company has to predict future sales in order to justify the investment.

6. Setting the objectives. Planning must do everything possible to ensure that once objectives have been determined, everything that is done assists in their realisation. In the small manufacturing company or the small store, objectives are likely to be simple and capable of easy communication to small numbers of staff. In the larger companies, whether industrial or retail, the organisation structures will be complex, and communications to the many activities contributing to the objective will involve management co-ordination and control. If the objective is to plan for greater profit, other lesser goals may also be involved, including:

(a) corporate growth;
(b) diversification of business;
(c) new product innovation;
(d) entry into new markets;
(e) increasing the share of existing markets; or
(f) economic integration by merger or acquisition.

7. The role of planning. Having set objectives, the role of planning is to decide how far they can be realised with existing resources. A sales manager's decision to enter a new market, to export, to introduce a new product, will require examination of:

(a) existing sales force;
(b) manufacturing capacity;
(c) financial resources; and
(d) advertising, or other promotional expenditure.

Sales management has a high degree of responsibility for planning, whether the objective is essentially a "sales" objective, or whether it is a production, or financial objective. Since the revenue of a company ultimately derives from some form of sale, the volume of sales is all important in judging the practicality of the objective.

A company has certain fixed costs which will be incurred whether the company sells or not, and they will not rise with increased sales. Other costs will be variable and will increase according to the amount of production or sales that are carried out, labour, transport, packaging, materials, etc. This will be seen by reference to the break-even chart in Fig. 28.

The fixed costs $(A–A^1)$ remain constant and start well above the point at which sales commence. The variable costs $(B–B^1)$ start from the line of the fixed costs and increase in proportion to

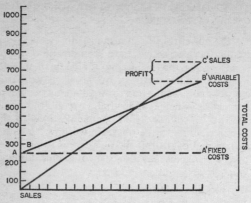

FIG. 28. *Break-even chart.*

sales (C–C¹). As sales increase the line crosses the fixed and variable costs; this is the break-even point, at which costs and revenue are equal, but beyond that point profits increase rapidly since the fixed costs are spread over a larger number of units of production.

Sales planning will endeavour to predict sales so that the level of profitability can be predicted. It will also predict the life of the product as the longer a product can be sold the greater the spread of the costs over production. The prediction of sales in terms of quantity, price and time is essential to setting realistic objectives and fundamental to the planning function.

FORECASTING

8. Sales forecasting. The central problem of forecasting sales arises from the need to predict consumer actions in buying goods at particular prices. A simple answer is that forecasting cannot do this accurately, but it can, by means of forecasting techniques, provide an indication of results.

It is important to make it clear that while emphasis is placed upon the importance of predicting consumer trends, forecasting is equally applicable to goods used by industry, to produce consumer goods or to make other manufacturers' goods: these are known as producers' goods.

It should be clearly understood that a fundamental difference exists between consumers' goods and producers' goods.

(a) Consumers' goods provide satisfaction in themselves: a television, a car, a washing machine, food or furniture.

(b) Producers' goods are a derived demand and are not wanted themselves, but for the use they have in making something else, ultimately consumer goods. A lorry is wanted only as a means of transporting other goods or materials; a lathe, to produce tools or other articles.

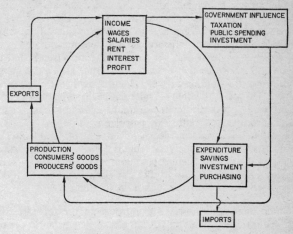

FIG. 29. *Simplified economic cycle.*

The essential point is that the strength of the economy and therefore the likely trend in purchasing is most clearly and readily indicated by consumer trends. If consumer spending on washing machines is rapidly declining, manufacturers of washing machines will need less of the materials and tools they use to make them. An understanding of this relationship between consumer goods and producers' goods is important to every sales manager and salesman and would save the latter, especially, a great deal of wasted effort in trying to persuade buyers with the wrong reasons. Figure 29 is a simplified model showing the relationships between consumption and production.

9. The time period of the forecast. Sales management's decisions on what can be sold, in what quantities, where, how, and when, have to be quantified in terms of time if they are to be of operational value. One may phrase the question as follows: "During what period of time will quantities of particular goods be sold in specific areas and at specific costs?" This will also need to include:

   (*a*) costs of promotion;
   (*b*) costs of sales; at
   (*c*) predetermined prices.

Once these answers have been determined, a projection of costs and income can be made. This, predicted as a break-even chart, will be essential for a valid control system. Clearly since all answers depend upon being able to predict the quantity of goods to be sold, the first step in the process is to determine that.

The object of the forecast is to predict future trends and the further into the future the forecast can be made the more helpful it will prove in planning the general and specific direction of the business. However, the dangers inherent in this type of prediction became very apparent after the dramatic economic changes that resulted from the escalation of petroleum prices in 1973. This sudden change showed very clearly how one factor could upset the established trend. Obviously the length of the forecast period will depend on the type of business and companies engaged in manufacturing products for day to day consumption, such as foods, will generally suffer less from such sudden changes.

10. Three forecasting areas. The purpose of the forecast is to predict the future trends but it should not be a static period. Forecasts should continually search ahead, and in this they

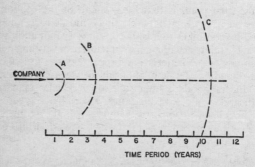

(A) IMMEDIATE FORECAST
(B) LONG-TERM OPERATIONAL FORECAST
(C) LONG-TERM OBJECTIVE FORECAST

FIG. 30. *Three forecasting areas.*

resemble a radar scanner before a ship, *see* Fig. 30. In order of time they are:

(*a*) long-term objective forecast;
(*b*) long-term operational forecast; and
(*c*) immediate forecast.

11. Long-term objective forecast. There are two aspects underlying the long-term objective forecast. It:

(*a*) makes no pretensions to accuracy, and
(*b*) seeks to indicate the general changes which are likely to occur in the future which could have a fundamental effect upon the company's operations.

To understand fully the company's objective it is necessary for the company to examine critically and systematically its capability, experience and marketing knowledge. In this critical analysis the company's long-term objective forecast is synonymous with its strategy, dealt with in Chapter XVII. Factors which may influence a company's operations are:

(*a*) population changes,
(*b*) economic trends, and
(*c*) technical innovation.

The main reason for the long-term objective forecast is to remind the company's executives of the purpose for which they are in business, and it should alert them at the earliest moment to forces which may cause changes to be made to their declared objectives. An example may be taken from the tobacco industry—the correlation between the smoking of cigarettes and the incidence of lung cancer. Is public opinion so affected that a cigarette manufacturer should diversify his products? This is a typical response to the findings of the long-term objective forecast.

12. Long-term operational forecast. Shortening the time scale to a period that is limited by the ability of executives to act on information determines how far ahead the operational forecast should scan. The manner in which industry has evolved has determined that operational forecasts are longer; Fig. 31 shows this.

The stringent regulations surrounding the automobile industry make forecasting very difficult. An example of the problem of forecasting demand is the way in which many millions of pounds may by spent over a period of several years in the development, pre-production engineering and promotion of a new model such

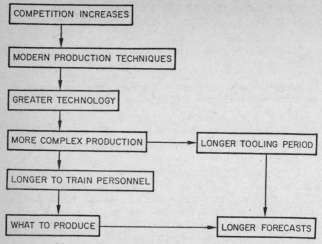

FIG. 31. *Development of longer operational forecasts.*

as Ford's "Capri". Built into the basic design was a capability for development along predetermined lines to enable the car to remain competitive for many years. The impact of and the results of energy policy will be to oblige manufacturers to reconsider many longer-term plans which could make it difficult to cover the "tooling-up" costs of the car.

Similar situations have existed in the aircraft industry, where attention is attracted because of the sheer size of the project. Nevertheless the rapid obsolescence of products is a factor all companies have to consider today, and long-term operational forecasts have to be modified from time to time. The degree of modification will depend to a large extent upon the way in which the project was initially conceived. A rigid commitment to a single objective may result in drastic re-appraisal of production, or marketing plans, whereas a plan into which a degree of flexibility has been built may permit of alteration without too much upheaval.

Modern industrial complexes have differing degrees of flexibility. At one end is the clothing industry in which the high level of operative skill and low degree of specialist machinery allow easy changes, to the other end of the scale, where the chemical processing plants are built to produce one product only and are wholly non-adaptive.

industry = process production = growth in investment = less ability to reallocate resources

13. Commitment to objectives. Under circumstances of rigid commitment to an objective, intuitive judgement has to be replaced by realistic appraisal of possible effects. The period of the operational forecast may be determined as the time required from the moment of decision to the time when the decision is finally implemented. To accomplish this, sales management must forecast objectives as shown in Fig. 32.

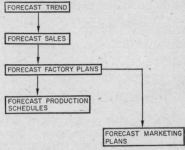

FIG. 32. *Objectives forecast.*

14. Bases of information. The amount of information needed to fulfil the task of forecasting objectives will vary according to the nature of the business but can be broadly classified into groups; economic and social.

(*a*) *Economic information*:
  (*i*) trading patterns;
  (*ii*) structure of the industry;
  (*iii*) use of resources;
  (*iv*) trends in population; and
  (*v*) level of income.
(*b*) *Social information*:
  (*i*) consumer trends;
  (*ii*) buying habits; and
  (*iii*) distribution of income.

15. A determined time period. Any major sales plan must relate the forecast to a determined time period, e.g. five years, and will concentrate on those areas likely to affect the company. Thus a company venturing into a new export market will wish for information on:

(*a*) the general growth of the economy;

(*b*) the increase in consumer spending;

(*c*) the development of various markets, e.g. food, consumer durables, specialised markets;

(*d*) the patterns of economic change, economy built on extraction industry, manufacturing, etc.; and

(*e*) population changes.

Only after careful collection of information, analysis and interpretation, can predictions be made enabling the forecast to be prepared that will assist in management's decision making. Figure 33 shows the bases of information.

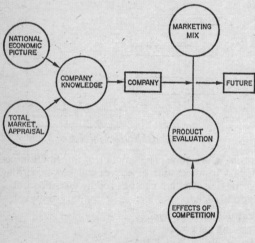

FIG. 33. *Bases of information.*

16. Short-term or immediate forecast. The immediate forecast is concerned with the period during which executives will be taking decisions continually, on a day to day basis. The control element will be most effective if the objectives have been clearly and precisely defined even if they have to be flexible.

Information for the short-term forecast can be obtained from salesmen's reports which will be of aid both in compiling the forecast and in modifying it during the duration of the forecast period.

It is usual to consider a period of one year divided into quarters, or months, to be the logical length for the forecast. The manner in which the forecast is calculated varies but *four* systems are most used:

    (*a*) extrapolation;
    (*b*) economic forecasting;
    (*c*) market research, and
    (*d*) sales-originated information.

17. Extrapolation. Extrapolation is a forecasting technique that is simple to use since it relies merely on the projection of past trends, as in Fig. 34. If a company by examining its past sales can find a yearly increase of 10 per cent then it can reasonably predict that the next year is also likely to produce a 10 per cent increase.

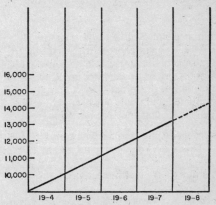

FIG. 34. *Extrapolation of next year's sales at 10 per cent p.a.*

Extrapolation can be effective and reliable in those areas where changes take place slowly, e.g. population growth or anticipated growth in demand for electricity. As a technique for forecasting sales it has limitations. Competitive activity is unpredictable, as new products may influence market trends. It has also to be understood that wholly dissimilar products may influence each other's sales. A revolutionary design in electric cookers may attract consumers to buy them, and the money spent might have been used otherwise, on cars, clothes, holidays, etc. Unexpected hazards may also influence sales, such as strikes, natural disasters, or international problems which interfere with supplies.

18. Economic forecasting. For the immediate future economic forecasting can be a guide to the expectancy of sales. It cannot be more than an indication of a trend and has the serious disadvantage that economic trends are difficult to determine in the short-term.

There are some areas nevertheless that can give the alert sales force an indication of likely trends. A salesman selling to the building trade may be alerted to a downward trend if inflation leads the government to slow down growth and cut back on capital projects. It follows that the converse will also apply; when the economy begins to recover, business will grow.

19. Market research. As an aid to forecasting in the short-term, market research has to be directed accurately at selected areas. A firm may use questionnaires to extract answers to specific questions.

20. Sales-originated information. The sales force is a valuable aid to forecasting trends in the short-term, and the information can be kept up to date and revised quickly in response to change.

Salesmen are required to submit a monthly sales report which will give information on actual sales achieved and this information will be collated and used for extrapolation. In addition they can provide the following information:

(a) What orders do you expect next month?

(b) What orders do you anticipate within the following two months?

(c) Information on competitive activity.

21. The year as a measurement. There are advantages to be gained from using the year as a period for the forecast. Most government reports, statistical surveys, etc. normally extend over months and years. The national budget also uses a year as a base and affects many business decisions.

Problems can arise from a commitment to the period of one year, especially in areas where the operation is known to extend over more than a year. It is disadvantageous to break these operations into periods of a single year.

(a) *New product launch.* The high investment in promotion at the launch of a product, to ensure an acceptance in the shortest possible time to achieve maximum profitability, will almost certainly entail a loss for the first yearly period.

(b) *Forecasting the results of export marketing* will certainly need to extend over a period longer than one year.

22. Elements of sales planning. Sales management's first responsibility is the planning and control of the physical selling effort, to ensure that company objectives for sales and profits are met. In order to achieve these targets, sales management:

(a) directs and controls *field selling activities*;

(b) determines the *channel of distribution* that will accord with customers' needs, and organises the physical distribution in accordance with company policy; and

(c) ensures that these activities are achieved *within the limitations of the financial budgets*.

23. The planning task. In any sales organisation, the sales force will be important in accomplishing objectives. Whether the sales force is predominantly a *selling* as opposed to a *merchandising* operation will not greatly change sales management's responsibility for its effective use. A great deal of planning and control will be needed to make sure that individual salesmen carry out their tasks efficiently and at an acceptable level of cost. In order to do this sales management's planning task will also include:

(a) setting up practices for sales reporting;

(b) determining standards of performance for sales personnel;

(c) evaluating sales results achieved against planned performance;

(d) establishing a system of statistical analysis and evaluation of sales; and

(e) establishing an adequate feedback control system to alert management to any necessary change in plans to correct deficiencies.

24. Objectives of sales planning. We have seen how forecasting will endeavour to predict likely trends. Planning is concerned with analysing the forecast and interpreting the results into operational requirements. It will be concerned with information and communication needs as much as it will with financial and sales results, in order to provide the necessary controls. Its objectives are:

(a) sales communication;

(b) sales reporting;

(c) statistical control, and

(d) review of manpower performance.

These essential management tasks will be dealt with more fully in Chapter XII.

PROGRESS TEST 4

1. "Implementing the results of planning is fundamental to the functions of organising, motivating and controlling." Discuss. **(1)**

2. Why is planning activity essential to effective sales management and in which directions may the activity be directed? **(1)**

3. What are the characteristics of objectives? **(3)**

4. What fundamental difference exists between consumers' goods and producers' goods? **(8)**

5. Define the three forecasting areas and describe their essential points. **(10–13)**

6. Sales management's first responsibility is the planning and control of the physical selling effort. How does sales management achieve these targets? **(22)**

CHAPTER V

Recruitment

FUNDAMENTALS OF RECRUITMENT

1. The problems of recruitment. Any organisation which takes on new staff is, to a varying degree, going to entrust its business operation to an unknown quantity. Inevitably there will, from time to time, be errors of judgment which can lead to difficulties with staff, customers, production, finance or some other area of the business operation. It is usual for staff to be selected on some logical basis of examination and acceptance, and on joining the firm they will normally be assigned to a responsible member of the staff for training or guidance, until such time as they are judged to be competent and reliable.

Sales people generally work in some degree of isolation. Even workers in a retail store will be left alone with customers at some stage or other, and commercial representatives, or outside salesmen, will by their jobs' requirements, be outside the company's immediate supervision. How effectively they will look after the company's interests, implement the company's policies and bring credit to their company will affect the relationships between the company and its customers. An untrustworthy salesman, or one who is insufficiently trained or otherwise unsuitable, can in a very short time undermine the jealously guarded goodwill that has taken many years to develop.

2. The cost of recruitment. The cost of training salesmen ever increases and apart from the basic money costs there is the cost of the wasted opportunity to have done something else.

EXAMPLE: A Scottish firm advertised nationally for sales representatives to sell industrial adhesives. Following the advertisement the company interviewed forty-three applicants and selected twenty-four. These were all recruited and sent to the company's regular induction training at a hotel in Scotland. For a week the group of trainees were introduced to the company's products, methods of manufacture, the way they were used, selling methods and documentary system. On the last night the management gave a party, and in due course the new salesmen left for their territories with supplies of stationery, samples, etc. The firm had paid the men their first week's wages, the cost of the week at the hotel, travelling expenses and the cost of samples. In addition it had borne the cost of taking company executives from their regular work to instruct the trainees.

After a month, of the original twenty-four only eight remained in the company's employment. Of the sixteen who had left, one had thrown away his samples on the return journey, and two had immediately resigned on their return. The others had been found to be quite inadequate and had been sacked.

We may enquire what was wrong with that company's recruiting, for the example given was not too dissimilar to many other recruitment campaigns it conducted over the years. Did the fault lie in:

(a) selection?
(b) training?
(c) general conditions of employment? or
(d) the trainees?

Whether the fault lay with the trainees or not is irrelevant, because they had been selected by the company and therefore were assumed acceptable. If blame could be laid at any specific point, perhaps it should be with top management for devising a system so open to fault, and for failing to recognise the faults and taking action to remedy them, even if it meant "shutting the stable door after the horse had bolted".

3. Limitations of recruitment. We are here concerned specifically with the recruitment of sales personnel, and if they differ to any great degree from other types of personnel it is because, as stated above, the company relies upon them so heavily and that they generally work away from supervision.

Selling is essentially a contest between two protagonists, the seller and the buyer, and in this we are dealing with aspects of human relations. It has been written elsewhere that in recent years there has been a general decline in the quality of service in a wide section of retail stores. This is the result of several interacting forces, including the better prospects in other forms of employment; the reluctance of many store managers to respond to calls for job enrichment, e.g. the introduction of variety in work and the increases in responsibility to create added interest in a job; the quite rapid change to less personal forms of selling which has reduced a skilled job to little more than shelf-filling in many stores. It might be argued that these forces have occurred because of the quality of labour available, rather than the reverse. That is a debate that will have to be argued elsewhere.

4. Technology and the need for salesmen. In the operations of the outside sales force, trends in certain trades have also detracted from the more personal aspects of the job; merchandising of much grocery and similar goods has also made the salesman's task more akin to shelf-filling. But, in the fields of industrial selling and exporting in particular, the needs for intelligent, self-motivated salesmen with an ability to sell grow ever greater. Economic pressures, the greater freedom of merchandise movement on an international scale, mean ever-increasing competition, and that means a need for better salesmen. The growing technical complexity of many articles also creates a need for salesmen with greater abilities for absorbing information and, even more important, the ability to pass it on to the customer.

5. Recruitment and human relations. There have appeared in the national press in recent years a glut of advertisements calling for salesmen to sell a wide variety of everyday products, and stressing that "only graduates need apply". Unfortunately many of the positions advertised are so mundane as to be incapable of holding the interest of high-calibre men or women for more than a few weeks. The job that offers "fantastic earnings", "outstanding opportunities", or similar, appears too frequently to be fulfilling the needs of employees.

It is fair to say that any sales force can only be as good as the manpower that it is built from. Sales management must recognise the limitations of both the job upon the man, and the man upon the job. If a job is dull, repetitive, too over-burdened with form-filling and without prospects of self-achievement, then it will fail to hold the go-ahead, self-motivated man; while if the man is basically lacking in confidence, age, education or skill, no amount of inducement—stick or carrot, threat or commission—will create an adequate, never mind efficient, salesman.

Selling as an exercise in human relations imposes its own limitations on what constitutes the right type of personnel. On the whole people feel happiest when they are with others whom they can recognise as being of similar status or background to themselves. It follows that a salesman has to be selected with one eye upon the sort of people he is going to have to sell to. A well-known chain-store, with a high reputation for quality and cleanliness, has undertaken a policy of carpeting its stores, because it was found that the "super-cleanliness" and the wide expanse of uncluttered flooring was indeed turning away a certain group of people who simply felt ill at ease in the store; a feeling of "we shouldn't be here".

Sales representatives have to reach a certain stage of maturity if they are to be accepted easily. However well educated and well trained a man might be, if he is to deal with older men he is at a disadvantage if he is too young. They either create a feeling of paternalism in the older customer that is evidenced by a polite condescension, or else they rouse feelings of blatant hostility derived from being "told their jobs by younger men".

6. Objectives of recruitment. The recruitment of sales personnel may be left to sales management to achieve, or in the larger firm may be undertaken by a personnel department, working with sales management. However the firm goes about the task it must undertake it in a logical way. The task will be undertaken with four objectives in mind. These are:

(*a*) to recruit personnel for the sales force;

(*b*) to select personnel by a recognised procedure;

(*c*) to bear in mind the training and operational needs of the firm; and

(*d*) to offer the job at a suitable remuneration.

7. Determining the sales objectives. In order to achieve these objectives the firm will determine its needs in exact detail.

(*a*) What will be the goals of the sales force?

(*b*) What degree of technical or specialised knowledge will be required?

(*c*) Does the firm have sources of information from which training can proceed?

(*d*) Can the firm so arrange the selection process that:

(*i*) the company will be able to assess the qualities of the applicant; and

(*ii*) the candidate will be able to obtain the correct ideas of the company?

(*e*) What procedures will have to be established to ensure that the new salesmen will receive their training on a continuing basis?

(*f*) Will the remuneration offered be satisfactory in terms of fulfilling the applicant's needs for:

(*i*) security;
(*ii*) status; and
(*iii*) self-fulfilment?

8. Matching man and job. In determining its needs for information about prospective salesmen, the company will decide the range of details it needs to assess the potential of each candidate. For an industrial salesman on a specific territory the following would be typical.

(*a*) Knowledge of the industry.
(*b*) Knowledge of the products.
(*c*) Knowledge of the customers.
(*d*) Technical skill.
(*e*) Experience in the particular trade or other trades.
(*f*) Type of customers previously called on.
(*g*) Knowledge of the territory.
(*h*) Any particular achievements.
(*i*) An indication of turnover.

The degree of technical knowledge that a prospective salesman should have will depend upon the type of job that he is to do. If the job necessitates a high degree of involvement with the customers' problems, then it is essential that the salesman be equipped to deal with them. Any shortcoming in this direction will have to be met by company training, both initial and on a continuing basis. It will also be affected by the ability of the company to give technical assistance to the salesman on a specialist, functional basis. In this respect a salesman operating near the head office, or works, will be in a better position than one working in isolated territories where a greater self-dependence will be called for.

9. Importance of experienced recruitment. In recruiting a force of salesmen, no amount of logic and systematic selection can replace the experience gained by matching the fundamental principles with practice obtained over a number of years. A sales manager in the clothing trade, after the personnel department had sent him yet another systematically selected candidate for the East London territory, remarked knowingly, "What we need is a good Jewish boy", and he was right. Recruitment of an adequate sales force requires five essential actions.

(*a*) A careful job analysis, to determine the exact nature of the job and its responsibilities.

(*b*) The preparation of a job specification to ensure the requirements of the man to fill it.

(*c*) Creating sources of supply of candidates.

(*d*) Developing a system of selection by means of application forms and interview techniques.

(*e*) Establishing an induction scheme to introduce new recruits to the firm.

THE SELECTION PROCESS

10. Job analysis. A complete study of a job constitutes a job analysis. In determining the needs for a salesman it will involve an examination of the job's purpose and objectives. What effect does this particular job have upon the over-all organisation?

A salesman's job is to sell the company's products or services. The purpose of the job is to provide a man or woman to visit customers on a regular basis; introduce them to the company's products or services; ensure they understand what they are for, and by finding out the customers' needs, show how the product or service can help them, either to make more profit or to solve a problem; obtain an order; ensure satisfactory delivery; ensure continuing customer satisfaction with the company. Undertaking a job analysis will involve:

(*a*) investigating the exact work to be done;
(*b*) the nature of the work;
(*c*) the optimum way to do it;
(*d*) essential characteristics of the person to do it;
(*e*) experience needed to do it; and
(*f*) the specialist training that is needed.

The completion of the job analysis will enable the sales manager to prepare a job specification, describing the particular nature of the work to be accomplished.

11. Job specification. The specification for a job is not information that can be borne in mind by the interviewer. It is an essential description that has to be documented and circulated to all those involved in the selection, appointment and training of the recruits. It is a specification that has to be written in considerable detail and must adequately cover all eventualities of the job. It will also assist in determining the placing of the job in the existing organisation structure and in making known the authority and responsibility pertaining to it. This will involve:

(a) the new appointment;

(b) the territory covered;

(c) the way the work is to be accomplished;

(d) hours to be worked;

(e) types of customer;

(f) salary, expenses and any commission;

(g) extent of paperwork, orders, sales reports;

(h) on-territory training and supervision;

(i) car allowances or vehicles supplied;

(j) special training events; and

(k) special problems relating to the territory.

Prepared in this way the job specification has several uses; it is an aid to filling vacancies by recruiting new personnel to the organisation, establishing the sort of tests best suited to locating personnel, and as an aid to transferring existing staff. It also establishes the limits to a particular job, by making clear the academic needs for the job and also by fixing the ideal age restraints, e.g. if it is found that a man of thirty will be the most suitable age, then the parameters can be established as being between twenty-eight and thirty-two. The job specification is used at the interview to check on the interviewee's suitability; any deficiency will be marked on the application form, and if the person is selected, allowances made in training to correct the deficiency.

12. Finding personnel. In Britain there is a fairly well established system of bringing the job-hunter and the job vacancy together. There is a well-established national press enabling an advertiser to bring his vacancy to the attention of a very wide range of people. Since the national newspapers also tend to have fairly well-defined customers, it is possible to choose a paper that is almost certain to be read by the kind of man the firm decides it needs. In this respect the process of selection has already begun. It is possible to predict with reasonable accuracy the sort of person who reads, say, *The Financial Times*, *The Times*, *The Daily Telegraph*, *The Economist*, and so on.

The jobcentres and employment offices operated by the Manpower Services Commission offer a Professional and Executive Register. Professional, managerial and sales people interested in seeking fresh employment can have their names placed on the register and will be notified of any vacancy that occurs.

Other sources are within the company itself, particularly the very large companies, by means of trade or professional journals and associations. Greater use is made today of the facilities offered by technical colleges and universities to bring jobs to the attention of likely candidates.

13. The selection process. It is important to remember that no matter how much thought, creativity and planning has gone into the design and production of a product or a marketing system, its eventual success will depend upon the way the sales force can get customers to buy it. If a company has an ineffective sales force, it will not create satisfied customers. The success of the sales force will in turn reflect the skill of the company in its selection and subsequent training of its sales personnel.

The responsibility for selecting personnel and their training lies in three directions in the medium to larger company; in the smaller company the three functions will probably be represented by a single person, or a management team.

(*a*) *Sales management* will be responsible for determining the needs of the sales force and for creating a job specification.

(*b*) *The personnel department* will be responsible for advertising the vacancy and for processing the applicants, at least at the stage of the final selection.

(*c*) *General management* will have a responsibility for the policy that enables people of sufficient calibre to be engaged.

14. Recruiting from within the company or not. The basic choice in selecting personnel for a sales force is between:

(*a*) selecting *existing* company personnel; and

(*b*) selecting *new* personnel from outside the company.

Obviously the first choice is limited by the size of the company, but where it is possible it offers the advantage of known and proven people with a knowledge of the company and its policies, its products and its customers. A person who has spent some time working in the sales office, despatch or some other department closely allied to the sales force will have a sound understanding of the manner in which the company handles the orders once the salesman has obtained them. This type of background is especially useful in developing export salesmen where a knowledge of the documentation and procedures for shipping is invaluable. But it is necessary that the person selected has the other qualities so necessary for a salesman.

15. The risk in recruitment. By selecting a person from outside the company one is undertaking a certain risk, which will be reduced as far as possible by the interview as a part of the selection process. The person may bring a wide knowledge of operations in similar companies which will be a distinct advantage in some areas, and may limit training to an introduction to the company's own particular working methods.

Training is an extension of the selection process and should be borne in mind when interviewing applicants. Any selection must be based upon a precise knowledge of the job to be done.

The interview is the focal point of the selection process and it is essential that this should be organised on a team basis. More than one interviewer should share in the selection process, particularly of sales personnel, where experience and ability is so open to interpretation. The advantages lie especially in the greater judgment it affords and, equally important, it gives the applicant a feeling of greater interest by the company and thereby stimulates his confidence in his prospective employer.

16. The bases of selection. There are a variety of "tools" which the interviewer or the panel of interviewers may resort to. These include:

(*a*) application forms;
(*b*) applicant's references;
(*c*) the initial interview;
(*d*) intelligence and aptitude tests;
(*e*) physical examinations; and
(*f*) final interviews.

Each of the "tools" is largely complementary to the others and no single one will accomplish as much as a sensible use of them all. Much of the doubt that is expressed about the selection process as a satisfactory means of recruiting personnel largely derives from interviewers differing as to the real objectives of the job. They also derive from a lack of real concern in interviewing, and disagreements on what constitutes the essential qualities needed to fill the job vacancy. It arises as well from divergent opinions as to what the information collected really means. These are faults in the interviewer and not the system, and can be largely eliminated by correct preparation and by clear objectives.

17. The application form. Application forms vary considerably and probably reflect the confused feelings of the interviewer more than the real needs of the task. They can vary between the non-existent, the interviewer makes "notes" on a convenient sheet of paper, to the "fully comprehensive", a document so offensive as to put off any sensible, self-respecting candidate.

The application form, like all the "tools" of selection, will be a means of obtaining necessary information. It will be drawn up after examining the job specification, and will seek answers to specific questions relevant to the job. Generally the form will require basic information about:

(a) name of the applicant and address;
(b) age/date of birth;
(c) education/qualifications;
(d) brief description of applicant's experience in work;
(e) applicant's leisure activities and interests;
(f) applicant's objectives; and
(g) present and expected salary.

The basic purpose of the application form is to aid in the elimination of the obviously unsatisfactory applicants as early as possible, and obviating the need to process more applications than are relevant. The larger forms will also include a variety of questions dealing with parentage, religion, health, military service, living conditions, etc.

18. Character. A salesman must be reliable and have a good character; he will be representing the company and to the customer he will be the company. His character has to be sound, honest, loyal, reliable, and he must have a likeable personality without becoming fawning or shallow; above all he must command respect. To achieve the correct degree of respect from his customers he will be well dressed, clean and evidence of the good company he works for.

The salesman's attitude of mind is important, manifesting itself in drive and determination and showing confidence derived from knowledge and a belief in his skill as a salesman.

It would be useful if all this evidence of character could be understood from a fairly brief discussion, but even the most experienced interviewer would find such a judgment decision impossible. The decision has to be supported by references from people who know the applicant better. It is usual to request references which may be from personal friends who know the applicant's character from long association, or from business contacts who will have an appreciation of his business standing.

19. Personal qualities of salesmen. The successful salesman is a man who can recognise the kind of person with whom he is dealing and who can vary his attitude with individual buyers.

This is not the same as being "shallow", a term not infrequently applied in accusation of salesmen's methods.

Occasionally a person, no matter how responsible a position he commands, fails to impress. Other people, while occupying quite a subordinate position, bring a dignity that commands respect. Salesmen frequently have to command a hearing by force of personality and this is often helped by their physical characteristics. However, it is obvious that so far as physical characteristics are concerned, there is little the individual can do beyond making the most of what he has.

It is not intended in this book to comment upon other sales manuals that set criteria for the height of salesmen. Certainly average height is better than extremes of short or tall, but it is equally certain that a man cannot write off a possible career because he is under the impression that he is the wrong height. In practical selling there are many examples of very successful salesmen among the very short and the very tall.

However, all salesmen must pay attention to their bearing, erect carriage and straight-in-the-eye manner for it is imperative to avoid any suggestion of shiftiness. Many people, by their manner, ask to be snubbed and they usually are. A salesman must be well dressed—a poorly-dressed person suggests poor products that cannot be sold—and must by his demeanour suggest that he is respectable, competent and not to be played with. The interviewer should consider the following aspects that are held by competent and successful salesmen.

(a) Pleasing personality.
(b) Physical energy.
(c) Nervous energy.
(d) Ability to eliminate worry.
(e) Capable decision-making.
(f) Self-faith and confidence.
(g) Knowledge of the goods.
(h) Self-reliance.
(i) Moral courage.

To a person considering selling, the list may appear impressive or perhaps pretentious. Does the average salesman really need to make such an introspective examination? For the average salesman, the answer is no. However, for the man who wishes to rise beyond the average and who aspires to eventual management, or at least greater responsibility the results of such a consideration can be of great benefit.

20. Interviewing. Faced with decisions about the suitability of an applicant for a job as a salesman, the interviewer is being asked to forecast the likely behaviour of a stranger in a certain job situation. A person interviewed during a period of, perhaps, an hour at the most will not necessarily display the same temperament or personality that he would during a hard day's work. In assessing the applicant's suitability for a job, the interviewer is faced with a psychological problem of determining his likely behaviour pattern under unknown conditions.

To achieve any kind of success, the interviewer must attempt to create a situation in which the applicant will behave as normal. This will then serve as a sample of what he might do in the future under operational job conditions. The aim of the interview is to educe the applicant's background as far as possible in the time available.

The conduct of an interview is very important; it should never become an interrogation in which the interviewer is waiting to catch the applicant out. It should be the interviewer's aim to establish as soon as possible a relationship with the applicant that will help him to talk freely and without fear. The experienced interviewer will not fire questions, or cut short an explanation, but rather will endeavour to steer the conversation to the topics that will be relevant and important, and to ensure that the information is obtained as quickly as possible.

Interviews can be supplemented by the use of aptitude tests. In these it is possible to put the applicant in a controlled situation where his behaviour can be assessed and compared with the results of other applicants. Aptitude tests usually take the form of problems which call for mental effort of a type likely to be encountered in the work situation. The tests will give pertinent information which can be combined with the information received from the personal interview.

21. Understanding the applicant. It has already been stressed that it is difficult to get a clear picture of an applicant's experience and life in a short time, but it will assist if we can get to understand his motivations.

Any person is subject to two broad influences in life; Rousseau summed them up as nature and nurture, the influence of the social environment and the influence of the family might be a more modern interpretation. Our applicant will have been influenced to no small degree by his family, home and upbringing, and also by the community in which he has lived. The way in which the applicant has developed and achieved his personal goals will reveal a great deal about his likely behaviour in the job.

Generally in life it is possible to choose, within limits, how one will behave. It is possible to be helpful and to carry out allotted tasks cheerfully and to the best of one's ability; or to be unhelpful and to avoid carrying out the tasks. The first behaviour pattern would suggest that the person is responsible and can be expected to behave in a mature and reliable manner which will suit him to a job requiring self-control and discipline. The second attitude would suggest a person not likely to accept responsibility and who will be unreliable.

22. The applicant's environment. By learning about the applicant's background we may understand him better and know what are his motivations. If a young person is successful in school, either academically or in sport, he will have shown a willingness to accept the situation imposed upon him and to have adapted positively to it. The achievement of status as a prefect, or captain of a sports team of the school will also be evidence of a hard working character. His working career will be evidence of the way he had adapted to a different situation. If the applicant has had four jobs in ten years, each with a greater responsibility, it may be supposed that he had worked hard and been capable. If he has had four jobs in two years, it may imply a personality not capable of adapting and lacking in positive drive.

The environment in which a person grows will exert a strong influence upon him. People who have spent their lives in one community will have absorbed much of the influence of that environment. All communities have their own standards of conduct and behaviour and a member of one will develop an attitude to life evidenced in the way he looks at events. If the applicant has spent his life in one type of community, it will have influenced his opinion and attitudes, and the interviewer will wish to determine whether they will be useful or harmful in the job.

23. Physical examinations. Selling is a hard job, calling for great stamina and good health. The salesman is likely to be out in all weathers, and the provision of a car is no help in today's city traffic conditions. Long hours, and the need for physical energy as well as mental effort often sustained over long periods, means that a salesman has to be physically fit.

24. Final interviews. The applicants will have been subject to two sorting processes by this time.

(*a*) Applications will have been sorted and some rejected.

(*b*) Application forms will have been assessed after the initial interview and some rejected.

Following the physical and aptitude tests the applicants will be subjected to a final interview. The purpose of these is:

(*a*) to enable a final assessment of each applicant to be made; and

(*b*) to supply additional information about the job to the applicants.

25. Profile charts. The information compiled from the application forms, initial interview, tests etc., will be correlated to give a profile of each applicant. It is usual to construct the profile in five aspects. These are:

(*a*) impact on others;
(*b*) natural abilities;
(*c*) motivation;
(*d*) adaptability; and
(*e*) qualifications.

For each of these five aspects points will have been awarded and registered on a profile chart, as shown in Fig. 35. Notes will have been entered as well, and the interviewing panel at the final selection each given a copy. After the applicant has been given the

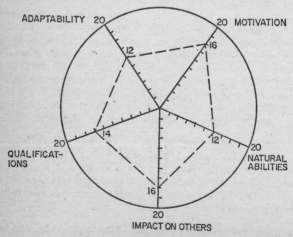

FIG. 35. *Applicant's profile.*

opportunity to ask questions, and has also provided answers to any points, the final selection will be made.

The successful applicant will then be recruited into the sales force, and a programme of training will have been prepared on the basis of his needs.

PROGRESS TEST 5

1. The recruitment of sales personnel is a task of sales management. It is undertaken with four objectives in mind. What are these? (6)

2. When considering remuneration, what other aspects of the applicant's needs should be considered? (7)

3. Distinguish between job analysis and job specification. (10,11)

4. Responsibility for selecting and training personnel lies in three directions. What are they? (13)

5. You are considering the appointment of a salesman. What personal qualities would you look for? (19)

6. During an interview it is necessary to create a situation in which the applicant's behaviour pattern is likely to be as near usual as possible. Which techniques can be employed to put the applicant in a controlled standard situation? (20)

CHAPTER VI

Training

SALES TRAINING

1. Type of training. How much training a salesman will need depends a great deal upon the type of selling he is called upon to do. However, the training will be based on two areas, which are:

(*a*) selling techniques; and

(*b*) technical knowledge.

The skilled salesman is the person who is accomplished in both these areas.

With the development of merchandising techniques, the need for personal skill in selling may well be less important than it was formerly. A product may be "sold" to the consuming public through the media of mass advertising and promotional campaigns, and the extent to which a product is available in the shops depends on distribution skills. The shopkeeper will stock the product because he knows that a demand will have been created for it by the manufacturer's advertising campaign. However, this practice is by no means universal: industrial selling and export selling, which can be of consumer goods or industrial goods, both call for a high degree of skill in selling and a deep product knowledge.

2. Product knowledge. Product knowledge is of the greatest importance no matter where the selling process occurs; department store, buyer's office or industrial plant. The only difference in knowledge will be in the degree, depth and the length of time taken to acquire it. Any training programme therefore must begin with an understanding of two essential points.

(*a*) How much will the customer need to know about the products?

(*b*) How do we ensure that our salesman has sufficient knowledge to inform him:

(*i*) about the product; and

(*ii*) about the company's policies of selling, administration and distribution?

Before any salesman can be entrusted with direct responsibility for his territory, or his department, it is necessary to make sure he fully understands the company's corporate policy, the sales function's operating policy and the company's administrative policy.

3. The basis of training. Until a few years ago, industrial and, to a great extent, commercial training was nearly completely informal in its concept and practice. The recruitment of new sales personnel in particular owed very little to principles of training, and relied more on experience.

A new salesman, whether a "commercial traveller" or within a store, was expected to work alongside a more experienced worker, usually older. This person might be disposed to train a newcomer or not, depending upon whether he regarded the newcomer as a threat to his position or not. Even if the older worker was disposed to pass on what knowledge he could, this was nearly always without a formal plan, and would depend largely on what circumstances dictated.

After a period of working with the older person, the new salesman would be expected to try himself, under supervision, and if he did not make too many mistakes he would be sent to work on his own.

Most of the knowledge that the new salesman acquired was empirical rather than theoretical and quite often he would know next to nothing about the company or its objectives, simply because the occasion to be informed never arose. The change to a greater appreciation of the sales function in industry, the mobility of workers, and the stronger competition have all created a need for formal training of sales personnel.

PSYCHOLOGICAL BASIS OF TRAINING

4. Understanding the recruit. In the training of sales personnel it is necessary to emphasise the reasons why a job should be learned and to see the job from the recruit's point of view as far as possible. Few people learn well if they can see no cause for doing so.

To help in understanding the recruit, and so make the training relevant to him, it is possible to hypothesise about his reasons for becoming a salesman. He may:

(*a*) regard his job merely as a means of making money;

(*b*) like a job where he is familiar with the standards to which he should work; or

(*c*) have no other options for making a living.

It is easy to over-simplify the salesman's reasons, however; they are likely to be a lot more complex than those presented above. For example:

(a) salesmen are unlikely to devote all their time to consider-ations of expected income as the only reason for their working;

(b) the standard of performance expected by the company may not be known to the salesman as many salesmen are allowed to develop their own level of sales performance; and

(c) the salesman may contemplate many other forms of employment; indeed it is likely he will have already done other kinds of work before taking up selling.

When the recruit's reasons for becoming a salesman have been determined, it is then possible to ensure that the training is presented from his viewpoint to maximum effect.

In training salesmen we are concerned with learning and in particular how to develop motivation of the sales force both during and, more important, after their training period.

5. Motivation in training. A new salesman can be expected to start his job with enthusiasm. He will probably have been through the process of recruitment, interview and selection, and will be pleased that he was finally selected from many. His enthusiasm may also be derived from the various aspects of the job, such as new products to learn about, new company car, and a new en-vironment in which to work.

People new to selling, perhaps from a commercial or industrial background, will find a new degree of freedom in their work, as they will be largely working on their own without constant supervision. All these factors combined will induce the salesman to create a new image of himself; this might be as a "top sales-man", perhaps eventually sales manager or even a tycoon of industry, all providing prestige, security of employment, en-hanced status and income.

During the first few weeks he will be strongly motivated by these complex and shadowy goals; prestige, security, income and status. It is only later when he finds that he is still only a part of a much bigger organisation, obliged to conform and perhaps find-ing difficulty in producing business that his motivation will decrease.

How long will a salesman devote himself conscientiously to his work and towards goals which have become remote and in-distinct? Before long he will find his customers increasingly difficult and his work a task rather than a challenge. He will begin to avoid work, take days off, or otherwise seek to escape supervision.

To keep a salesman enthusiastic over a long period, especially when he may be breaking into a new territory, ways have to be found of strengthening his motivation.

6. How to augment motivation. Having recognised that the initial enthusiasm of a new salesman will begin to weaken when he is up against the realities of his job, it becomes necessary to augment his motivation and sustain his effort. This will depend on:

(*a*) the type of selling, status of the salesman and the degree of remoteness from the firm;

(*b*) the salesman's own concepts of his job and vague individual goals, being replaced by a precise valuation of the knowledge and skills he needs to acquire; and by

(*c*) the provision of precise goals to replace his own shadowy idea of becoming a "top salesman".

Precise goals are important for they are within the salesman's ability and will be reached fairly easily and quickly instead of being too remote. They will also be personal and related exactly to his job and role within the organisation.

Therefore, one purpose of training is to augment motivation by a process of replacing remote ideas with precise goals and supplying precise performance standards instead of indeterminate levels of achievement.

7. Skill. Any training programme must be based upon an appreciation of two distinct kinds of learning process. These are:

(*a*) *gradual development of skill* in a simple operation, which is characterised by a slow but steady improvement in performance; and

(*b*) *rapid intuitional understanding* of a problem which allows a swift advance in performance after a few attempts.

Any training programme will include situations in which both these forms of learning will be apparent so that a salesman's performance will be characterised by periods of rapid improvement with periods when performance is more slow.

The development of a salesman's skill, either in total or in part. e.g demonstrations, will result from his practising the same actions over and over again. This practice integrates the habit-patterns formed for each part of the selling process. With different customers different parts of the selling process will be accentuated and will become clearer. Eventually, after repeating a particular pattern of selling with many customers, the salesman will be adept in all areas. The presentation will become smoother when all the parts are integrated into the selling process and as the understanding between the salesman and the customer increases, the salesman will feel more confident.

A successful training programme must allow for adequate practice. This can be accomplished by sending a new salesman with an older salesman who is experienced in training. Sometimes it can be accomplished by providing facilities for the salesman to practise with a tape-recorder.

Providing a salesman with a chance to learn is difficult in selling as there is always the danger of upsetting established customers. Many customers will be sympathetic to a new salesman and not put too much pressure upon him, but not all will, and even the best customer when busy cannot be expected to provide facilities for other companies to practise. A means has to be devised of overcoming this difficulty, for without practice skill cannot be acquired. Often a salesman can spend the first few weeks going around firms which are unlikely to become customers. This has several points of merit. First if the firm is unlikely to become a customer, for whatever reason, it is not so important to avoid upsetting them. Secondly they will probably throw more arguments against the products than convinced customers and this is good practice, making for a quick mind and a development of skill. Against this practice, however, it must be said that too many refusals, particularly if accompanied by a lack of sympathy or even rudeness, will be a big disincentive to a new salesman.

8. Training salesmen. Sensible training will result in:

(a) greater efficiency of performance;

(b) the promotion of conformity to company regulations and the reduction of errors which might lead to customer complaints;

(c) by creating better job performance; increased earnings and more job satisfaction;

(d) a more stable sales force with less turnover in manpower; and

(e) a reduction in the amount of supervision required.

The quality of training will depend upon the extent to which the company is anxious to protect its position in the trade. Some firms provide little or no training and expect a high turnover on the sales force. In turn they offer high remuneration to those who can achieve it. If a company has a low regard for training and cannot see any profitable result obtaining from it, little training will result. Companies with a reputation to defend will usually have a high regard for training and this will often be reflected in the care given to selection of personnel.

ORGANISED TRAINING

9. Centralised and decentralised training. Centralised training is carried out solely by the department responsible for training. It does not always follow that personnel are sent to a single store or centre for training, although this frequently happens, but often that a central department devises the training programme. Some companies engaged in industrial selling will recruit salesmen at various times through the year and provide on-the-job training to begin with. Later all the new salesmen will be sent to head office or some other centre for formal training on a centralised basis.

Decentralised training is growing in favour at the expense of centralised training. It relies upon new salesmen learning their jobs by performing under operational conditions and under the care of some responsible person with a knowledge of local conditions. The system has much to commend it so long as the essential training in the products performance, methods of manufacture, and matters relating to company policy can also be given on the decentralised basis.

10. Training programmes. Most companies have formal training programmes of varying complexity which consist of:

(*a*) *initial* training; and
(*b*) *continuous* training.

Often the salesman will receive simple initial training amounting to little more than an introduction to the firm. A visit to head office, interview with the sales manager, a tour of the production facilities and a meeting with head office staff whom he might later need to liaise with. He will then return to his territory and proceed to undergo on-the-job training with an area manager or even another salesman. Later when he has learnt some of the problems and the basic needs of the job he will be given intensive training at a centre in all the facets of his job. This will last a week or two and training will continue on a periodic basis after he returns to his territory.

11. Consumer training programme. A typical training programme for a company selling consumer products would be as follows.

(*a*) *Initial induction training*. The trainer must first identify the duties of the salesman so that a suitable training programme can be arranged. The trainer must be aware of the knowledge and skills to be acquired and the attitude of the salesman which is required. The salesman will be given sufficient knowledge to begin working until a training seminar can be arranged. He will learn about:

(*i*) the company's background, including its history, organisation structure, policy towards customers and merchandising policies;

(*ii*) the merchandise;

(*iii*) documentation;

(*iv*) care of stock and samples;

(*v*) selling techniques, such as methods of contact, types of customer, presentations, closing the sale, company policy on payments and credit.

(*b*) *Continuous training*. Following the induction training the salesman would receive additional training as a part of a regular programme throughout his period with the company. This would consist of:

(*i*) operational training;

(*ii*) motivating sessions; and

(*iii*) training seminars.

All the training would have as its basic aim the upgrading of the salesmen's knowledge and the creation of a strongly-motivated sales force.

12. Industrial training programmes. The needs of industrial selling require a comprehensive knowledge of the industry in which the salesman is selling, in addition to a knowledge of his own products. He also needs to know about the products of his competitors and those products which may be used as substitutes. The training programme will need to provide a wide range of training including:

(*a*) the company's policies;

(*b*) the use and application of the products;

(*c*) the methods of manufacture;

(*d*) administrative procedures;

(*e*) the nature of the industry in which the company operates; and

(*f*) competitive products.

13. Training seminar. A typical training seminar might be along the following lines.

(*a*) *Day 1.*

(*i*) Welcome to the seminar.

(*ii*) Introduction to senior executives and functional heads.

(*iii*) Tour of works and production facilities.

(*iv*) Discussion on the aims of the company, its policies and plans.

(*v*) Introduction to the product range.

(*vi*) Syndicate discussions on the products.

(*b*) *Day 2.*

(*i*) Lecture on the problems of the industry.

(*ii*) Detailed lecture on the construction/composition of the product or products.

(*iii*) Salesmen's practice on the use of the products.

(*iv*) Group exercises about the products, followed by discussion.

(*c*) *Day 3.*

(*i*) Introduction to selling techniques.

(*ii*) Lectures by sales manager and senior salesmen on their particular techniques.

(*iii*) Salesmen practise selling techniques with tape-recorders followed by discussions, and criticism.

(*iv*) Test questions set for salesmen on product knowledge, use and selling techniques.

(*d*) *Day 4.*

(*i*) Introduction to main competitive products, their use and price.

(*ii*) Methods of combating competition.

(*iii*) Commission and bonus details.

(*iv*) Distribution, ordering, accounting procedures.

(*v*) Issue of stationery, sales manuals, literature and samples.

(*vi*) Winding up by sales manager.

PROGRESS TEST 6

1. What are the two basic forms of training, the accomplishment of which will lead to better motivated salesmen? **(1)**

2. There are two distinct kinds of learning process that must form the basis of any training programme. What are these and how may they be employed in a training programme? **(7)**

3. What is the difference between centralised and decentralised training? **(9)**

4. What should be the basic aims of a training programme? **(11)**

CHAPTER VII

The Role of Salesmen

IMPORTANCE OF SALESMEN

1. Salesmanship. It is a truism of selling that the process consists of:

(*a*) sales management; and
(*b*) salesmanship.

We can postulate that the sale is not complete until the goods are in the hands of the user and are giving satisfactory service.

The salesman carries the ultimate task of discovering the customers' needs, interpreting them into clear needs for his company's products or services and ensuring that the goods delivered provide continuing satisfaction.

2. Influencing customers. The salesman fulfils one of three important forces which influence customers:

(*a*) advertising;
(*b*) experience of customers; or
(*c*) the sales force.

Advertising will inform the customer of the existence of the company and its products or services, and then motivate him to want them.

Experience of the customers will stem from satisfactory service enabling satisfied customers to influence other would-be purchasers.

The sales force, by their skill in display and presentation, will effectively introduce the product to would-be customers and will so create new customers by making new sales.

3. Basis of salesmanship. The term selling, implying the making-over of a product or service in exchange for money, has many unfortunate connotations. Past experiences of some consumers have caused fear and resentment to surround the implication of "salesmanship".

That this is unjustified need not be argued, but firms have had to recognise it, and there have come into use many euphemisms for salesmen: consultants, advisers, counsellors, etc., even the common term "representative" is being frequently used to disguise a salesman's real occupation. Selling is a matter of dealing with people and the salesman will be effective if he:

(*a*) acts from common sense; and

(*b*) has a basic understanding of psychology.

A basic knowledge of psychology helps the salesman to understand why people behave as they do. In particular he must have an appreciation of:

(*a*) the mental processes;

(*b*) the elements of motivation and people's needs;

(*c*) the way in which people are likely to react to propositions; and

(*d*) the psychological bases of leadership.

To fulfil the needs of salesmanship, the salesman must also understand completely the business in which he is occupied. He must:

(*e*) be familiar with the business;

(*f*) comprehend the policies of his firm;

(*g*) be aware of the policies of his competitors; and

(*h*) endeavour to create a harmonious relationship between his company and their customers.

It will become apparent that while some men will have natural advantages in selling over others, good salesmen are nevertheless created by training.

4. Satisfactory service. Satisfactory service is the most important element in the completed transaction.

Many so-called "super salesmen" who are able to boast of being able to sell anything fail to realise their high pressure selling results in dissatisfaction. If you work hard and sell an article to a customer that is *not* what he really wants, then he will not be a satisfied customer. He will not become a repeat buyer. A reaction begins:

(*a*) the customer will not buy again; and

(*b*) the salesman has to create further dissatisfied customers.

In the distributive industry:

(*c*) the retailer will not buy more of that product from the wholesaler;

(*d*) the wholesaler will not re-order from the manufacturer; and

(*e*) the manufacturer may eventually cease production.

The product has failed, but worse, no goodwill has been created for further transactions.

5. Dependency upon the salesman. Advertising's job, in general terms, is to promote knowledge and acceptance of the product to potential customers. The salesman has the task of personally introducing the consumer to the product, thus ensuring completion of the cycle from knowledge to satisfaction of the consumer's needs.

We can, in the selling process, talk in terms of "pushing" and "pulling", whereby advertising "pushes" goods to consumers and the sales force "pulls" goods into consumption. A good salesman–customer relationship is vital to the completion of a sale. The necessity for the success of this relationship is clear when it is realised that the impression the customer receives from the salesman will usually form the opinion he has of the company. This in turn may affect the customer's decision on buying the product.

6. Example: point of sale. The manufacturers of hedge-trimmers may spend considerable investment in time and finance in perfecting a machine. They will spend further effort in marketing activities, i.e. market research, advertising, publicity, distribution, transport costs, to put the machine into widespread stockists. If the machine is not "sold" in the correct manner, the entire process collapses.

A customer goes to a merchant for a hedge-trimmer. He asks the assistant's opinion of hedge-trimmers and requests information. The assistant mentions a brand by name but makes no move either to take the customer to the machine, or the machine to the customer. The customer gives the assistant every opportunity to introduce the machine, but the "salesman" remains apathetic and negative. The customer leaves.

It is important to separate the two aspects of getting goods into users' hands and getting them sold. Until they are the responsibility of salesmen, everything that has happened to the goods is *distribution*. The selling does not begin until the salesman takes over and confronts the customer.

In the past the salesman was either:

(*a*) an order-taker; or
(*b*) a persuader.

Today he has to become more of a consultant in his dealings with customers who are becoming more knowledgeable, and less credulous. The modern salesman, if he is to be successful, has to more than equal his customer in knowledge.

MAXIMISING SALES EFFICIENCY

7. Selling by proxy. The manufacturer who recognises his dependency upon the salesman will have a more competitive position, and a healthier growth. There are basically two types of selling.

(*a*) Speciality selling, selling direct to customer.

(*b*) "Commercial travelling", selling to a distributor before the product reaches the final consumer and users (industrial selling).

In some circumstances salesmen may be called upon to do both types of selling, e.g. in a builders' merchants, but it is more usual for salesmen to specialise in one form only. It is necessary to determine the differences, otherwise poor results only will be achieved, and as an example we will take the selling of floor coverings in a firm of contract carpeting specialists.

8. Speciality selling. Consider selling it directly to a customer—speciality selling. What advantages do we think will make him buy? We can make a list of benefits for an imaginary carpeting:

(*a*) hardwearing and durable;

(*b*) simple to lay and match;

(*c*) no underfelt needed;

(*d*) good range of colours;

(*e*) easy to clean; and

(*f*) washable.

There may be many other advantages that can be interpreted as being of direct benefit to the customer, appealing as satisfaction of his needs. He wants an easy life, comfort, as few worries as possible. No mention has been made of the price; the benefits must be made to *appeal* to the customer—any price is a disadvantage.

9. Selling to intermediates. Consider now the distributor, retailer or contractor. The requirements of the distributor are fundamentally different to the consumer/user. The customer is interested in benefits related to the satisfaction of his needs. The motivation of the distributor is increased profits and enhancement of his reputation.

Having decided what type of selling is appropriate to a

particular customer, we can then turn our attention to the manner in which our products should be presented.

The manufacturer must ensure that the salesman is familiar with important selling points of the product and can present them to the customer.

This is what is meant by "selling by proxy".

Recognition of the need to sell by proxy enables manufacturers to determine characteristics necessary in their choice of salesmen. They must:

(a) be able to give good service to the customer;

(b) possess an accurate and full knowledge of their products; and

(c) know and understand their customers.

If the customer who enters the shop, or the buyer in a distant part of the country who meets the salesman, is to form the correct assessment of the company, its policies and products, the salesman has to meet exact requirements in knowledge, character and training.

10. The salesman. There exists in every sale two variable factors, who are:

(a) the seller, or his representative; and

(b) the buyer.

Any study of the effectiveness of salesmen as part of the science of business and distribution must include to a large degree a study of these two factors.

We have already determined that there are two basic types of salesmen, the commercial traveller and the speciality salesman. The latter may be either employed in travelling to customers, or in a shop or other place of business awaiting the customer. In either case the personality of the salesman will influence the type of selling he undertakes.

It must be understood that between the extremes are all types of salesman, and sometimes a man or woman may progress from one to the other.

A person may be a successful commercial traveller but lack the single-mindedness and aggressiveness to be a successful speciality salesman. In the simplest form the salesman may be little more than an "order-taker"; this can apply to either the "traveller" or to the shop assistant.

Having obtained business the salesman's task is to retain it. He will therefore adopt a different attitude towards his customer.

11. Retaining business. In retaining business the main task of the salesman will be to make it easy for the customer to keep his business with the company. A buyer will, on the whole, tend to keep buying from a known and trusted supplier, rather than risk changing. A salesman can ensure that customers are retained and service maintained by:

(*a*) a good relationship;

(*b*) quantity, quality and grade of the orders; and

(*c*) familiarising himself with delivery details.

By attention to detail a salesman may succeed in changing a buyer's source of supply, or having a specification altered. The salesman's success is also his weakness. If the buyer has changed once—he can change again. The salesman must be alert to competitors' activity and defeat it by diligent attention to detail.

12. Intensive and extensive selling. It is possible to determine two types of selling, intensive and extensive.

(*a*) *Intensive selling* is employed where a product is high priced and of limited appeal. With intensive selling the salesman must under-take a high degree of preparation and it calls for a high order of salesmanship.

(*b*) *Extensive selling* is necessary where the product appeals to a wide range of people. In this type of selling the product is usually low priced and the salesman cannot profitably occupy more than a few minutes trying to sell.

13. Two-way representation. Within the structure of the selling process the salesman occupies an important position, interposed between customer and company. Communication of information, knowledge and opinion between customer and company is of vital importance in the salesman's work. Figure 36 shows the two-way tasks of the salesman and the intricacies of his responsibility.

EXAMPLE: A manufacturer of large valves for oil refineries had difficulties in finding a material for coating the steel casings of the valves to resist certain chemicals. The salesman from a manufacturer of plastic coatings was informed of the problem and undertook to find a solution, using, of course, his firm's products.

The salesman was given two of the steel valve casings to experiment with. He took the valve casings to a shot-blaster for cleaning and priming. Following this the salesman arranged for his company's chemist to coat and experiment to determine the suitability of various alternatives.

After a few weeks the salesman was able to return the valve casings together with his recommendations. Once it was approved by the company the salesman assisted in the setting up of the plant.

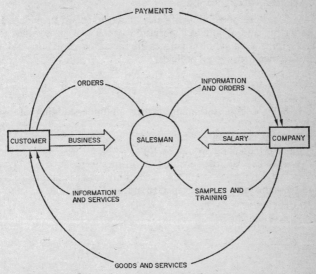

FIG. 36. *Salesman's two-way communication model.*

At other times a salesman may find himself having to advocate changes proposed by his company even when he believes they will cause dissatisfaction to his customer and ultimately lose the company business.

14. Management's responsibility. Salesmen, by the nature of their job, must work away from their company, home and family. An expert salesman may find it particularly onerous to be away for very long periods at a time. It is claimed that because a salesman works alone he is unable to express opinions and confide problems to family or firm.

Good sales management will be aware of this problem of isolation and will make provision for the sales force to meet at regular intervals. On these occasions the salesman will make contact with colleagues, management and production and will be able to discuss problems and collect information from the experience of others. Management will endeavour to assist the salesman to enjoy successful personal salesmanship by developing:

(a) proper attitudes;
(b) knowledge; and
(c) practical application.

It will be a responsibility of sales management to provide alert leadership and adequate supervision which will ensure that the sales force as a whole operates in the same direction and in accordance with agreed policies.

PROGRESS TEST 7

1. Why does a salesman require an understanding of psychology? **(3)**

2. What is the difference between "pushing" and "pulling" as applied to the selling process? **(5)**

3. How can salesmen ensure that business is retained? **(11)**

4. What is management's responsibility towards salesmen, and how can the salesman be helped to success? **(14)**

CHAPTER VIII

Salesman's Knowledge of Goods

UNDERSTANDING SALES

1. The need for knowledge. Developments in self-service, mail order and other non-personal selling techniques have led some observers to believe that the time of well-informed creative personal selling in the distributive and retail industry is past. It is suggested that we are in a period of impersonal selling.

However it can easily be shown that, with only a few exceptions, the salesman's knowledge of the goods he is employed to sell is of paramount importance. He is employed for the purpose of *selling* and his purpose and objective will be to persuade someone to *buy*. The question of whether the person will buy will depend upon the prospective customer's consideration of the goods he is offered—are they suitable for use or for reselling?

To be able to face his prospective customer with confidence the salesman requires a high degree of merchandise knowledge. This depends upon his own ability to equate his needs for merchandise knowledge with:

(*a*) the need for *sources of information*; and
(*b*) his selection of *selling points*.

2. Industrial selling. The salesman has to understand that all industrial goods are a *derived demand* and that buyers are interested in what the products will do. His knowledge must be related to this and he must recognise that dissimilar products may serve the same ends. To improve a bad floor surface, a customer could:

(*a*) lay a new cement screed;
(*b*) lay granolithic concrete;
(*c*) lay an epoxy-resin screed;
(*d*) lay quarry tiles;
(*e*) lay thermo-plastic tiles;
(*f*) lay linoleum;
(*g*) paint with polyurethane; or
(*h*) lay a wood-block floor.

The salesman's knowledge must also include costs, duration of work and the advantages and disadvantages of each type.

3. Retail selling. With the exception of self-service stores, vending machine purchases or mail order sales, a salesman–customer relationship is of the greatest importance. Without the salesman's knowledge there can be no accomplishment in retail selling. The knowledge of the salesman is required in:

    (*a*) an understanding of customer motivation; and

    (*b*) a knowledge of the merchandise he has to sell.

4. Extent of product knowledge. A wide knowledge of his products broadens the scope of the salesman to sell them, enabling him to:

    (*a*) satisfy customer needs;

    (*b*) innovate on product uses; and

    (*c*) assist customers to innovate.

When a salesman's knowledge extends to a critical analysis of his competitors' products, it becomes his best defence against competition, enabling him to present a rational counter-argument. This knowledge must extend beyond the narrow limits of his products alone, and can be represented as a model as in Fig. 37. He will know about:

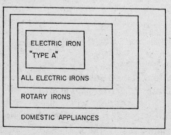

FIG. 37. *Product knowledge model.*

    (*a*) competitive products which are *closely similar*;

    (*b*) all products which although not closely similar could compete as *substitutes*; and

    (*c*) all products which may compete for *customers' scarce resources*.

SALESMAN AND BUYER

5. The buyer's knowledge. The buyer keeps his job by his ability to buy only those goods which can be resold at a profit, or used to profitable or economic effect by the user. He must have the widest possible knowledge of the types of merchandise or materials he handles. A good buyer is:

(*a*) aware of what his company is interested in, or needs;

(*b*) aware of what new development will benefit his company; and

(*c*) one who recognises that it is essential for the buying department to welcome new ideas.

6. Meeting the buyer on equal terms. Both the buyer and the salesman use their product knowledge to gain advantages over the other. If the salesman is ignorant of his products he will be competing on less than equal terms. In many cases, particularly in industrial selling, the selling process becomes a contest in which the two protagonists (buyer and seller) aim to overcome each other's arguments, and whoever gains the advantage over the other will be better able to create a good deal for himself.

Therefore the salesman, and to a lesser extent the buyer, should prepare himself by finding out about the product and the conditions under which the selling will take place.

7. Reciprocal information needs. The buyer and seller need to know about each other. They both have to know about the industry with which they are involved and they have a reciprocal need to know about each other both as individuals and as companies. For example, the salesman needs to know the buyer's idiosyncracies while the buyer needs to know the character of the salesman. When these reciprocal information needs have been satisfied, a sound working relationship can be built up between buyer and seller. Figure 38 shows the type of information needs that must be satisfied.

8. Knowledge develops confidence. All knowledge develops confidence, the ability to converse and to express an opinion. There is no substitute for the salesman. A glib-talking salesman might bluff his way along for a while, but in time the buyer will realise he doesn't know what he is talking about.

That persuasion still has its place is true, but it must be directed towards needs which may be satisfied by the purchase of particular goods and services.

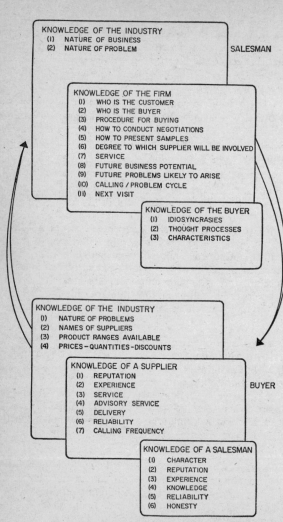

KNOWLEDGE OF THE INDUSTRY
(1) NATURE OF BUSINESS
(2) NATURE OF PROBLEM

SALESMAN

KNOWLEDGE OF THE FIRM
(1) WHO IS THE CUSTOMER
(2) WHO IS THE BUYER
(3) PROCEDURE FOR BUYING
(4) HOW TO CONDUCT NEGOTIATIONS
(5) HOW TO PRESENT SAMPLES
(6) DEGREE TO WHICH SUPPLIER WILL BE INVOLVED
(7) SERVICE
(8) FUTURE BUSINESS POTENTIAL
(9) FUTURE PROBLEMS LIKELY TO ARISE
(10) CALLING / PROBLEM CYCLE
(11) NEXT VISIT

KNOWLEDGE OF THE BUYER
(1) IDIOSYNCRASIES
(2) THOUGHT PROCESSES
(3) CHARACTERISTICS

KNOWLEDGE OF THE INDUSTRY
(1) NATURE OF PROBLEMS
(2) NAMES OF SUPPLIERS
(3) PRODUCT RANGES AVAILABLE
(4) PRICES – QUANTITIES – DISCOUNTS

KNOWLEDGE OF A SUPPLIER
(1) REPUTATION
(2) EXPERIENCE
(3) SERVICE
(4) ADVISORY SERVICE
(5) DELIVERY
(6) RELIABILITY
(7) CALLING FREQUENCY

BUYER

KNOWLEDGE OF A SALESMAN
(1) CHARACTER
(2) REPUTATION
(3) EXPERIENCE
(4) KNOWLEDGE
(5) RELIABILITY
(6) HONESTY

FIG. 38. *Reciprocal information needs.*

If salesmen are lacking in product knowledge, the responsibility lies in two directions.

(*a*) *Salesmen* are to blame for failing to equip themselves adequately to meet their customers.

(*b*) *Sales management* are to blame through the proprietor or training department, when they neglect to impress personnel with the importance of product knowledge. They have:

   (*i*) failed to provide instruction, or

   (*ii*) failed to follow-up initial training to determine that products are being presented to customers in a satisfactory way.

SENSIBLE USE OF KNOWLEDGE

9. Fact as opposed to opinion. One of the worst mistakes a salesman can make in the course of an interview is to express an opinion: "I think this will solve your problem . . ." or "I imagine you can sell a lot of this . . ." The buyer is neither interested in nor impressed with the salesman's opinion.

The buyer wants advice and product knowledge which the salesman must provide to help the buyer form his own decisions.

To present a sound case, the salesman should be as familiar with his competitor's products as he is with his own. If on occasion he has to accept defeat, it can enhance his technical reputation in the eyes of the buyer and prepare the way for next time.

10. Merchandise knowledge requires fluency. Merchandise knowledge requires fluency with technical terms. The salesman must be capable of understanding technical terms and be able to express an idea in a simple but accurate manner to the non-technical customers.

The salesman must have all the pertinent facts enabling him to give a complete explanation of the product, be familiar with its maintenance, and must also be aware of the opportunities being offered by competing firms.

11. Industrial salesman's knowledge. The industrial salesman's interest and knowledge can be stimulated by sound technical training. This should include:

   (*a*) background to the product;

   (*b*) related industrial problems;

   (*c*) product research and development;

   (*d*) manufacturing methods;

(*e*) methods of use; and

(*f*) service and servicing.

The salesman will make greater progress and obtain increased job satisfaction if he has an interest in his products and a knowledge of his customers. Whenever possible, the objective should be to build on the salesman's personal experience, performance appraisal, cost analyses and experiments so long as he keeps within the broad parameters of corporate policy.

12. The kinds of knowledge. The salesman must appreciate that buyers will have differing degrees of knowledge about the product he is selling.

Basically three kinds of product knowledge are important to the salesman and he should ascertain he is in possession of, and can distinguish between, them. They are tangible qualities, intangible qualities and behaviour of the product in use.

(*a*) *Tangible qualities* are the facts that can be quite definitely proved or equally disproved, e.g. "polyurethane", "stainless steel", "solid oak". They are statements which can be proven and for this reason they are the most convincing.

(*b*) *Intangible qualities* are facts claimed for a product but which can be neither proved or disproved by test. They have to be supported by warranty or a certificate, e.g. "made in England", "this season's fabric" and so on. They imply a quality and the declaration is proof of the standard.

(*c*) *Behaviour in use* would be the most important group of facts to the speciality and industrial salesman. The majority of speciality or industrial products are sold not for what they are made of but rather for what they will do.

A buyer of electric sanding machines is concerned with the appliance's ability to sand, or buff, and its qualities in terms of capacity and power to remove wood or metal; he is not likely to be concerned with the quality metal used in its construction.

The speciality salesman who relies to a great extent upon demonstration is concerned with this last aspect almost to the exclusion of the other aspects.

13. Sources of information. There will be many and varied sources of information, and the determination with which the salesman pursues that knowledge to its sources will largely be the measure of his success. A salesman should always be hungry for knowledge. Product knowledge may be obtained:

(*a*) by examination of the products themselves;

(*b*) by trying out the products;

(*c*) by consideration of the method of manufacture;

(*d*) by asking others, including those who made, or distribute, the products, other salespeople and superiors;

(*e*) from the consumers', or users', experiences;

(*f*) from catalogues, brochures, reports and other company-originated literature;

(*g*) from trade journals and press reports;

(*h*) from advertisements;

(*i*) from books; and

(*j*) through information on labels and tags.

The sources and amount of information required will vary according to the nature of the product and the kind of people it is sold to. A simple criterion is that salesmen should always be able to give concise information about the product.

14. Comparison of products. To be able to give a comparison with competitors' products is an important selling point.

EXAMPLE: A salesman is selling a single-coat paint for outside application.

Salesman: ". . . and '*Weathertex*' is a single-coat emulsion that is weatherproof and will cover seventeen square metres to five litres."

Buyer: "Seventeen square metres? That's not much. I'm using '*Plasti-tex*' and that gives twenty-five square metres to five litres, and it's the same price as yours."

Salesman: "That is quite true, Mr. Brown. '*Plasti-tex*', an excellent product, does give twenty-five square metres to five litres, but are you aware that the film thickness is only 300 microns compared with 800 microns with ours? Since these products are sold to cover cracks and be weatherproof, you need that extra thickness. The extra thickness also means longer life . . ."

Buyer: "Hmmm, I see your point; I hadn't thought of it that way . . ."

Salesmen must know how to expose points of superiority; these might be: economy; durability; safety; colour; taste; scent; cost; service; convenience or beauty.

The example is a hypothetical situation using imaginary

brands, but it is the sort of situation and information a good salesman would make himself aware of. It is not over-stating the point to say again, that the good salesman will know as much about rival products as his own.

A salesman must also be familiar with problems arising from the use of the product. A salesman selling metallisation treatments to a shot-blaster will do better if he familiarises himself with the process and complications of shot-blasting.

15. Selection of selling points. The purpose in investigating the product, and its competitors, is to select selling points. The salesman must be aware of the limitations in applying knowledge. The inexperienced salesman must beware of not "teaching grand-mother" by offering information to a man who should and probably does know all about his job.

> EXAMPLE:
>
> Salesman to a painting contractor: "I would suggest, sir, that you apply the material with a 100 millimetre brush, taking care to cut in first . . ."
>
> Buyer: "Yes, yes; get on with telling me about the material!"

Main selling points might be:
  (*a*) materials used;
  (*b*) construction;
  (*c*) visual appeals;
  (*d*) performance;
  (*e*) maintenance; and
  (*f*) reputation.

16. Tactful use of knowledge. The salesman's knowledge of his and other products is acquired to put him at least on equal terms with the prospective purchaser. If his knowledge is superior to the customer's, it may be tactful to conceal the fact. A typical opening might be: "As you will be aware, the chemical reaction to this would be . . ." The customer may or may not be aware. The words will either flatter him, because he doesn't know; or it will put him at his ease because his capability has been acknowledged.

It is wrong to offer too much information. If the buyer is told everything, it may exhaust the argument before convincing the prospect. You may then have to repeat yourself. Whether the information is offered or not, it must be known as a question may be asked.

PROGRESS TEST 8

1. The salesman faced with a prospective customer needs a high degree of merchandise knowledge. What are his needs for merchandise knowledge based upon?   (1)

2. Why should a salesman have a wide knowledge of his products?   (4)

3. "In many cases, particularly in an industrial setting, the selling process becomes a contest in which the two protagonists (buyer and seller) aim to overcome each other's arguments". How can the salesman prepare himself?   (6)

4. If salesmen lack product knowledge, where does the responsibility lie?   (8)

CHAPTER IX

Techniques of Selling

THE SELLING PROCESS

1. The correct technique. In this chapter we will deal with selling techniques in general terms. Aspects of selling specific to export selling and retail selling will be dealt with in subsequent chapters. The techniques employed are very much dependent upon two factors:

(*a*) the type of product or service; and
(*b*) the type of customer.

It must also follow that if the salesman is travelling to meet his customers in their places of work, a different technique will be called for than that used when the customer visits a shop or showroom. The reasons derive from the considerations about the product's importance to the customer in terms of time and place.

EXAMPLE: A travelling salesman calls at a house at 11.30 a.m. to sell cleaning materials. The woman of the house is busy with her cooking. To her the salesman is an interruption of work which she considers more important at that time and place and the salesman is "choked off". At 2.30 p.m. the woman goes shopping and may be prepared to visit several shops and spend time in each selecting the same type of products which she refused in the morning.

We can generalise that in selling, *product, time* and *place* are important considerations to both buyer and seller. Figure 39 shows this.

2. Levels of preoccupation. From the graph certain conclusions can be drawn.

(*a*) The customer is most likely to buy *when the needs are highest and the preoccupation is lowest*; the converse will also apply.

(*b*) The salesman's likelihood of selling is greatest when the *customer's preoccupation is lowest, but will rapidly diminish as preoccupation grows.*

(*c*) This tendency will hold true in most circumstances as it can be assumed that *the greater the level of preoccupation the lower the level of immediate need.*

(*d*) *Elasticity of demand does not influence the general assumptions* because the degree of elasticity is implicit in the level of pre-occupation.

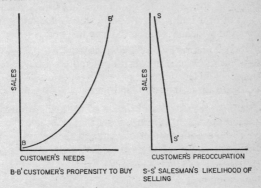

FIG. 39. *Effect of customer's preoccupation on sales.*

The greatest influence on the customer to lower the level of preoccupation at a given time will be the ability of the salesman to stimulate the level of immediate need. If he is to succeed in doing this he has to give consideration to several important points.

(*a*) When will be the best *time* to see my customer?

(*b*) Where will be the best *place* to see my customer?

(*c*) What will be the best *product* to show my customer?

If inadequate attention is given to these fundamental points all the subsequent steps in the selling process will be negated.

3. The buyer's needs. The buyer is often considered, certainly in relation to industrial goods, as buying for logical or economic reasons. This attitude unfortunately ignores the fact that the buyer is human and in making his institutional buying decision he will encounter the same kinds of personal doubts that he does in his private buying.

If the buyer is young, or new to the firm, he will feel less confident than if he is well established with the company, i.e. a long-term buyer with a proven record of success. If the buyer has recently moved to the firm's locality, has a young family and is totally dependent on the firm, his response to sales pressures will be different from that of an older man, with no mortgage and a grown-up family.

The salesman must recognise these human factors in the industrial buying decision. He will appreciate the buyer's need for reassurance, especially if the product is new to the company. The buyer may in turn have to "sell" the new product to works management or a senior buyer and must be adequately supplied with facts and evidence of success. These will be:

    (a) specialist reports by well known users;
    (b) test reports by scientific institutions;
    (c) samples and test pieces;
    (d) accurate, up-to-date cost analysis data.

4. The selling process. The objective of the selling process is to persuade customers to buy products that will give them satisfaction. There are four major elements in the process which are fundamental to all other factors in the process:

    (a) the company and its policies;
    (b) the customer;
    (c) the products or services; and
    (d) the salesman.

It must be a prime responsibility of sales management to ensure that the sales force has an appreciation and clear understanding of these four major elements in the selling process before they embark upon the subsequent steps in the process.

5. The steps in the selling process. These will be:

    (a) approach and greeting;
    (b) determining the customer's needs;
    (c) effective presentations of the products;
    (d) countering objections;
    (e) closing the sale; and
    (f) developing goodwill after the sale.

In some forms of selling one can interpose an additional step between (e) and (f); that of suggestive selling of related products, e.g. selling sewing cotton to the person who has bought cloth, or brushes to one who has bought paint. When the objective of the selling process is the satisfaction of a specific need or the winning of a substantial order, as much industrial selling is, this additional step can have unfortunate results and is best omitted.

6. Describing the selling process. It is important to state that:

(a) *a classification of steps* must by the nature of the process be arbitrary;

(b) *some steps may be unnecessary* in accomplishing some sales; and

(c) *the actual sequence is variable* according to customer and salesman.

7. The mental processes in a sale. The buyer may progress through a series of stages before he decides to buy the product. We can identify seven of these as follows.

(a) Arousal of interest.
(b) Increase of knowledge.
(c) Adjustment to needs.
(d) Appreciation of suitability.
(e) Desire to possess.
(f) Consideration of cost.
(g) Decision to buy.

(a) *Arousal of interest*. Figure 39 shows that a customer has a higher propensity to buy when he has a low preoccupation level. It follows that the salesman's first task is to arouse the interest of his customer. Until this has been achieved the customer will not give all his attention to the salesman's proposition.

(b) *Increase of knowledge*. If the salesman has accomplished stage (a), the customer will be receptive to further information and will wish for further knowledge of the product.

(c) *Adjustment to needs*. A customer may find a salesman's product information is interesting, but unless it can be shown that the product fulfils his needs, the sale will not be accomplished.

(d) *Appreciation of suitability*. Following the adjustment to needs the customer will consider whether the product is suitable to solve his particular problem.

(e) *Desire to possess*. If the customer has been successfully taken through the preceding stages the desire to possess should arise naturally and lead to (f).

(f) *Consideration of cost*. If the selling process has been conducted sensibly, the customer will wish to consider whether he can afford to buy the product he now desires.

(g) *Decisions to buy*. The decision to buy should not be a sudden confrontation but should have gradually become larger in the customer's thoughts until the right moment for the decision is arrived at. The salesman's knowledge and skill is aimed at making this stage as natural as possible.

These mental stages in the selling process are important to the successful conclusion of a sale, but it must be remembered that they exist only within the wider context of the selling interview.

THE SALES INTERVIEW

8. Creating the right environment. A relationship exists between the company and the customer. The relationship might be favourable, unfavourable or completely neutral depending upon the knowledge each has of the other. When the company's salesman and the customer's buyer meet, as representatives of the two parties, a confrontation results. These two people will exchange arguments, views, information, opinions and finally both will make a decision.

(a) The salesman's decision will be on the prospect, and whether it is worth continuing and for how long with the sale.

(b) The buyer's decision will be on the suitability of the product.

In reaching their respective decisions seller and buyer will alter the relationship between them. The manner in which this is brought about is illustrated in Fig. 40; from this the complex chain of decision-making may be understood. For the seller it is a simple consideration of continuing with the sale or not; but for the buyer it is the seven mental stages expressed as decisions.

9. The sales interview. The mental stages are only a part of the sales interview which itself is a more complex process. It is possible to identify fifteen steps in the typical sales interview.

Opening
- (a) Exchange of courtesies.
- (b) Salesman's opening.
- (c) Interest aroused.
- (d) Interest developed.

Body
- (e) Commencement of selling proper.
- (f) Demonstration:
    - (i) presentation of product,
    - (ii) explanation of selling points,
    - (iii) operation of product by salesman, and
    - (iv) operation of product by customer.
- (g) Discussion of price.
- (h) Countering of objections.

Close
- (i) Commencement of close.
- (j) Persuasion and trial close.
- (k) Decision-making.
- (l) Order taken—purchase completed.
- (m) Completion of details.

Departure
- (n) Closing courtesies.
- (o) Departure.

10. Opening remarks. The opening remarks in the exchange of courtesies are the beginning of the selling process. The customer may well draw conclusions about the salesman from his first words.

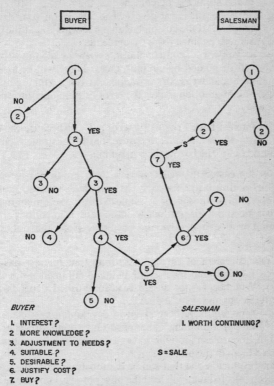

FIG. 40. *Decision-making complex.*

EXAMPLE: A man from Yorkshire called on a customer in South Wales during a period of prolonged bad weather. The bluff Yorkshireman in an attempt to be jolly began: "Good morning, sir, I always knew Wales was wet but you must be enjoying this . . ." The results were a foregone conclusion, as this was a tactless and rather stupid remark.

A little prior knowledge can help. Does your customer play

golf, garden, suffer from gout, watch birds? The salesman will help himself by being observant. On entering a customer's office the successful salesman can take in the room at a glance and learn about his customer. The opening remark should succeed in getting the customer's agreement at the outset. "It's rather wet. . . ." "It's a nice morning" "The flowers on your desk are magnificent. . . ." If the customer can agree with you at the outset he may be more inclined to go on agreeing.

Seek to guide and control the interview at all times but be prepared to be guided by circumstances. There will be a certain amount of manœuvring for advantage in the beginning and the younger salesman often makes the error of plunging into the sale too quickly.

11. Get interest first. Frequently sales are lost because the salesman is over-eager and fails to ensure that his customer's interest is aroused before he begins the real selling.

12. Get the customer's point of view. It is important to get the customer enthusiastic as early as possible—interest must be developed into enthusiasm. To achieve this the salesman must be enthusiastic about his products—enthusiasm is infectious and the salesman who can involve the customer from the outset will succeed.

13. Commencement of selling. Assuming that interest has been aroused the salesman reaches the point to commence the selling proper. Whether or not a sale is accomplished depends upon what the salesman says and does!

Some time will have been spent in developing product knowledge, and by combining experience and sound pre-sales preparation the salesman will have assessed selling points and arranged them in the best sequence.

If the product is one that can be demonstrated a sequence will have been selected that will lead the buyer to the point at which he will be prepared and keen for a demonstration.

Sales talk should be standardised but standardisation should concern facts, and it should not degenerate into a parrot-fashion talk. At the beginning of the selling process, endeavour to inspire confidence by:

(a) sincerity of manner as conveyed by voice and bearing;
(b) capitalising the good name of the firm and its prestige;
(c) product knowledge;
(d) basing selling techniques upon sound customer investigation.

14. The demonstration. The demonstration will have two effects. It will show the customer:

(a) the performance of the product; and
(b) the product is as good as the salesman says it is.

To ensure maximum effectiveness the demonstration should be practised frequently and new techniques incorporated where possible.

The demonstration must be informative and it is important that the customer should be told what is happening at every stage. Too many salesmen are unsure of themselves when it comes to the demonstration and so they work too fast. Learn to develop the demonstration so that natural pauses will give effect, allow the customer to digest what he has seen and ask questions if he wishes. Remember that the customer hasn't seen the product before.

15. Finding the customer's needs. The demonstration on occasion may be less specific than that indicated in the last paragraph. Determining the customer's needs and presenting the merchandise may sometimes be two aspects of the same operation. Among commercial travellers the presentation may be the means by which the customer finds the products he needs—this is particularly true in the grocery and general wholesale trades. It is also typical of retailing and this will be developed in subsequent chapters. To be effective a demonstration involves:

(a) the knowledge of location of products, in bag or showcase;
(b) a sensible selection of what is to be demonstrated;
(c) a careful selection of selling points;
(d) the correct display of product; and
(e) an effective presentation.

16. Price. In any sales interview there is a correct time to mention the price. More sales are lost by the incorrect handling of price than by any other aspect of selling. The following points should influence the way in which price may be dealt with.

(a) Price is only *one* factor in the consideration of a purchase.

(b) The right price will not sell the wrong goods—the wrong price will not prevent the sale of the right goods.

(c) *Do not fear price.* So long as it is approached in the same way as any other selling feature, the salesman should be equipped to deal with price and counter any criticism.

(d) If price is mentioned at the outset it should not be dodged;

the counter is to *stress the value*. Nothing is cheap—you get what you pay for.

(*e*) All prices can and should be *related to the article* and to what the article can do.

It must be remembered that on its own, price means nothing. It is always considered in relation to other factors.

EXAMPLE: Selling a paint treatment for chemical tanks.

Buyer: "£90! That's rather more than I bargained for. No, I think I'll have to leave it for the moment."

Salesman: "Perhaps I should explain the product's ability to solve your particular problem once more . . ."

Buyer: "There's no point in your doing that. You see we have had our budget cut and just don't have as much money as that available. We will use our own product."

Salesman: "If I may take you up on that point, sir. You will agree that price has to be related to other factors. The most important factor today will be labour costs. This product has greater durability and protective capacity than an ordinary paint. By its use you will make considerable economies in the very expensive element of labour. . . ."

MATTERS ARISING FROM THE INTERVIEW

17. Disposal of objections. Even if a sale is presented effectively and efficiently, there are still likely to be objections. Objections should be treated as opportunities for further explanation.

Meeting objections correctly constitutes the most difficult part of the selling process. Many objections can be anticipated and countered in the presentation, but the unexpected can also occur; they can be of three forms:

(*a*) general objection;
(*b*) specific objections; and
(*c*) excuses.

The experienced salesman will have the knowledge and ability to deal with the first two and will ignore the last. There are several general "rules" for dealing with objections.

(*a*) Do not argue with the customer.
(*b*) Anticipate objections.
(*c*) Counter objections firmly and completely.

(*d*) Inspire confidence, by mannerisms.

(*e*) Do not denigrate competitors.

18. Concentrating on decision. The objective of the selling process is to make a sale. Salesmen must not become too interested in the conversation and lose sight of their objective. No attempt should be made to "rush" the customer as it will certainly fail. The sequence of the salesman must be to:

(*a*) state his case;

(*b*) demonstrate; and

(*c*) dispose of objections.

Following this sequence the salesman will direct his efforts to closing the sale.

19. Closing the sale. Closing the sale is the most delicate point in the selling process. To achieve success the salesman needs to be aware of the buyer's behaviour and must be able to make decisions at the correct moment. One of the most useful ways of closing a sale is to suggest a finish.

"Now, how much material will you require?"

"We can deliver by Friday morning."

"Will you be sending the order, or can you place it now?"

"I should think blue is the most suitable, do you agree?"

Remember the entire selling process is working to the objective of closing the sale and should progress naturally towards it.

20. Arranging further interviews. Industrial selling can be a protracted business and a sale is not always possible on each occasion. Frequently it requires repeat calls to secure an order, or to develop further business. It is important to leave on terms that will permit a return visit, and the method will depend upon circumstances.

21. Departure. Having completed the selling process, finalise any arrangements, ensure there are no outstanding matters and allow the customer to depart or make your own withdrawal. Both customers and salesmen are busy people.

PROGRESS TEST 9

1. How can the salesman succeed in overcoming the prospective customer's preoccupation? **(1)**

2. What are the seven stages of the mental processes in a sale? **(7)**

3. Faced with the need to standardise a sales talk, how can the salesman inspire confidence at the commencement? **(13)**

4. What points should influence the way in which price may be dealt with? **(16)**

CHAPTER X

Export Selling

ECONOMICS OF EXPORTING

1. Exporting and the economy. In Chapter IV, Fig. 29 illustrated, in simplified form, how the circulation of money in the economy works. It is not the place of this book to explain the complexities of "money" and so we shall leave it in simple terms. It will be seen that production gives rise to income which in turn flows back into production through savings, investment and consumer spending.

If this was all that happened in the national economy, it would be reasonable to suppose that income and production would grow very little and a country would have to rely upon its own resources. Since this country relies upon buying tropical products, like bananas and coffee; industrial raw materials, such as rubber, iron ore and uranium; and also buys much of our consumer products abroad, Japanese radios, German cars, French wine, etc., then it becomes clear that the economy is complex. Goods bought abroad have to be paid for from the earnings of the goods we make and sell abroad.

2. Balance of payments. The balance of payments is the difference between our overseas earnings and our overseas expenditure. Payments fall into two broad categories.

(*a*) *Merchandise exports*, which include all the manufactured goods, processed materials, raw materials and other merchandise such as livestock or antiques that are distributed abroad.

(*b*) "*Invisible*" *exports*, which include the payments for services, banking, sea and air freight, insurance and investments.

The earliest records of the U.K. balance of payments date from 1816 and show a fluctuating surplus until 1840 when a deficit of £2·3 million was recorded. Surpluses were made in 1842 and 1847 and these continued until the General Strike in 1926 when there was a deficit of £26 million. 1931 and 1937 were also deficit years but there was a surplus of £8 million in 1938. Since the war the record has not been very favourable:

1946	deficit	£298	million
1947	,,	£443	,,
1948	surplus	£ 1	,,
1951	deficit	£403	,,
1955	,,	£ 78	,,
1960	,,	£457	,,
1964	,,	£744	,,
1965	,,	£252	,,
1966	,,	£ 48	,,
1967	,,	£417	,,

With the escalation of oil prices the deficit increased sharply.

1974	deficit	£5,195	million
1975	,,	£3,205	,,
1976	,,	£3,510	,,
1977	,,	£1,607	,,

3. Reasons for the imbalance. Over the last hundred years the over-all trend has been to a deficit on merchandise exports, although in most years the addition of the "invisible" exports has resulted in a final surplus. The reasons for this tendency towards an imbalance are:

(a) the growth in the number of industrialised countries;
(b) the decline in the traditional "Empire" trade;
(c) Britain's loss of traditional markets in two World Wars;
(d) generally increased competition;
(e) a lack of satisfactory investment banks in Britain;
(f) rapid technological advances;
(g) the general uncertainty in world trade which has put off many U.K. firms from exporting;
(h) the high level of consumer demand on the home trade; and
(i) U.K. firms' generally uncompetitive stand in world trade.

In addition to these reasons must be added the changed relationship between the Western economies and the oil producers, together with the inflationary trend that has damaged their economies. But of all the reasons which may apply to British companies (and to some companies in other countries), it is (i) over which export management can by itself exert the most influence.

REASONS FOR EXPORTING

4. The purpose of exporting. "Why should we export?" is a common question asked by firms who have never exported, or who had little success in doing so. Harold Macmillan, when Prime Minister in the early 1960s, once declared, "Exporting is fun!" but this is hardly sufficient cause for companies to engage in the extremely demanding task of selling their products abroad. Many failures and disappointments are the almost constant running mates of success in international trade. It is an uncertain business, but a vitally important one for a number of reasons.

5. To aid the nation. Throughout the years since 1945 successive governments have exhorted firms to export with phrases like: "We must export or die!" No matter how emotive the message it is unlikely to persuade many firms to try. There have to be sound economic reasons for management to export.

6. Increased company profits. It is often claimed that exporting is not as profitable as home sales. This is often true. One small car manufacturer used to pay his agents' commission from the 2 per cent export rebate allowed by the government. Many firms have found it necessary to trim their export prices in order to be as competitive as possible.

As will be seen in Chapter XIV, the maximisation of profit is an erroneous objective. Companies should be looking to a longer-term resilience, and in this aim, exporting is a valuable aid. So long as exporting is not undertaken at a loss, then it is contributing to over-all company profitability.

7. Increased company growth. Companies that have pursued export sales as a deliberate policy have generally found more rapid growth. A company making consumer durables had ten home trade salesmen who totalled £350,000 sales per year. An export department was established with a basic export unit. Within two years exports amounted to over £100,000 per annum, or almost two-thirds of the home trade, and total company sales, allowing for growth in the home market, was over half a million pounds.

If a company can sell its products in Britain with a population of around 55 millions, then by selling in Western Europe it can increase its market to over 200 millions, without going outside Europe.

In general, companies cannot afford to remain stable. If they cease to grow, they stagnate and eventually decline; exporting, by involving firms in the most dynamic and competitive areas of trade, is a great stimulus to growth.

8. Exporting supports the cost of research and development. The enormous increase in the costs of research and development is often just too much to recover by selling in Britain alone; consider the costs of aircraft development. But many products could achieve greater developments if the cost could be spread over larger sales. Cheaper research is yet another spin-off from exporting.

9. Exports cushion fluctuations in demand. Most companies experience some fluctuation in the demand for their products, either seasonal or climatic. Not many bikinis are sold in Britain in winter, or de-misters in summer. There are less obvious trends; more menswear tends to be sold in winter than summer.

It is not only seasonal fluctuations which occur. Recent economic difficulties such as restrictions on hire-purchase, credit, etc. have made it difficult to sell domestic appliances. Of course seasons and economies fluctuate in all countries, but not all at once.

Companies that export to seventy or eighty countries in the southern and northern hemispheres have a wide range of economies, seasons, climates and consumer trends which all lead to a more constant production at home.

10. Exporting aids corporate development. The demands of international sales make challenges to executive skills and call for a high-calibre businessman. Executives who travel frequently and meet international businessmen are made aware of and involved in the latest management methods.

It is not only in marketing that a company learns from exporting. Techniques of production, distribution, research and mechanical handling are all improved from experience in exporting.

11. Exporting supports home sales. Most countries have export programmes and their efforts can be seen on our home markets. Over the years competition at home has increased enormously and, with better communications and enlarged trading communities, the days when a clear distinction between domestic sales and international sales could be drawn has gone.

PRACTICE OF EXPORTING

12. The essentials of exporting. Exporting is by no means as simple as home sales. Government policies, both at home and abroad, distances and financial exchanges all complicate exports —while they do not fundamentally change the commercial considerations they are all causes of commercial friction. Essentials of exporting are as follows.

(*a*) *Comprehensive market research.* The fundamental difference between the home market and the export market is simply that the latter may mean a large number of different countries each with varying needs, economies and practices.

Market research must be undertaken systematically on the basis of one market at a time, and, most important, the sources of information must be up to date and reliable.

(*b*) *The right sales organisation.* In exporting there are many firms and agents who can help, but they all need payment. There is no one method and each problem has to be dealt with on merit. It is fair to say that the fewer intermediaries, the better will be communication and the lower the costs.

(*c*) *Distribution.* Distribution should be tackled with a view to optimising cost and time. The cheapest method is often the slowest and competitive markets will not wait. Distribution must be examined and costed to determine which method will satisfy the customer most. Above all else export distribution must be reliable and efficient. Late deliveries cost future sales.

13. Sale of goods abroad. The conduct of export transactions can be divided into two categories.

(*a*) An exporting company may complete a Contract of Sale with a buyer abroad.

(*b*) An exporting company may establish a permanent office abroad and complete transactions there through appointed representatives. This may be an office, or a subsidiary company or agents.

Decisions as to the method employed will depend upon the firm's appraisal of export business. The first method is more appropriate when exporting is subordinate to the home trade, or when business is limited to occasional orders. The second method is suited to the medium or larger company when exporting assumes an important place in the company's sales objectives. Within this basic choice considerable variations can exist and an exporter will choose that which fulfils his needs most suitably.

(a) Exports may be conducted through regular Contracts of Sale.

(b) Exports may be isolated orders received from abroad.

(c) Company representatives may be appointed to conduct overseas sales, and who will remain under the direct control of the home enterprise.

(d) Business may be conducted on the basis of arrangements where overseas representation is in the hands of independent agents who represent firms other than the British principal.

14. Defining the customer. Exporting is a complex process and there are many ways of securing an order, arranging payment and completing its despatch to an overseas destination.

Export merchants have been an important factor in the export process for a long time, fulfilling an important and traditional function. Export merchants carry out their business under an assortment of descriptions, such as:

(a) export merchants;

(b) merchant shippers;

(c) confirming house; or

(d) buying office.

None of these descriptions has any precise legal or established commercial meaning and it is important that the seller should determine on each occasion whether the exporter who buys the goods is acting in the capacity of a principal or as agent for a client abroad.

(a) *Principal:* his profit is made from the percentage added to the purchase price and taken when the goods are re-sold to the overseas importer.

(b) *Agent:* his profit is taken from the buying commission which the overseas buyer has agreed to pay him.

The importance of this distinction arises out of the legal implication of the term "agent". This book makes no attempt to be an authority on the legal aspect and interested readers should consult specialised works. The essential point is that when goods are purchased by agents acting for an overseas client, the manufacturer is not in direct contractual relationship with the customer abroad, although his contractual party is the overseas importer who will re-sell the goods to the customer in his own name.

15. Merchant houses. Much trade is still undertaken by merchant houses. They have been of great aid and importance in enabling the manufacturer to devote his attention to production and leave the special export marketing in the hands of the merchant. It may be that the reliance on merchant houses has also tended to limit the expertise of exporting in the belief it is a business best left to "experts". It has been customary that:

(*a*) the manufacturer;
    (*i*) produced the goods, and
    (*ii*) sold them to the merchant house;
(*b*) the merchant house;
    (*i*) visited and otherwise undertook market research into foreign markets,
    (*ii*) was responsible for financial status,
    (*iii*) distributed orders from customers to manufacturers,
    (*iv*) paid for goods, and
    (*v*) shipped goods.

The advent of large companies undertaking direct exporting, aided by ease of travel and communication, enables contact to be maintained with overseas companies. Most exporters now establish their own market research and shipping departments and this generally reflects the more complex marketing techniques and stringent competition prevailing.

16. The export transaction. Once an export order has been received and processed, it is important, from the legal viewpoint, that the contract of sale, the objective of which is the export of merchandise, should be separated from other contracts of sale which will relate to the same merchandise, but which are not the reason for the shipment of merchandise.

The export transaction is the immediate cause for the export of the merchandise from the country, and there may be other contracts of sale leading up to this point.

EXAMPLE: A firm of export merchants sends its representatives abroad in search of business. In due course an order is received for shoes from a customer in Kuwait. The export merchant now places an order on his account for the shoes with a manufacturer in Britain. The manufacturer completes delivery to the export merchant, sending the shoes to his London warehouse and invoicing them accordingly.

The order placed by the export merchant with the British manufacturer and duly executed by sending the merchandise to a warehouse in London and invoicing to a firm in Britain for payment in Britain is a *home transaction*.

When the export merchant re-sells the same shoes to his customer in Kuwait and despatches and invoices them accordingly, it is an *export transaction*, as shown in Fig. 41.

FIG. 41. *Home and export transactions.*

When an overseas buyer places an order direct with a manufacturer, or with his agent, then in precise terms this is an export transaction. Again in the legal view, there is a considerable difference between whether the contract is completed by delivery of the merchandise ex works, or if the order is completed by sending the merchandise free of charge to an address supplied by the buyer.

Normally there is no difficulty in determining whether the contract of sale is to be completed by exporting the goods as the conditions of the contract will state:

(*a*) the place to which the goods are to be delivered;
(*b*) the manner of transportation; and
(*c*) who the buyer is.

Export transactions by their nature are more complicated than home transactions. The many variations possible and the wide choice of delivery methods have been embodied in a stereotyped set of clauses.

17. Additional contracts. Export orders are characterised by the contract of sales by which the goods are delivered abroad, being interwoven with other contracts.

(*a*) Contract of carriage, by air or sea.
(*b*) Contract of insurance.
(*c*) Delivery of the shipping documents, which in many export orders play an important part in the accomplishment of the transaction.
(*d*) Bank contracts: if payment is made by banker's credit, two additional contracts are involved.
   (*i*) Contract of the bank with the buyer.
   (*ii*) Contract of the bank with the seller.

18. Shipping documents. Once the goods are shipped it will be necessary for the exporter to deliver the shipping documents in accordance with the instructions. The shipping documents comprise:

(*a*) the Bill of Lading (or the Air Way-Bill);
(*b*) marine insurance policy; and
(*c*) the commercial invoice.

It is customary to refer to these documents as the elements of the three prime contracts.

EXPORT SHIPPING CLAUSES

19. Special clauses in exporting. The complications of exporting have necessitated the use of special clauses which are not used in the home trade. These clauses have been developed by international mercantile custom and have simplified sale of goods by standardising practice.

There are a number of alternatives the exporter can choose from depending upon his experience, size of orders and their frequency. These are:

(*a*) ex works, ex store, ex warehouse;
(*b*) F.O.R., F.O.T.;
(*c*) F.A.S.;
(*d*) F.O.B.;
(*e*) C. & F.;
(*f*) C.I.F.; or
(*g*) domicile.

Each of the clauses is specific, not only in the definite information it communicates to the buyer about how much the goods will cost him, and why, but also in legal terms it places responsibility for particular aspects of the transaction upon either the buyer or the seller. As a generalisation it may be said that at one end of the scale, under the ex works clause, the buyer has most responsibility for shipping the goods, while under the "domicile" clause the seller has most responsibility. Since the seller is not going to undertake work for nothing, the cost will rise as he undertakes greater responsibility. Accordingly the buyer has a more accurate knowledge of total cost of the merchandise when he is quoted a C.I.F. price than when he is quoted an ex works price.

20. Ex works, ex store, ex warehouse. For the inexperienced exporter, or for a firm that exports infrequently, this clause is most favourable as it keeps the transaction as near as possible to a home transaction. Under the terms of the clause, the buyer is responsible for arranging documentation, other than commercial invoices, and shipment. The seller, however, must inform the buyer when the goods are ready for shipment, and, of course, they must be in accordance with the conditions of the order.

21. F.O.R. free on rail; F.O.T. free on truck. This is specifically a named point of departure and some confusion can arise as in the United States this can be interpreted as equivalent to F.O.B. and in France it is equivalent to "Franco Wagon". Essentially the seller is responsible for seeing that the goods are loaded on to a railway wagon, although acceptance of the goods by a railway lorry at the seller's factory or other premises does constitute fulfilment of the conditions.

Problems can occur over the responsibility for providing packing, particularly where a wooden crate may be needed, and also for the cost of providing tarpaulins to cover consignments in open railway trucks. To avoid confusion it is best to come to an understanding with the buyer in advance. Responsibility for the goods after loading on to the railways vehicles is the buyer's.

22. F.A.S. free alongside. This names a vessel in a port of shipment at a given time. It is the responsibility of the buyer to arrange for the vessel and to inform the seller when his goods should be presented for loading.

The seller should determine that his goods can "go alongside". In some ports, particularly small ones, it may be necessary to arrange lighterage, i.e. have goods taken out to the vessel which is standing off-shore, in a small vessel, or lighter.

23. F.O.B. free on board. Perhaps the most widely used export clause, F.O.B. can nevertheless be subject to many variations. Basically it is a named port of shipment and normally includes the named vessel. It is important that the port is mentioned at the outset. A firm in South Wales normally shipped from Newport and it costed the transport to that port. When it received an order from Norway for shipment from Newcastle upon Tyne, it found itself out of pocket.

Many disputes have arisen from the F.O.B. term and users are recommended to the British Chamber of Commerce leaflet, *F.O.B. Vessel.*

24. C. & F. cost and freight and C.I.F. cost, insurance and freight. This is essentially a named port of destination. Responsibility for packing, insurance (C.I.F.), arranging shipment, placing goods aboard, and documentation is the seller's. The buyer is responsible for the landing of the goods and their delivery to his premises.

25. Domicile. The seller quoting a "domicile" price and conditions is undertaking all charges and risks until the goods are delivered to the buyer's premises.

26. Export clauses as a basis for quotation. The importance of export clauses is not only in clarifying responsibility for delivery of the goods but also for quoting export prices.

It will be seen that the exporter quoting a C.I.F. price needs a great deal more information than he does for quoting F.O.B. or ex works. A problem can arise quoting C.I.F. New York, or some other port of destination, if delivery is to be extended at a time of inflating freight charges. In these conditions it is usual to place a time limit on the quote, e.g. "£256.00 C.I.F. New York, delivery within three months".

EXAMPLE: Goods quoted three different clauses:

	Ex Works	F.O.B. Cardiff	C.I.F. New York
GOODS	£153·00	£153·00	£153·00
PACKING	—	3·00	3·00
RAIL FREIGHT	—	6·00	6·00
DOCK DUES	—	2·00	2·00
WHARFAGE	—	1·50	1·50
LIFTING	—	50	50
SEA FREIGHT	—	—	24·00
INSURANCE	—	—	4·00
PRICE	£153·00	£166·00	£194·00

Quoting a C.I.F. price is much more helpful to the foreign buyer who has a better understanding of what he is expected to pay. Many exporters take the view that by quoting the lower "ex works" price, the goods will appeal more to the buyer. They perhaps fail to appreciate that the placing of export orders is not an "impulse buying" decision, but one that is subject to careful scrutiny and evaluation. The buyer faced with alternative offers, one quoting a price at a port in his own country, and one quoting a price at a factory in a town he has never heard of, has little to decide.

MARKET ORGANISATION

27. Selecting a market. One of the common faults among companies new to exporting is to attempt to sell in all markets at once. There are now more than 150 independent countries in the world and they vary considerably in living standards, social order, technical ability, allegiances, language and finance.

An export manager's prime objective is to select the markets in which the company's products should be sold. The majority of companies concentrate their efforts on only those markets in which the business prospects are known to be best. The problem then is to select markets.

Management decision-making must be based on information; the first task therefore is to determine a method for market identification and selection.

28. Decision process. If a company is not to waste time and effort in pursuit of export markets, a process must select the correct market by sound analysis.

Figure 42 is a model of a selection process, which identifies seven stages.

(*a*) *Product analysis/customer analysis.* If a company is to avoid wasting valuable time it must know:

(*i*) what are its products for; and

(*ii*) what kind of people use them.

For example, a cutlery firm with a new line of steak knives will not waste time on a Hindu country. Once it has an understanding of its role in providing for the needs of its customers it has a measure to apply in the next stage.

(*b*) *Screen world markets.* By applying its basic "measure" to world markets the export company can effect a quick screening of world markets.

(*c*) *Reject unsuitable markets.* Those markets not meeting the conditions of the company are rejected, although from time to time they may be subject to review as conditions may change.

(*d*) *Select particular markets.* Markets which have passed the initial screening are all potential markets, but since the company tackles all of them at once, it will refine the analysis to determine the most profitable market to concentrate upon.

(*e*) *Research into particular markets.* The purpose of this activity is to appraise conditions in each country.

(*i*) *Economic structure:* is the market a "free" economy or a controlled economy? Is the country's economy growing,

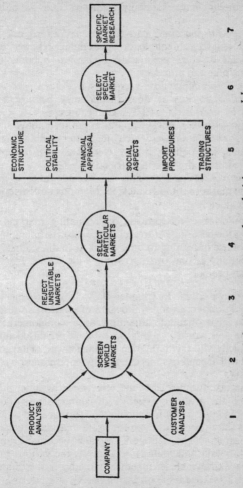

FIG. 42. *Selecting an export market: decision process model.*

stagnant or declining? Is it a manufacturing country, or agricultural?

(*ii*) *Political stability:* many "sound" markets, subject to much investment, have suddenly vanished due to political change.

(*iii*) *Financial appraisal:* can the country afford our merchandise? Does it have adequate foreign exchange reserves?

(*iv*) *Social aspects:* population dynamics, religion; legal restraints, customs and practices.

(*v*) *Import procedures:* licences, quotas, free entry?

(*vi*) *Trading structures:* does the country belong to any trading organisation; E.E.C., EFTA, Comecon, etc.

(*f*) *Select specific market.* The appraisal outlined above should produce one, or two, countries which offer better trading potential than the others. This country is now selected as the prime export market where initial effort is concentrated.

(*g*) *Specific market research.* This will be undertaken to determine how the market should be tackled. Methods of distribution, payment, agent, etc.

Having undertaken the process of evaluating markets and decided upon the best market to tackle, the information amassed will also be of use in turning to other markets in due course. The process essentially is one of "narrowing" the choice from the general to the specific.

29. Market organisation. In Chapter III we saw how there are physical limitations to an indefinite span of control; so also no manager can give adequate attention to a conglomerate of markets. The 150 world markets have to be organised into a structure which will facilitate their management. The actual organisation will depend to some extent upon interpretation of the term "market".

During the last twenty years the emergence of independent countries, and the grouping together of countries into trading blocks have made distinction difficult. The former East African territory has now become three separate markets; Uganda, Kenya, Tanzania. "The Rhodesias" have become Zambia, Zimbabwe-Rhodesia and Malawi. Conversely the various European states have drawn closer together. We have now a changed system of markets. (See table on facing page.)

There is no single solution to this problem of organisation and decisions will largely reflect a company's appreciation of the importance of a market. It will aid organising to:

(a) list all world markets;
(b) determine which can be considered separate markets;
(c) design an organisation structure; and
(d) establish future reviews upon the structure.

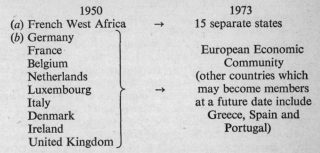

The organisation will determine responsibilities for each group of markets under a specialist manager. In the small company it may need only a responsible member of staff to look after a particular group under an export manager, as illustrated in Fig. 43.

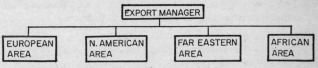

FIG. 43. *Market organisation.*

30. Bases for market departmentalisation. There are several methods in fairly general use by experienced exporting companies. These are:

(a) geographical;
(b) trading structures;
(c) established and potential; and
(d) dynamic structures.

(a) *Geographical organisation* will relate countries in the same geographical area and group them into one department in the organisation structure. The system will vary in effectiveness as it frequently groups together countries of a very different social, economic and political structure. Thus in an "African" area, one would include "white" South Africa; the central, west and east African areas, essentially "black" Africa, and North Africa, which is predominantly Arab. In a similar "Middle Eastern" area, the Arab States and Israel would presumably be lumped together.

(*b*) *Trading structures* may well be the most convenient method of organising in the future. The growth of trading communities throughout the world has created associations of countries with the same social and economic structures, and, most important to the exporter, the same general trading conditions.

(*c*) *Established and potential markets* consist of those markets which are developed and important to the company, together with the remaining markets. Although the system is in use, in general terms it tends to contain certain anomalies. Clearly the developed areas need as much attention as the potential markets if they are to be retained; presumably they were selected and developed at the outset because of their greater potential.

(*d*) *Dynamic structures* will be those which are most suited to the needs of the company and being subject to constant review will be most receptive to change. Since conditions in export markets are continually in a state of flux, any system will have less than maximum effectiveness if it is rigid.

31. General considerations. Market organisation must, if it is to function properly, encourage within the company a constant appraisal of its exporting effectiveness. It will seek to:

(*a*) separate actual and potential markets;

(*b*) physically separate existing markets in accordance with the organisation; and

(*c*) determine into which department in the organisation the remaining markets can be placed.

32. Knowledge of geography. Organisation of exports requires as a fundamental that the people responsible must have a sound knowledge of geography. There are criteria for determining how markets should be graded. These are:

(*a*) physical;

(*b*) social;

(*c*) financial; and

(*d*) economic.

Exploiting a market once it has been determined as being profitable is subject to certain considerations. Some markets because of their distance, size and complexity will necessarily take more effort than others. Developing a market in Belgium will be easier than Australia, if only because communication and travel will be so much easier. The United States is so big and diversified as to constitute many markets. The *New Yorker* published a book some years ago entitled *The 50 primary markets of the United States*. Dealing with such complex markets is as difficult as with many independent countries.

33. Size and location are important criteria in market selection. In the social aspect population is an important consideration, but only in relation to purchasing power. Faced with a choice between 4 million Norwegians and 23 million Ethiopians the relevant purchasing power must be obvious. At the same time however one can also recognise that 50 million Germans are a better proposition than 6 million Swiss in spite of how wealthy the latter are.

Language, custom and convention are equally important, and one does not have to go to the more remote parts of the world to offend local custom. A company making ladies' blouses once shipped a consignment in blue and yellow checks to Sweden and offended them considerably; no Swede wears his national colours.

There are several countries, which although having large populations, are so short of foreign exchange as to have very poor development potential at this time; India and Pakistan both fall into this category.

Many contradictions occur. One would expect underdeveloped countries with little or no manufacturing capacity to be important markets for consumer goods, but instead we find that the important markets are the industrialised exporters of those goods; Germany, Japan, the United States. Thus the best customers for industrial goods are other industrialised countries.

EXPORT SALESMANSHIP

34. Export salesmen. The objective of an export salesman is to obtain orders for his company's product from customers in other countries. The objective may be achieved in several ways by, for example:

(*a*) meeting overseas customers when they visit Britain;

(*b*) visiting the buying offices of customers in Britain, or by visiting merchant houses, etc. in this country;

(*c*) visiting overseas customers in their own countries; or

(*d*) attending exhibitions or trade shows abroad.

Techniques of selling and the need for product knowledge are not only as important in export selling, but because the company

is competing on a world-wide scale, they need to be better than is
general on the home market. The fact that a salesman is dealing
with customers from, or in, another country complicates matters
but does not basically alter them.

35. Fulfilling the needs of the company. An export salesman will
spend a considerable part of his time away from the company, and
during that time not only will he represent the company, he may
well be the only contact the overseas buyer ever has. The opinion
the buyer has of the salesman will largely form his opinion of the
company.

It is important that the export salesman should fulfil the
needs of the company and inspire confidence in his own company
and among his company's customers. To ensure satisfaction in
the appointment of an export salesman, an export manager
should consider the following points.

(a) Knowledge of the company, its policy and products.

(b) Familiarity with the company's production and marketing
processes.

(c) Ability to communicate ideas and convictions.

(e) Self-reliance and ability to take effective decisions.

It is worth while to enlarge upon certain of these considerations.

(a) *The ability to satisfy a customer's needs* for technical assistance is a significant factor in overseas selling. At home it is
normally possible to compromise between the choice of a salesman or a technical man by supporting the salesman with technical
assistance. An export salesman cannot call for technical assistance
and has to be self-reliant, but at the same time the demands for
selling ability are high. Often the choice is between training a
technical man to sell, or training a salesman to be technical. The
choice will be a management decision based on the needs of the
market.

(b) *It is often difficult to communicate ideas* without resorting
to idiomatic expressions. Literal translations can frequently be
cold and unhelpful, if not positively harmful! An export salesman
should not only have a working knowledge of a language, but
should also have a fluency that will enable him to communicate
ideas and encourage enthusiasm. Where this is not possible it is
feasible for the salesman to resort to an interpreter, but it cannot
be stressed too strongly that such a person must be technically
competent; fortunately such people do exist and are very useful.

(c) A salesman working thousands of miles from home can be

faced with many decisions: "Should I stay another day and make certain of the order?" "In the face of strong competition, should I offer a discount?" "Can we deliver in only three months?" A salesman, if he has been properly briefed and trained, can take such decisions confidently and correctly.

Export salesmen also need to be good researchers and capable of compiling concise, informative reports. After every trip he should be able to give his export manager detailed information that will help in assessing the market.

36. Personal qualities of export salesmen. It has been said, "The person to do the job is a function of the job." There can be few areas of business where this is more appropriate. The precise needs of the company when applied to personnel will produce a person who will fulfil the requirements. But apart from the qualities necessary to satisfy the company, an export salesman will need many personal characteristics.

(a) *Physical fitness and stamina.* Export selling is a costly business and a salesman must make the most of his time. Frequently after a day's business a salesman will travel by night to his next scheduled appointments and will have to be fresh early in the morning.

(b) *Self-reliant.* Apart from the ability to take decisions, the export salesman will spend a great deal of time on his own. He must not get lonely or bored.

(c) *Self-discipline.* There are many attractions to a lonely salesman in most countries. It is important that he should always be conscious of his responsibilities. Overseas customers can be over-hospitable and frequently will encourage heavy drinking.

(d) *Compatibility.* Working abroad with peoples of many nationalities, races, religions and political persuasions creates a need for compatibility. An export salesman frequently has to listen to complaints and criticisms of his own country. His reaction to them will be a measure of his standing as a businessman.

(e) *Integrity.* All salesmen must guard their reputations jealously but never more so than when travelling abroad. The salesman who spends his time sightseeing when he should be seeing customers is wasting the company's money.

(f) *Enthusiasm.* On many occasions a salesman may be called away at short notice, and he will often be away from home and family for long periods. He must be enthusiastic about these journeys.

37. Basic export knowledge. Apart from these personal qualities, an export salesman needs basic export knowledge, which can be provided by company training.

(*a*) *An understanding of export administration*, in particular documentation, finance, shipping and insurance.

(*b*) *A knowledge of languages* can be vital in some forms of selling. While many executives and managers in Europe have a good knowledge of English, it is good manners to be able to speak their language. In selling some goods, especially industrial goods, it is important to instruct workers at shop floor level, where it is not usual to find people speaking anything but their own language.

Since the principles of selling apply to export selling, it is almost impossible to control a sales interview with a poor knowledge of the customer's language.

OVERSEAS JOURNEY

38. Planning an overseas selling trip. The crucial factors of a successful overseas selling trip are cost and efficiency. Too many non-exporting staff regard the overseas business trip as a "joy ride", whereas in reality it is a period of intense concentration on detail, and great physical and nervous energy.

The decision to send a salesman overseas is reached after due investigation into the results likely to be achieved. It is rarely a quick decision and is a culmination of much preparatory work.

Clear objectives are as vital to the sound planning of an overseas trip as to every other area of business planning. The reasons for making the trip must be precise and to fulfil a purpose. The vague notion of "researching the market" is not a rational approach. Export business trips should be the outcome of market research, not its purpose. Nevertheless, once market research has determined the existence of a market it may well save a great deal of time to send an executive to check on information, "get the feel" of the market and explore the best way of tackling it. The appointment of agents is a risky business and one can reduce the risk by meeting the agent and forming a personal assessment of him.

Before making any trips abroad, the export manager or salesman will spend time familiarising himself with customers' records, and getting to know of any outstanding problems they

may have. It is fruitful to discuss his visit with other departments
and see if they have any particular needs as design, production
and accounts may all have a problem that can be rapidly cleared
up by a personal visit.

39. Planning the itinerary. Once the decision to make an overseas
trip has been taken and the objectives determined, the planning
of the itinerary can take place.

In planning the itinerary it is important to bear in mind any
local conditions. The author once arrived full of plans in Han-
nover on Corpus Christi day to find it a public holiday with
everyone away. In Greece and Egypt the afternoons are given
over to rest and business begins again when the day has cooled. In
Germany work begins early and one's agent may call at the hotel
at seven o'clock in the morning.

It is wrong to try to do too much or to be away too long
without a break. Even the fittest executive may be ill after a
month of living in hotels, travelling, late nights and early
mornings. It is better to do a little thoroughly than break down
trying to do too much. The following is the itinerary of a trip the
author made in 1963.

Day	Itinerary
1. Sunday	Leave by car to take samples to preview showing for British Week in Düsseldorf.
	Air ferry to Le Touquet, drive to Brussels; discuss possible agency with "M" at 15.00. Drive to Düsseldorf.
2. Monday	Attend opening of show with agent Herr "S" and colleague Mr. "E".
3. Tuesday	Attendance on stand: afternoon visit Hertie and Karstadt with Herr "S".
	Evening, departure by air 18.00 for Geneva, Switzerland. Change flights at Zurich, meet agent Herr "Z" for general discussion 19.30. Continue to Geneva.
4. Wednesday	Appointment 09.30 at firm "X" to show new season's ranges. Lunch with Mr. "A". Afternoon visiting customers. Evening depart by air for Milan 19.00.
5. Thursday	Appointment with Signor "A" to sign agency agreement covering Northern Italy. Remainder of day visiting customers. Depart 19.00 for Paris.

6. Friday   Appointment 09.00 with M. "T" our agent in Paris to discuss details of promotions.

Visit company "L" concerning recent complaint about faulty goods.

Depart for London 18.00.

40. Ensuring routine work continues. While the export manager is away, the routine work of the office must continue. A meeting with the export office staff at which problems and queries can be discussed will usually take care of routine matters. It is not difficult to keep in touch by telephone from Western Europe, and by letter from further afield, provided the itinerary is known and hotels booked in advance.

EXPORTS AND FINANCE

41. Payment of exports. It was once said to a young salesman: "The customer who places a large order too easily is probably not going to pay for it." Getting paid for orders delivered abroad is a complicated business, and to reduce the risks certain practices have evolved. Payment of goods exported is generally by:

(*a*) letters of credit; or
(*b*) bills of exchange.

42. Letters of credit. Once an importer has decided to buy goods he will open a letter of credit with his bank. To do this the importer will deposit a substantial part of the total amount with his own bank. The bank will hold this money until the credit is paid. The importer cannot use this money which is committed to the exporter. Letters of credit exist in three categories which are:

(*a*) revocable;
(*b*) irrevocable;
(*c*) confirmed irrevocable

(*a*) *A revocable letter of credit may be revoked at any time* by the importer notifying his bank accordingly. To the exporter it does not provide very much protection, although if the customer is known it may be all that is needed to show he is serious in his intent to honour his order.

The reason for opening a revocable letter of credit lies in the system of discounting bills of exchange, which in this case would be at a keen discount, thereby saving the importer money.

(*b*) *An irrevocable letter of credit cannot be revoked by the importer* at any time and the exporter knows his money is secure.

(*c*) *A confirmed irrevocable letter of credit is confirmed by the negotiating bank* and implies that, no matter what happens to the customer, consignment, etc. the bank will pay—provided the exporter has complied with instructions. The conditions under which the letter of credit is opened are usually the result of a proforma invoice sent by the exporter. The conditions stated on the confirmed credit therefore are usually those implied by the exporter. The exporter must ensure that his documents, bills of lading, or other approved evidence of shipment, and insurance documents, are in complete agreement with the negotiating bank's instructions. Particular attention must be paid to closing dates as documents presented after that day will not be met. Any extensions to the credit will then cost the customer extra money.

43. Bills of exchange. This method of payment requires the exporter to prepare a Documentary Bill of Exchange, a system frequently known as "cash against documents" (C.A.D.). This method permits the exporter to release the shipping documents in return for payment, or for the promise of payment within a certain period of time. The system has two alternatives:

(*a*) D.P. (documents against payment); or

(*b*) D.A. (documents against acceptance).

(*i*) In D.P. transactions *the documents will be sent to the exporter's bank or shipping agents* and handed to the customer only after payment.

(*ii*) In D.A. transactions *they are handed over when the customer "accepts" the bills of exchange*, which he does by signing the bill.

The exporter will send to his bank a complete set of documents either to be paid at sight, or so many days after sight, this being expressed usually in multiples of thirty days.

PROGRESS TEST 10

1. What is the balance of payments and what two categories do payments fall into? (2)

2. How do exports cushion fluctuations in demand? (9)

3. How many forms may export transactions take? (13)

4. "The seller should determine on each occasion whether the exporter who buys the goods is acting in the capacity of a principal or as agent for the client abroad." How would you distinguish between the two? (14)

5. What documents constitute the shipping document? (18)

6. Distinguish between the different special export clauses. How is the quotation affected by the various terms? **(19)**

7. What are the two broad methods of securing payment for exports? **(41)**

CHAPTER XI

Retail Selling

1. Retailing: its place in society. Retail selling may be defined as the activities concerned with selling consumers' goods to final consumers. If it is considered as a part of the economic system of production, exchange and distribution, it is that part of the chain that seeks to predict consumers' needs, calls the goods into production and ensures their ultimate distribution.

RETAIL BUSINESS ORGANISATION

2. Retail shops. Marketing specialists when considering the retail trade distinguish different classifications of retail shops. The following headings are generally accepted.

(*a*) Independent retailers.
(*b*) Variety chains.
(*c*) Departmental stores.
(*d*) Consumer co-operatives.
(*e*) Multiple chains.

3. Independent retailers. These generally represent all the sales outlets not included under the other headings. They are the small shopkeepers who operate within the limits of their own capital, frequently take all the risks and have independent policies of buying and supply. They vary considerably in the level of the turnover, but a simple classification is that of small, medium and large.

4. Variety chains. These are groups of stores operating in different areas or different towns but with a common policy and, increasingly, their own branded goods, although they also sell other popular branded goods. They offer a wide variety of merchandise and this has in the past tended to appeal to lower income groups. Since the early 1950s, however, the better-known chains, Marks & Spencer, F. W. Woolworth, Littlewoods and British Home Stores, for example, have all traded up and have widened their area of appeal considerably. Marks & Spencer in particular have not only established their own brand, "St. Michael", as a leading national brand in clothing, but have also expanded into a considerable export trade.

5. Departmental stores. These are large stores with at least five distinctive departments under one roof, i.e. clothing, hardware, furniture, foodstuffs, and soft furnishings. The larger stores are usually located in the main cities with smaller stores emulating them in less densely populated areas. In recent years the situation has changed somewhat, as the major groups have tended to expand through acquisition and imparted to their new subsidiaries something of their own image. Independent department stores have grown up and can be quite large even in the smaller towns, but generally lack the sophistication of the older stores.

6. Consumer co-operatives. These are societies formed by an association trading for the benefit of its members. The co-operative movement developed in the nineteenth century from socialist concepts, and has developed to include the wholesaling function as well as the retail; it has also sought to manufacture its own products, including clothing and food in particular, and has spread into banking and services such as funerals and weddings in some areas. The movement has traditionally been strongest in "working class" areas but has endeavoured to penetrate the markets dominated by the department stores. Its success in this area has been helped by the adoption of "store names", e.g. Fairfax House, Cavendish House, etc. which have overcome resistance by many customers to the co-operative movement.

7. Multiple chains. These are organisations controlling at least five retail branches. It is usual for the multiple chain to restrict its trading to fairly narrow lines; clothing, foodstuffs, hardware, chemists and so on. The multiple chains have been the foremost in changing to supermarkets, particularly in the grocery trade, and this has often led to a broadening of merchandise stocked.

For the sales function of a manufacturer, these general classifications will have differing degrees of importance according to the product he makes. It will also vary in terms of his sales policies. For the manufacturer of hair lacquer the variety chains may be the most important, and the departmental stores may be relatively unimportant. But for the manufacturer of good quality shoes, the multiple chains specialising in footwear will be the market to pay most attention to.

RETAIL DISTRIBUTION

8. Shop distribution. Sales management will find shop distribution its most important consideration in arranging distribution of its products. This term denotes the number of shops stocking the product and not the way in which the products are physically moved.

Shop distribution is an important concept for sales management to ensure that the company's investment in advertising to the consumer will not be wasted. If the manufacturer spends a large amount of money upon his advertising, he may create a demand for his products by many people over a wide area; it is vital that consumers, motivated to buy the product, can find it stocked by as many shops as possible. If the consumer cannot find the manufacturer's brand, he may buy a competitor's. Shop distribution may be considered as:

    (*a*) "actual"; and
    (*b*) "sterling".

There is an important distinction between the two and this is evident in the disparity in the sales turnover between various retail shops.

> EXAMPLE: A town has forty grocers' shops. Of these, ten larger shops account for 75 per cent of the business while the remaining thirty shops account for only 25 per cent of the business. The supplier will have achieved 25 per cent "actual" distribution, i.e. ten out of forty shops, and 75 per cent "sterling" distribution, i.e. the ten shops will do 75 per cent of the business.

For the sales manager "sterling" distribution is the most important.

9. The changing pattern in retail distribution. Retailing has in the past been rather static in its form; what sufficed at the end of the nineteenth century survived with little change until the period of the Second World War. Since 1945 the retail business has become more and more dynamic. The reasons for this lie in:

    (*a*) greater affluence among consumers leading to demands for a wider range of goods;
    (*b*) wider consumer knowledge of goods available through mass advertising;
    (*c*) more mobility of population by:

(*i*) personal cars allowing a wider freedom of shopping; and

(*ii*) a general tendency to move residences more frequently;

(*d*) an increase in nationally known branded goods and increase in competition generally; and

(*e*) escalation of costs in terms of buildings, maintenance, transport and labour which, coupled with the greater competition, has reduced margins.

The mobility afforded to individuals by the motor car has not been the only factor influencing shopping habits; the increased use of deep freezers and refrigerators has also exerted an effect and led to the "once-a-week" shopping trip.

Urban renewal schemes constantly upset the balance of shopping centres. Frequently the demands for motorways or urban highways and bypasses cause the destruction or isolation of established shopping centres. Many smaller towns that relied upon through traffic for the bulk of their business have found themselves forgotten when a bypass has taken the traffic away. All too often retailers have to take decisions on whether to stay in existing premises with the accompanying risk of a declining trade, or take the alternative risk of moving to a new shopping centre, not all of which have been successful.

10. Trends in distribution. It is important to analyse the trends that have led to the change in retailing, and to do this one must examine two factors: economic, and the relative standing of different classifications of retailers.

Since the early 1950s the various factors outlined in **9** have combined to bring about a concentration of the retail trade in a pattern reflecting the concentration of industry in general. The factors causing this concentration have been:

(*a*) the decline of certain types of trading and smaller traders;

(*b*) the disproportionate growth of certain firms and forms of trading;

(*c*) the absorption of many older and declining firms by acquisition, which has sometimes led to their closure and sometimes to their incorporation into a more dynamic business organisation; and

(*d*) the tendency, also evident in industry as a whole, for the number of firms going out of business to be greater than the number of new firms being established.

The concentration as a whole has been evident in two ways.

(*a*) The development of larger stores.

(*b*) The considerable expansion of supermarkets and self-service stores, originally in the grocery trade but now spreading to other businesses.

11. Social factors. The trends in distribution may also reflect social changes in the country which have occurred in a parallel development. These are:

(*a*) a greater demand for leisure activities and free time;
(*b*) the influence of television;
(*c*) an increased pressure of living pace; and
(*d*) a much larger number of women at work leading to demands on shopping time.

None of these social factors alone has brought about the changes in retailing, any more than single economic factors, but combined they have produced a social development within the framework of which retailing has a part. It is not too great an exaggeration to say that Britain in the 1980s will be vastly different to Britain in the 1940s and early 1950s; that this change has been recognised by retailers is seen in the rise of new forms of retailing; those that have failed to perceive the changing tide of society or resisted it have gone out of business. Retailing is now a dynamic business in a dynamic society.

12. Multiple chains: advantages over independents. The multiple chains have secured advantages over the independent retailers by their ability to take advantage of the changing situation, and have promoted more rapid growth by the use of improved techniques such as:

(*a*) mass production for mass markets;
(*b*) bulk buying for all the stores in the chain; and
(*c*) pre-packaging and own branding.

All these techniques have enabled them to reduce their costs and pass this on to the consumer in more competitive prices.

A multiple chain has another important advantage over the independent; whereas the latter is dependent upon his single, or maybe two, stores for his livelihood, the multiple can spread his risk over the entire chain, often covering wide areas of the country. This ability has allowed the multiples to experiment with new techniques, often in only one or two stores at a time. If the new techniques are seen to be of value, then they will be exploited on a national basis. The multiple will generally be better known than the independent, and will capitalise his name and also offer a wider range of well-known and reputable branded goods.

There are some disadvantages to the multiple chains arising from the wide areas over which they operate which makes communication difficult. Some branches may be much smaller than others and be insufficiently profitable to enable a satisfactory salary to be offered to the manager; this can lead to poor management.

13. Changing role of department stores. Department stores originated as independent stores, but in the last twenty years amalgamations have led to the grouping together of large numbers of stores. This group organisation has led to many department store groups operating along the lines of the multiples with group bulk buying and branding of their own goods. Nevertheless they are at a disadvantage by being generally too distant from their customers, and they tend to have high operating and maintenance costs. They also have an obligation to continue many of their special services, such as deliveries, alterations, credit facilities, in order to maintain a competitive advantage.

The department stores were essentially founded on the premise that women liked shopping and had sufficient time to do it. They were large stores where women could circulate around different departments, and to a large extent relied upon impulse purchasing by their customers. To this end they:

   (a) *concentrated a wide range of merchandise* within one store;

   (b) *emphasised customer service* and maintained well-trained staff; and

   (c) *frequently offered a free delivery service* and undertook alterations of garments, curtains, etc.

The changes that have taken place in the social sphere have reduced the appeal of many of these factors. Over a third of women work and have limited shopping time during lunch break, and perhaps a quick dash into a shop for a particular item or items on their way home. This restriction of shopping time has made women turn more to the self-service store which is faster and frequently cheaper. The department stores have been unable to operate in the same way as the multiples simply from the sheer competition and need to reduce costs.

To cope with the increased costs of labour and overheads since 1973, many stores are having to forgo the personalized service traditional to them, and introduce a large measure of self-selection. In order to broaden their appeal to a wider range of social classes, many stores have done away with their characteristic window displays in order to allow passers-by to see into the stores, so attracting their custom.

14. Mail order. Mail order has had a major impact upon the operations of the department stores in particular, but while it has been growing rapidly—an 80 per cent increase in the four years from 1957 and an estimated future growth of 12 per cent per year—it has not had much impact on retailing otherwise.

Mail order businesses originated in the United States, largely as a means of enabling consumers in the remoter western areas to buy good quality merchandise from reputable suppliers on favourable terms. They grew rapidly, and some firms, e.g. Sears Roebuck, became enormous companies with huge catalogues offering a far wider range than any ever seen in Britain. The rise of the motor car, better communications and the spread of other forms of retailing into the remoter areas as the towns grew has caused many of the mail order companies to establish their own stores; Sears Roebuck again was foremost in this.

In Britain mail order has fulfilled rather different needs, and the benefits have derived from its credit facilities rather than its customers' remoteness from the market. The advantages lie in the fact that it:

(*a*) is less time-consuming than shopping around;

(*b*) means people buying from mail order catalogues in the security of their homes are less price conscious; and

(*c*) has easy credit terms.

While the service offers advantages to consumers, there are areas of disadvantage to the operating companies. These are:

(*a*) the long-term planning of catalogues;

(*b*) inflexible pricing;

(*c*) stocking problems arising from inaccurate forecasts; and

(*d*) no personal contact, except by the agent.

That mail order has had an effect upon retail business cannot be denied, but it could be combated by more flexible attitudes on the part of retailers, particularly in shopping hours. One could question the need to open at nine o'clock in the morning. Certainly tobacconists, newspaper shops, perhaps grocers, but need menswear shops or furniture stores be open first thing? Why not open at 11.00 a.m. and remain open until 7.00 p.m.? Many of our big cities "die" at 5.30, unlike continental cities which are active until late. It is an area for exploitation, but it needs concerted action by a Chamber of Commerce or similar; it is no good one shop opening in isolation.

15. Co-operatives. The co-operative movement was founded in a particular period of our history and under certain economic and social conditions. These conditions have changed and the co-operative movement has had to change accordingly. That it has lagged in the change can be seen from the decline in its percentage of total retail sales since the war. This has been a feature of co-operatives in the United States as well as Britain. Recently the movement has begun to improve its image by the adoption of a new corporate image that plays down the regional nature of the "industrial co-operatives".

16. Voluntary chains. The growth of the voluntary chain probably owes more to the declining fortunes of the wholesale function than it does to the uncompetitive stand of the independent retailer.

Manufacturers' greater investment in brand names and the need to shorten the lines of distribution to their stockists, so exerting greater influence and reducing margins, has contributed to the decline of the wholesaler. This movement has been further exacerbated by the more effective transport facilities obviating the need for the regional wholesaler.

Wholesalers have in some instances arrested their declining importance by means of the voluntary chain organisations. Under this system a number of independent retailers undertake to buy all their supplies from a certain wholesaler. This enables the wholesaler to reduce his operating costs and frequently to dispense with the personal salesman. Often it will lead to a brand name being used, and this is reflected in the title of the retailers who will trade under that banner rather than their own names. The economies achieved by bulk buying and less risk in distribution are passed on to the retailer in lower prices and also in the form of market guidance.

RETAIL PLANNING

17. Strategy in retailing. It will have become apparent from what has been said already that retailing today is liable to sudden change arising from social and economic needs. The decline of the independent retailer in the face of competition from the larger organisations, and their own problems in competing with mail order and other forms of selling, make long-term strategy necessary.

It has been the practice for firms in retailing to watch the trends of the trade cycle for indications of the future prosperity of their sector of the market. Since the trade cycle itself is now questionable as an indicator of prosperity due to the influence of social payments, trade unionism and government action, it is not satisfactory as a means of judging levels of investment or stocks. The complex nature of the modern economy with its large-scale operations, greater technology and competitiveness makes increased demands on investment decisions. The trend towards a more positive strategic planning instead of simply watching the trade cycle creates a need for better management.

Better management is really a demand for more scientific management. Frederick W. Taylor summed the situation up in his testimony to the Special House Committee of the American Senate; although he was not speaking of retailing, it nevertheless applies: "Exact scientific knowledge and methods are everywhere, sooner or later, sure to replace rule-of-thumb." For retailing, beset with the pressures of the modern economy, the "sooner" has come.

18. Aims of strategy in retailing. Strategy is inseparable from objectives. The aims of it can be found from the answers to these questions.

(a) What do we want?
(b) How do we get it?

The objectives in retailing will naturally vary according to the firm and its management or proprietor, but for the positive company interested in long-term security and success they will resolve themselves as:

(a) ensuring a satisfactory level of return now and in the future; and

(b) determining a sound long-term competitive position.

Having resolved the objectives to some acceptable formula, the retailer will embark upon long-term planning to ensure the achievement of his objectives.

19. Long-term planning in retailing. Long-term planning in retailing denotes the preparation of plans for at least five years ahead, and in the present state of flux in retailing perhaps that is about as far as is sensible, although the strategy may project further. Figure 44 examines the structures of long-term planning in retailing.

(*a*) The company will, through the medium of research, endeavour to explore the areas of:

(*i*) marketing research to determine the needs of the market, now and in the future; by economic research to predict what conditions will apply, e.g. will the general level of income rise, fall or remain stagnant? and by consumer research to anticipate consumer needs, greater leisure and sporting activities; and

(*ii*) internal assessment to determine whether the existing organisation is suitable for the anticipated future needs, management, financial resources, marketing skills and staff abilities.

(*b*) From the results of marketing and internal research combined with the company's concept of what its policy should be, the objectives will be determined.

(*c*) The company's over-all policy will be broken down into departmental objectives which will be subject to departmental planning to achieve their particular objectives. The plans will be devised, a time scale for achievement established, a feasibility study made, and from this the plan will either be accepted or subjected to revision.

(*d*) If the plan is accepted it will be incorporated with other departmental plans into the operational plan and put into effect.

(*e*) The operations will be subject to continuing review and the experience of the operation will be the starting point for further forecasting, both in the short- and long-term.

20. Planning for growth. If a retail company does not advance, it will stagnate, for in retailing as in other spheres of business there can be no standing still. Long-term planning must make provision for growth, and growth may mean a company has to think in terms of products or customers other than those it sells to at present.

If a company plans for growth or a more stable market position it may need to broaden its operational base. This process, usually known as "diversification", need not in fact take a company outside its known operations.

Figure 45 charts ways in which a retail firm, in this case a decorator's store, can move into quite different areas of selling and still retain a strong link with its existing operations. Basically its operations can be in the field of related marketing or unrelated marketing techniques. Its customers can be the same, similar to itself or different, but with the exception of the final area of

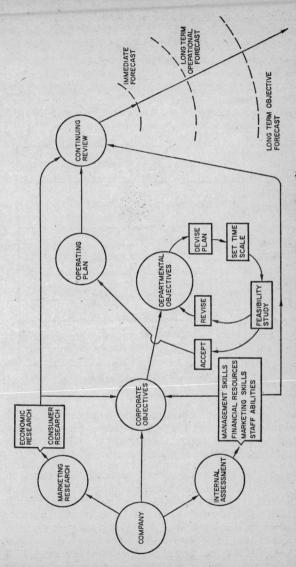

FIG. 44. *Structure of long-term planning in retailing.*

different customers and unrelated marketing, it is maintaining a
link with its present known abilities. The thinking behind long-
term planning should be along the following lines.

(a) The improvement of market share and continuance of
profitable operations.

(b) To ensure the firm competes in growing markets rather than
deteriorating ones.

(c) To maintain cash flow at a level compatible with the needs
of existing resources and building new ones.

OPERATIONS / CUSTOMER	RELATED MARKETING	UNRELATED MARKETING
SAME CUSTOMER	FORMICA SHEETING	CURTAIN MATERIALS
SIMILIAR CUSTOMER	INDUSTRIAL PAINT FOR LOCAL AUTHORITY HOUSING	PLUMBING ACCESSORIES
OWN CUSTOMER	MAKE PAINT, LADDERS, FIREPLACES	ESTATE AGENCY (PROPERTY REPAIRS)
DIFFERENT CUSTOMER	CHEMICAL RESISTANT COATING FOR ROAD TANKER INTERIORS	MOTOR ACCESSORIES FOR GARAGES

FIG. 45. *Decorator's store—suggestions for
different areas of selling.*

The needs of long-term planning force management to think
objectively and rationally. They also emphasise the demand for
co-operation between different departments and ensure they
are all working to common objectives.

21. Organisation needs of long-term planning. The retail organisation, if it is to function effectively in its task of long-term
planning, has to undergo modification to ensure continuity and
direction of effort. A massive effort to understand the corporate
need and its satisfaction, and to produce a long-term plan and
implement it, must be done on a continuous basis if it is to be of
any use. This means that organisation must make provision for
planning on a permanent basis and this can rarely be achieved by

part-time application from senior managers already busy with their jobs. It requires retail organisation to provide for:

(*a*) corporate planning groups;
(*b*) management services departments; or
(*c*) research and development departments.

The organisation must be on a functional basis in relationship to the remainder of the organisation structure. This shows the research and development responsible to the managing director, but available for consultation to all other functional heads.

LOCATING THE RETAIL STORE

22. Retail store location. Retail stores rely upon customers visiting them and making purchases. For this to be a reliable and continuous feature, the location of the store is of vital importance. The location will determine the volume of sales and the eventual level of profit. With the rebuilding of many older areas of towns and the gradual decline of other areas the location of a shop cannot be seen as of permanent value. The factors listed in 23 illustrate the phases any store location will go through, the only doubtful point being—how long will the process take? The problem is making itself felt in Britain, while in the United States it has reached major proportions. Large department stores that used to be in the main shopping streets of New York and other big cities have now been re-located outside the towns, largely due to the needs of a car-conscious population, congestion in the cities, and the changing status of certain areas of the cities. It is reasonable to state that not enough attention is given to the implications of retail shops. The basic factors in location are:

(*a*) those that influence the decision to locate in a *particular city or shopping area*, and
(*b*) those that determine a particular *site within the chosen city*.

23. Location decision-making. There are several factors which must be considered before deciding upon the location of a store, even in the broad terms of a city or a shopping precinct. There must be considerations in the area of:

(*a*) the existing population;
(*b*) the population trend;
(*c*) the age structure;
(*d*) levels of income;

(*e*) the degree of competition;
(*f*) future urban plans (developments for roads, etc.); and
(*g*) the anticipated sales volume.

All these factors will exert a degree of influence, or pull, in the location decision. ~

24. Selecting a specific site. The selection of a specific site is a matter of estimating the likely return from the investment in the site. Early in the appraisal the retailer will estimate what the potential sales are likely to be as volume of sales will be the decisive factor in the choice of a site.

Clearly any decisions on the potential sales volume have to be related to the buying habits of the population in relation to the goods that the proposed store will sell. A simple distinction would be between groceries and consumer goods. On the whole consumers will want to buy their groceries as close to home as possible, or in a shopping centre where there are facilities for parking cars. For consumer goods, which include clothing, furnishings, electrical goods, etc., an area containing a wide choice is desirable, as people will wish to shop around before making a buying decision.

Planning the location of retail outlets is becoming more hazardous as the trend to movement of populations continues. It was at one time relatively safe to establish a store in a city centre, and less certain to open one in the suburbs. Today the situation has altered. With the immense building programmes and more particularly the expansion of the car-owning public, the entire concept of shopping has altered. The consumer now moves further afield. Where once a housewife would take a bus to a town centre and walk around a fairly compact shopping area, she can now go by car to out-of-town shopping areas. Many towns now have extensive markets situated on their outskirts. From the store's viewpoint this is good. Not only will rates be lower than town centres, but the shopper who takes a car to the shop door will certainly be persuaded to buy more. This has been shown by the development in size of the trolley which is larger and can be taken out to the car.

25. Predicting the volume of sales. The prediction of the sales volume is a problem of forecasting, and as such cannot be a precise figure. It can only be arrived at by consideration of such factors as are likely to influence the sales, and by combining them attempt to calculate what might happen under the known conditions. One method of attempting such a prediction is the *traffic count system*.

26. Traffic counting. Traffic counting refers to the counting of pedestrian traffic passing a specific shop or site. In particular it is used to determine:

(*a*) numbers of people;
(*b*) kinds of people;
(*c*) time of day with the greatest volume of people; and
(*d*) days of the week with the greatest volume of people.

It is based upon the supposition that a heavier volume of pedestrian traffic will, other things being equal, lead to a greater volume of business.

Difficulties arise from determining the following.

(*a*) Which people shall be counted?
    (*i*) All the people?
    (*ii*) One sex only?
    (*iii*) By age groups?
(*b*) On which day of the week shall they be counted?

EXAMPLE: A bakery was interested in a site for a new shop in a town of some 18,000 inhabitants in South Wales. Like many valley towns, the shopping area was essentially a single street, with a few smaller shops in the side streets.

Local knowledge indicated that the peak shopping period in the town was between 12.00 and 2.00 p.m. on a Friday. In order to assess the relative merits of two possible locations, a traffic count was undertaken at two points in the town during the peak shopping period.

One census point was outside the proposed premises and the other outside the local branch of Woolworth's at an intersection a little way off.

It was found that the pedestrian traffic did not favour any particular side of the road, although at point (2) the traffic was 2,480 pedestrians per hour, while at point (1), the proposed site, it dropped to 946 pedestrians per hour.

As a result of other enquiries combined with the traffic count it was decided to locate elsewhere.

27. Model simulation of the shopping process. From government census returns on the distribution of goods and services, the annual Family Expenditure Survey, and the Annual Report of the National Food Survey Committee, it is possible to assess the shopping needs of a given population, and these can then be translated into over-all shopping floorspace requirements. The information is not of direct use, however, when deciding about locations of sites. It has to be supplemented with market research.

28. Market research. To supplement the enquiry stated in the example given above, a questionnaire was used which asked respondents which type of shop they would definitely use as local shops rather than going elsewhere; the shops selected are listed in order according to the percentage of those who said they would definitely use one.

(a) Chemist.
(b) Post Office.
(c) Grocer.
(d) Baker.
(e) Butcher.
(f) Greengrocer.
(g) Newsagent/tobacconist/confectioner.
(h) Fishmonger.
(i) Bank.

This type of information is an aid to understanding what types of shops are preferred to be near home, and what types will induce people to travel further from home.

Market research will also answer questions about "who shops in a particular town and why?" A market research survey conducted by students to aid in the re-location of an off-licence revealed the following information about pedestrian traffic:

(a) *Percentage who shop in "Tiny-town" regularly*   82
(b) *Percentage buying take-home drinks at*:
    Supermarket   49
    Off-licence   43
    Public house   8
    Chemist's shop   0
(c) *Reasons for buying at a particular place*:
    Convenience   59
    Cheapness   32
    Selection   5
    Service   4
    Free delivery   0
(d) *Services required*:
    Cheaper drinks   26
    Wine sampling facilities   19

Wide selection   17
Wine information   15
Free delivery   0

The information has been put into graphical form in Fig. 46
and makes it clear that the answers to the questions "Where do
people like to buy alcoholic drinks, why, and what do they
want?", in this case are "in a supermarket, for convenience and
cheapness".

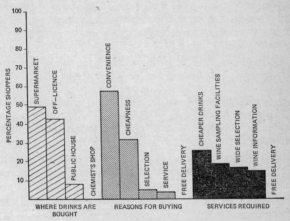

FIG. 46. *Making a decision on location.*

29. Inducing shop entries. Customers have to be induced to enter
the shop before they will be persuaded to buy. While the skill of
the sales personnel can be brought to bear once a person has
entered a shop, the inducement to enter is the result of impersonal
appeals. There are factors which will influence a passer-by in his
intention to enter a shop, and the retailer must consider what he
can do to make the factors more effective. The factors are location, pulling power and price.

The location's suitability should already have been determined.
The pulling power is less easy to define. Some have determined the
length of window as a basis for measuring effectiveness; there are
many boutiques which have had the windows completely painted
out, so the length on its own is not a reasonable criterion. Clearly
the pulling power of the window is related more to its effective use
than its dimensions. Many of the most attractive displays are
small but appealing, many are simple and certainly not the result

of using the entire length of the window in the strictest sense. In Amsterdam in the 1960s I was much impressed by the simplicity of display which had tremendous pulling power. Price is an ambiguous criterion. What appeals in price? One can turn possible customers away by its incorrect handling, as much as encourage them by its correct use.

30. Layout. The manner in which the equipment, merchandise, fixtures, sales aids, displays, aisles and supporting departments are organised is known as the layout. They must be laid out in accordance with a prearranged plan determined by an examination of customer needs and appeals. Factors which will influence layout are:

(*a*) dimensions of the building, including number of floors;

(*b*) types and quantities of merchandise to be handled;

(*c*) known characteristics of the customers;

(*d*) location of permanent features, i.e. stairs, lifts, escalators, loading bays, etc.; and

(*e*) design and size of the intended fixtures and ancillary equipment.

All these factors will be combined to produce the best solution in accord with the management's preferences. These preferences should be based upon the ideas that:

(*a*) the store should be made as attractive as possible and should invite customers to enter; and

(*b*) the layout should make the most effective use of available space and is an allocation of scarce resources.

RETAIL PERSONNEL

31. Dealing with complaints. All enterprises are bound to encounter complaints from time to time. They may arise from the firm's operations, or by some fault of suppliers, or others entwined with the firm's operations. The retailer will regard complaints as occasions to build goodwill for the firm and enhance its reputation. This does not imply that the policy should be to give way to the customer every time. Management has to see that its staff are appraised of the firm's policy in dealing with complaints and be able to distinguish between different kinds, such as:

(*a*) complaints made by customers who feel they have a real cause for complaint; and

(*b*) those who would take advantage of the firm's policy.

However a complaint is handled, a record should be kept, and the data so compiled should be used to classify complaints so that they can be avoided in the future, as far as possible.

32. Techniques of selling. In retailing today there are two broad classifications of obtaining sales. These are:

(a) personal selling using *trained salespeople*; and
(b) impersonal selling using *self-selection means*.

The techniques of personal selling have been dealt with in Chapter IX, and here we are concerned with self-selection only.

33. Change to self-selection. The conversion of a conventional shop or wholesalers, whether a food, non-food or even a specialist business such as a builder's merchants, to a self-selection or cash and carry store is often undertaken for the purpose of economising in the sales operation. Rising labour costs generally encouraged the growth of the self-service operation as a means of reducing the labour costs aspect of store management. In the present day context, however, this can be a misguided belief. A self-service store may easily require as many sales staff as the conventional store; indeed it is generally vital not to cut down on staff.

34. Sales staff are more important than ever before. A builders' merchants changing to self-selection with check-outs should not cut down its sales staff. In this type of operation, the sales staff can be a vital factor in increasing sales—provided the training is such that it will ensure their full effectiveness. In a self-selection store, sales staff have increased time to give attention to customers as:

(a) sales staff are no longer obliged to serve customers;
(b) the customers will prefer to serve themselves, and this permits the assistant to give attention to several customers at once; and
(c) the sales staff become specialist selling staff and are no longer involved in cash handling, giving change and wrapping goods.

The purpose of the self-selection system is to maximise the use of sales staff; because they are no longer required to attend to non-selling activities they are more effectively used. During the busiest selling times, the sales staff are able to attend to more customers and give an immediate service. They will be concerned solely with creating customers, the prime function of sales staff.

35. The need for a new understanding. The following incident happened in a builders' merchants that had recently been converted to a self-selection store.

> EXAMPLE: A builder, who had been looking around for some while, asked the manager where he could find putty. The manager was both eager to help and to show his staff how to deal with customers. Although there were other customers in the vicinity, he took the builder to the appropriate shelving and then, instead of leaving him to select, and returning to the other customers, the manager selected a tin of putty and chatting amiably in his usual manner, led him to the cash desk. There he continued to talk while he wrapped the tin and, taking over from the cashier, rang up the cash, gave change, and finally walked to the door with the customer.

A change to self-selection has to be accompanied by the correct mental adjustment on the part of sales staff; this applies particularly to older staff. In the example given above, the manager was behaving in a way in which he had been trained many years before, and to him it was helpful and polite, the essence of good salesmanship. Unfortunately it was not appropriate in the new setting. In the self-selection builders' merchants, he made two serious mistakes.

(*a*) The builder whom he served was politely led out of the store without being given the chance to make impulse purchases.

(*b*) While he was giving his personal attention to the one customer the other customers left.

36. Self-selection must aid circulation. The essence of the self-selection operation is that while a customer may enter the store to make a single purchase, by a careful grouping of related products the customer will be stimulated to buy other goods on impulse. The manager, by attending to routine matters, had taken the builder out of buying circulation and himself out of selling circulation.

It is vital when undertaking conversions of this kind that the activities of selling or servicing customers are separated from the activities concerned with after-sales, e.g. cash, wrapping.

37. Basic steps in training staff. There are five essential points in developing a natural and efficient manner in self-service dealing with customers.

(*a*) *Welcome customer*. When customers enter it is only necessary to welcome them; this establishes a friendly relationship and tells customers the salesman is available. Unless customers ask for help, the salesman does nothing and allows the customers to circulate. This enables the salesman to deal with all customers and customers to select merchandise.

Selling in a self-selection store is accomplished by the merchandise in the manner it is displayed, arranged and promoted.

(*b*) *Readiness to give service*. When a customer is in need of help, it can usually be deduced by attitude. The salesman will then make himself available to assist.

(*c*) *Correct approach*. "Can you find what you want?" and not "Can I help you?" is the correct approach. "Can I help you?" obliges the salesman to give help, and it may be unnecessary.

Supposing the customer answers, "Yes, I want a 100 millimetre brush", the sales assistant will be obliged to serve the customer by getting the brush.

The question "Can you find what you want?" only obliges the salesman to point out where the merchandise is. It may be that the customer will need additional information as he may not be sure exactly what he wants, and in this instance the salesman will provide the information. The essential point is that the customer is free to continue shopping.

(*d*) *Make the sale*. When it becomes apparent that the customer is interested in an item that needs a little more selling, the salesman gives all the information, advice or demonstration that is needed.

The need emphasises again the importance of product knowledge. It is important that the customer is assured of the salesman's adequacy to fulfil his needs. The builder who wants a plasticiser and asks: "What ratio do I use for a 1 : 4 cement–sand mix?" and gets the answer . . . "Er . . . what?" or "Just a moment, sir, I'll read the can. . . ." is not likely to waste further time.

It is important for the salesman in a self-selection store, as much as any other form of selling, to make himself familiar with the product. He is not there only to fill shelves, he is there to sell by providing convincing answers.

(*e*) *Let the customer continue in circulation*. It is important that the salesman can distinguish between closing the sale and allowing the customer to go on shopping. He will put the customer back into circulation by suggestion: "While I have the paint taken to your van, sir, you might like to have a look at our new line of paint brush cleaners."

The examples have been taken from a builders' merchants; they will be appropriate in their right form in any self-selection store.

38. Basis for improvement. When the sales staff of a self-selection store, no matter what the business, consumer or industrial, are familiar with the appropriate techniques, it will be found that:

(*a*) volume of sales will increase;
(*b*) salesmen will sell more;
(*c*) service is improved at the busiest time;
(*d*) it becomes easier for the salesman to provide a service;
(*e*) there is a diminution of selling costs; and
(*f*) the business will be more profitable.

PROGRESS TEST 11

1. What are the types of retail establishment distinguished by marketing specialists? (2)
2. Define "actual" distribution and "sterling" distribution. (8)
3. What techniques aided the multiple chains to secure advantages? (12)
4. What should be the aims of strategy in retailing? (18)
5. What are the organisation needs of long-term planning? (21)
6. What is "traffic counting" and how would you use it in locating a store? (26)
7. What factors if any may influence a passer-by in his decision to enter a shop or not? (29)
8. What factors will influence shop layout? (30)

CHAPTER XII

Sales Management

Sales management is concerned with the management of the selling function; since this work is concerned with the entire selling function it must follow that many of the activities are the subject of separate chapters. This chapter therefore is concerned with the broad responsibilities of sales management, excluding those activities dealt with in depth elsewhere.

1. Scientific management. Before devoting time to the specialist sales management as a function of the business operation, it is important to understand what the principles of management are and how they relate to sales management. It is easy to think of "management" as a general term covering certain work in the business administration, a mere title awarded arbitrarily. It is accepted that solicitors, doctors, accountants, etc., must conform to certain rules of their professions, and so too must management be guided by specific principles; it is important that these are understood so that management ceases to be the result of personalities and instead is based upon recognisable fundamentals which are common to management in all its aspects. Management's role can be determined as a responsibility combining four essential elements. These are:

- (a) planning;
- (b) co-ordinating;
- (c) controlling; and
- (d) motivating.

These four elements of management are interrelated and each exerts an influence on a particular situation. When that situation alters, the manner in which the elements are used will also change. Management's skill is in the recognition of the situation and in responding with the correct action to rectify the situation.

ELEMENTS OF MANAGEMENT

2. Planning. Planning is an essential element of management and will be carried out in all management's differing functions. It is an answer to the question, "what must be done", and will determine also "who will do it". The basic requirements of all plans are that:

(*a*) they must be based on fact, or upon rational assumptions;

(*b*) they must be realistic;

(*c*) they must be comprehensive;

(*d*) they must incorporate sufficient flexibility to allow for reasonable variation; and

(*e*) they must be known to all involved in carrying out the task.

3. Application of planning. A firm of menswear manufacturers planned to develop a market in Western Germany. The plan was based upon extensive market research and personal visits by the export manager to verify facts. The plans were evaluated after investigating the total market for the particular type of menswear, the total imports from Britain, and all the other information for producing a reasonable target for sales. The plans included contingencies for material supplies, production capacity and shipping. Flexibility was provided by establishing a specialist production line to allow for variation to production, and the plan itself was to be subject to continual review. The details of the plan were discussed with all the departmental heads and their subordinates who would bear responsibility for fulfilling their parts of the plan.

4. Co-ordination. Co-ordination may be described as the essence of management. It is a concomitant of planning and consists largely of what a manager makes of it. It derives from the manager's personal sense of co-operation and requires tact, understanding and guidance. Co-ordination helps the staff to see the total picture of the task and in turn to co-ordinate their activities accordingly with the rest of the team.

The following points should be noted about it.

(*a*) It will encourage direct personal contact within the organisation, particularly in lateral relationships.

(*b*) The co-ordination concept must be fundamental to the business operations and will be basic to, and arise from, the planning element.

(*c*) It will encourage the free flow of information that is relative to the objectives of the business.

(*d*) It will see that no personal problems arising from the business operation are ignored but will endeavour to help through a free exchange of ideas.

5. Co-ordination and sales management. Managing a team of salesmen presents particular problems of co-ordination which are a challenge to sales management. For example a salesman selling protective coatings determined a possible need for the products treating oil storage tanks on an admiralty tank farm in Wales. On attempting to sell the idea to the engineers the complexities of the transaction emerged. He contacted his sales manager, who by co-ordinating the activities of those members of the sales force and head office staff who could help, brought about a successful conclusion. This involved:

(*a*) *sending the works chemist to Wales* to investigate the technical nature of the problem and then produce a suitable specification;

(*b*) *directing the Midlands salesman to a firm of specialist shotblasters* and metal sprayers to enlist their aid in working out the cost and eventually to apply the materials;

(*c*) *directing the London salesman to the head office of the Department of the Environment*, the authority responsible, to find out their recommended specifications and obtain a ruling on whether they would accept the company's;

(*d*) *directing the South Wales salesman to the regional office of the D. of E.* to see the District Officer to "sell" him the scheme; and

(*e*) *visiting the site himself with the local salesman* to ensure that all the details were appropriate.

6. Controlling the sales force. Controlling arises from the activity of planning and ensures that set targets, budgets or schedules are attained. It will also instigate procedures to bring to light a failure to attain targets. Sales management's role in controlling is especially onerous as many of the targets are the results of forecasts. Salesmen's targets are predictions based upon estimates of their forthcoming sales. Not only does the control system have to determine whether targets were achieved but also whether the system of prediction is accurate enough. It must:

(*a*) prepare sales and market forecasts;
(*b*) determine the level of the sales budget;
(*c*) determine the sales quotas for each salesman;
(*d*) continue the review and selection of distribution channels;
(*e*) organise an efficient sales office;
(*f*) establish a system of sales reporting;
(*g*) establish a system of statistical sales control;

(*h*) establish a stock control system;
(*i*) establish a delivery control system;
(*j*) continue the review of performance of the sales force; and
(*k*) establish periodical training programmes.

EXAMPLE: A force is established to sell industrial cleaners on a national scale. From the sales manager's prediction of the size of market, determined by marketing research, the size of the sales force is decided. Each salesman is awarded a territory which has been calculated to be sufficient to cover the salesman's total costs, but not so big that it cannot be adequately covered. Each salesman has a target set for a specific period, and from his weekly sales results a control system is established that will reveal whether he is working efficiently.

The sales office will be responsible to the sales manager for the receipt and processing of orders, for statistical records and for ensuring the correct despatch of the goods.

7. Motivation. Motivation may be described as an important role of leadership (*see* **17**) and as such is essentially a human relations concept. The ability to motivate requires a knowledge of industrial psychology as a means of understanding behaviour patterns. The sales manager's responsibility for motivation may be summarised as follows.

(*a*) If the members of a sales team are not motivated to the achievement of the goals of the company, then the goals will not be reached.

(*b*) Motivation is accomplished only by the fulfilment of the needs of those whom it is intended to motivate.

ROLE OF SALES MANAGEMENT

8. Management responsibilities. Management, unlike many professions, lacks any formalised rule, but then management pervades all forms of enterprise and it is not strange that it should be difficult to find many common denominators. Management itself must be in the nature of a derived demand; it exists to fulfil the needs of the enterprise. A study of management in its many aspects reduces the areas of responsibility to three fundamentals.

(*a*) Ensuring the work gets done.
(*b*) The economic use of scarce resources.
(*c*) Decisions requiring judgment.

9. Ensuring the work gets done. Responsibility for ensuring the work gets done is an involvement with the total problem of motivating workers. For the sales manager there is a concern to see that those personnel reporting to him accomplish their goals efficiently. Further than this, however, the sales manager has a task of ensuring that his staff will do more than the compulsory minimum allowable.

A salesman will cost £x per year to employ. To break even, the profit on sales emanating from that salesman will have to be at least £x. The sales manager will be responsible for so motivating the salesman that he will sell over that lower limit, which does not reflect the potential of the territory, but only the cost of employing the salesman.

The degree of motivation required by the salesman can be measured in terms of the difference between the salesman's present attitude and the one needed to perform effectively to reach the potential of the territory. An understanding of the need to motivate people according to their attitude to their work obviates the use of the "stick" attitude of many employers. A sales manager who periodically confronts his sales force and admonishes them with threats of dismissal, etc., as a means of improving performance probably needs motivating more than they do.

10. Motivating the sales force. There was a marketing company that sold industrial products very well. It had a team of around twenty-five salesmen, many of whom had been with the firm for more than eight years and were mature, reliable and very competent men. In order to raise funds to launch a subsidiary company that would operate in a non-industrial field with a completely new sales force, at that time not recruited, the company had a sales drive. It acquired a supply of power tools of somewhat indifferent design and at a regular sales meeting ordered its salesmen to cease selling their other products for two weeks and concentrate on selling the power tools. The market was in a new area which meant very hard work breaking into a market in which they had no future, with a product many salesmen expressed serious and sensible doubts about. They were also anxious about appointments they would have to break, lost business and lost income from commission. The sales manager did not explain in any detail the reasons for the operation nor did he listen with any patience to reasonable doubts. It was stated categorically that any salesman who did not sell his quota would be in trouble and any who refused to co-operate would be sacked! No-one denies the right of a sales manager to pursue a policy agreed by his directors but such a complete lack of imagination and concept of motivation had the inevitable results. No-one was sacked in spite of refusals, but many left voluntarily as soon as they were able.

The job specification discussed earlier (*see* V, 11) will have determined the characteristics of the man most suited to do the job, and the resulting tests at interviews will have determined the level of training needed. Motivating the salesman will need a further understanding of aspects of human behaviour.

11. Hierarchy of needs. People differ in their physical and mental make-up. It is almost impossible to devise a system that will work for everyone, but by understanding something of the general characteristics of workers it makes it possible to determine the way in which motivation might apply.

The hierarchy of needs lists the needs of people in an ascending scale of importance. As one need is fulfilled, so the next becomes more important to the person.

> 5　self-fulfilment needs
> 4　egoistical needs
> 3　status needs
> 2　security needs
> 1　physiological needs

A man who has been unemployed for a long period of time will begin at the lower end of the scale, but in the modern welfare state even his physiological needs, those of shelter, food, warmth, clothing, will have been largely attended to, at least to a minimum degree. If an employer thinks he is doing a man a favour by employing him at a low wage or on some other lowly terms and that the man has no alternative to taking the job, he must not be surprised if the man thinks little of him, or of his job. Once the basic, physiological needs have been met, a person will think of his security needs as being of prime importance. The need for security is related to the way the man feels about the future of himself and his family and is satisfied basically by provision of a satisfactory level of income. The next need to assume importance will be the status need.

If a man has been unemployed or otherwise unhappy in his previous work, he may be satisfied with a particular level in the organisation for some while. The need for status may express itself in a wish for a better car, or a title. A man appealing to his manager for a rise has been known to go away quite happy with a title; it has satisfied his need for status which more money would not necessarily have done. Egoistical needs are those related to a man's feelings about himself, they will relate to the way a man believes his company regards him. Finally, when he has achieved as much as is necessary to satisfy his other needs, he will seek self-fulfilment, which may be found outside his work entirely, e.g., gardening, painting, writing, or some other activity.

12. Need for recognition. The nature of the hierarchy is such that a sales manager should be capable of recognising in his staff the reasons for discontent. A man who feels he is not appreciated may have a very general feeling of discontent that manifests itself in a "chip on the shoulder". The sales manager may interpret this as dissatisfaction and genuinely seek to alleviate it. Increases in salary, a later model company car, more petrol allowance are tried but after each attempt the man resumes his attitude. Perhaps all that is needed is a recognition that he is appreciated, something that could cost very little. If a man is good at his selling job, why should he have to have periodic training like the less experienced salesman? Professor Hertzberg, professor of psychology at Western Reserve University, has summed up the man who is given a rise when all he needs is recognition, "He's not *unhappy*, but he isn't happy either."

13. A new approach to the job. It is important for the success of the sales force that a sales manager should recognise that the old views regarding motivation, "stick and carrot", may under modern social conditions no longer be appropriate. Even if we consider the older concepts of the nature of work, in terms of their historical and social environment, they may have been incorrect. The following points may form a beginning for another way of looking at the difficulties of motivating.

(*a*) *Work is an indispensable part of a man's life* and is the part which gives him status and his links with his community.

(*b*) *Generally men like their work* and those instances when they do not are frequently attributable to the conditions of the job in terms of the prevailing psychological and social attitudes in the firm.

(*c*) *The worker's morale does not of necessity have a positive relationship with the physical conditions of the job.* Although poor physical conditions may have an adverse effect on health and well-being, if a worker is sufficiently motivated his morale will not be affected.

(d) *Money is not necessarily the most important incentive in motivating a worker.* Recent research has shown that job satisfaction and job security are regarded as more important than remuneration. Unemployment is regarded as a strong negative incentive as it removes the worker from his particular society.

What has been said so far in relation to salesmen also applies to the whole field of retail and distributive workers. The conditions in many stores today , in terms of rest facilities, cloakrooms and working areas, may be superb, but if the attitude of management to its staff remains embedded in archaic ideas of master and servant its staff will not give their best and this will be revealed by bad customer relations.

If sales management is to fulfil its essential responsibility of seeing that work gets done and, more important, that sales people do their best over and above the minimum requirements, it must understand the problems of motivation and the needs of people to realise personal goals.

14. Management and objectives. If salesmen do not know the objectives of the company they cannot be expected to exert themselves to attain them. It has been shown time and again in industry generally that workers make more effort when they know and understand the objectives of the firm and themselves.

The corporate strategy of the company will provide the objectives of the company and that in turn will decide the goals of individuals. A company seeking a 10 per cent increase in sales will be more certain of attaining its objectives if it tells its sales force what it wants and why. Management has to define the objectives and see that the sales force is aware of them and also that the conditions under which they work are favourable to their accomplishment.

15. The economic use of scarce resources. Management's task is to ensure that resources are used in such a way that the return on their use is at least equal to what could have been realised in any form of use. In all economic decisions the manager must consider the opportunity cost, i.e. the cost of doing something else with the money. The opportunity cost of mounting an advertising campaign costing £10,000 is whatever could have been done with the £10,000 instead.

The selling function of a company should be the first to discern changes in the environment in which it operates. No commercial firm should be so committed to a single purpose that it cannot change its purpose when all the evidence suggests that it should. The manufacturers of motor-cycle sidecars no doubt kept a keen eye on each other's developments and forgot to watch the rise of the mini car. Another example, this time more positive, is the way in which the Dutch equivalent of the Coal Board realised the limited life of coal as a predominant fuel, closed its few mines and became instead one of the biggest chemical producers in the Netherlands. It recognised its essential skills and how it could use its limited resources to get the best return from them.

A sales manager with a limited budget and faced with many alternatives must consider the return from each possible alternative and make decisions on them. Many times he will be able to quantify the problem in terms of pounds and pence, or units sold, but other times he has to take a decision that is part intuitive, part derived from experience and part very much a value judgment.

16. The manager's judgment. It is in the aspect of decision-making that the responsibility of management is greatest. Managers may delegate work to subordinates but they retain the ultimate responsibility for their work and they cannot delegate their essential decision-making role.

Decisions cannot be made until clear objectives have been determined. These will have been derived from the policy of the company and the sales manager will translate them into departmental, group, or individual goals. The decision-making process may be summarised as:

(a) specifying the objective;
(b) analysing the objective;
(c) selecting the information;
(d) collecting the information;
(e) evaluating alternative solutions; and
(f) deciding on the solution.

The final decision may not be a precise decision allowing no doubt, it will be that which on the evidence available and in the sales manager's experience will be better than any other.

APPLICATION OF SALES MANAGEMENT

17. Leadership. The whole concept of leadership is complex and subject to wide differences of opinion among industrial psychologists. This treatment is intended to make those interested in the problems of selling aware of the effects of leadership.

It does not necessarily follow that when we talk of the "leader" of a group we are talking of the formally appointed "head" of the group. A sales manager is undisputed head of the sales force, and because of his formal position will be accepted as the man who is in charge and who must be obeyed; failure to obey could mean dismissal. His ability to "lead" the group will, however, depend upon qualities that are independent of his formal appointment. The confusion between "headship" and "leadership" is one that has created problems in industry for many years.

EXAMPLE: The sales manager of a firm of flooring specialists was a Mr. "O". Mr. "O" was very short in stature, completely casual in approach and entirely sympathetic towards the idiosyncrasies of his sales force. He also possessed a very wide experience of selling and product knowledge. He requested the minimum of reporting so long as essential information reached the company, and he was not concerned too much how the salesmen worked. He once remarked to a salesman, "I don't mind if you work with a telephone from bed, so long as you get the business." He had a hardworking sales force who accepted his leadership without question and maintained a high volume of business. Mr. "O" left the company to start his own firm, and his place was taken by Mr. "M". Mr. "M" was tall, distinguished looking and a stickler for attention to detail. Perhaps to "make his mark" he ordered the sales force to complete daily returns accounting for their every movement, accompanied them each month regularly to comment upon their methods and ensure they were competent. Within a few months sales had fallen off, the sales force were displaying signs of frustration and many left. It is dangerous to draw conclusions from such value judgments as these but the fact that Mr. "O" had qualities of leadership not possessed by Mr. "M" is fairly obvious.

18. Types of leader. It is recognised that three basic types of leader exist:

(a) *Autocratic* leaders:
   (i) strict autocrat;
   (ii) benevolent autocrat; and
   (iii) incompetent autocrat.

(*b*) *Democratic* leaders:
    (*i*) genuine democrat; and
    (*ii*) pseudo democrat.
(*c*) *Laissez-faire* leaders.

Autocratic leaders give orders which they expect to be instantly obeyed, their attitude is that orders should go down the structure and reports come back to them. Policies are determined without consulting the group and he will give no information about future plans. He remains outside the group and gives praise or criticism on his own judgment. The distinction between autocrats is only in the way they pursue their beliefs; the benevolent autocrat will have a conviction that he knows better than anyone else in the group and it is his duty to "lead"; the incompetent autocrat is frequently in his position by virtue of influence rather than capability, his autocracy derives from sheer incompetence and a lack of knowledge.

Democratic leaders are those who will consult their group to solicit their views and opinions and will, where possible, act accordingly. It is important that the democrat retains his responsibility for decision-making and does not relinquish it to "the vote". The pseudo democrat, on the other hand, will often make a pretence of "sounding opinion" but has already determined what he will do anyway.

Laissez-faire leaders let do; they simply let the group carry on without attempting to co-ordinate or control. They are frequently found on the golf-course or some other locality of similar vein.

19. Importance of leadership in selling. A salesman is frequently a lonely person, in the sense that he works away from the company and his home. It is important for him to feel trusted and not to feel neglected. Salesmen are frequently "characters" and have their own ways of working. A good leader will blend these distinctive personalities into an efficient team. While the company must ensure that they comply with its policies and provide evidence of their efforts in terms of the required levels of business, meeting their goals and supplying a steady flow of information, too much rigid control will frustrate good salesmen. Leadership, by inspiring confidence in the company, the sales manager, the management team, the sales force and the salesman himself, will ensure that the whole operation is well co-ordinated, and the team well motivated.

A sales manager should have imagination in determining objectives and frequently can inspire the team to greater effort by his vision of achievement expressed in his leadership and enthusiasm.

20. Direct selling. The sales manager has to be a good salesman, and since it is usual practice to promote the "best" salesman to be sales manager this is generally so. Being a good salesman is not, however, the only criterion of a good sales manager as we have seen. A sales manager's tasks may be seen in two broad areas.

(*a*) *Administration* of the sales function.

(*b*) *Responsibility* for selling.

21. Responsibility for major accounts. The sales manager will not only be responsible for the recruitment, training, motivation and supervision of the sales force, he will also be responsible for the company's major accounts. In this he will need to be more than a good salesman; the big accounts of one company are likely to be the big accounts of other companies too and the competition will be stronger there than elsewhere. It is sometimes apparent that many think the sales manager's main purpose in this area is the wining and dining of the major accounts, a view strongly held by the accounts themselves; indeed if they are loyal buyers of the company's products they are entitled to the best customer treatment. The wining and dining, however, should be the result of good business, not in anticipation of it. Good business is obtained by good salesmanship and all that it entails in after-sales care of the customer and his order.

22. Sales manager's expert knowledge. The sales manager needs to know more about the products, their capabilities, competitiveness and success than anyone else. Unlike the production manager, who, faced with a problem, can consult his records, files, manuals or colleagues, the sales manager has to have the knowledge at his finger-tips. To be faced with an unexpected question from a customer and have to resort to bag rummaging, or note scanning, does not instil confidence. The only exceptions might be highly technical questions related to the customer's business rather than the product generally; then the sales manager might be excused for having to admit he cannot give an unqualified answer.

EXAMPLE: The sales manager of a coating firm visited an oil refinery. The products were used there regularly and the two companies were on good terms.

Maintenance Engineer: "I have a problem which I hope you can help me with."

Sales Manager: "We will do our best. What's the problem exactly?"

Maintenance Engineer: "We have an impeller which is inside a tank, it is becoming corroded and needs protection. It's made of mild steel."

Sales Manager: "What chemical is it used for?"

Maintenance Engineer: "It's a strong solvent, called toluene. Can you do it?"

Sales Manager: "That's a problem. I haven't treated for protection against toluene. I'm sure we can evolve a system for you, but I must consult our chemist, who will probably run a few tests. It won't be a cheap job and neither of us wants any breakdowns. . . ."

Maintenance Engineer: "Excellent, I was hoping you would help; I'll have a sample of the chemical prepared and you can take it with you."

23. Aid in training. A sales manager will not only visit the major accounts on his own but will also pay periodic visits with the members of his sales force. For the newer members it may be to assist in training while for the more experienced it may be merely routine or simply an opportunity to see the customers. A problem does arise on these occasions in that the customers do tend to talk to the sales manager rather than the salesman. This is difficult to overcome and the sales manager has to be careful not to let it develop into a two-way conversation that ignores the salesman.

24. Sales manager's authority. Frequently problems arise that cannot be left to the limited authority of the salesman. The sales manager will be able to bring a greater authority to bear and take immediate decisions where the salesman would have to refer back. These might arise from negotiations for a very large order where details of special discounts, deliveries or modifications are to be settled. They may arise from a difficult complaint. The sales manager carries the ultimate responsibility for the selling operations and it is his job to solve any matters beyond the ability or authority of the salesman. Apart from his greater authority, he is often able to bring to the situation an experience the salesman cannot have achieved.

EXAMPLE: This company made building fixtures and had a regular contract with a firm of nationally known construction engineers. One structure developed a fault which was traced to the fixtures. The engineers blamed the product, but after investigation the manufacturers said it was the fault of the people who had fixed them. The salesman visited the firm several times to explain the attitude of the manufacturer and to try to come to an amicable arrangement. The engineers were adamant that it wasn't their fault and that the manufacturer would have to accept full blame. At this point the sales manager stepped in. He went to see the engineers to discuss the matter with their managing director. He was greeted icily.

Sales manager: "Good morning, Mr. J. We have a nasty problem, haven't we? Well now, you and I are going to sort it out, and I want to make it clear that whatever we say to one another, we will find a solution and part good friends. Now, I cannot accept any responsibility. . . ."

A solution was found that satisfied all parties to some extent, but most important, good-will was kept and they remained good friends.

25. Handling the sales force. A sales manager's skill in diplomacy must extend not only to the customer, but also to his sales force. There are times when visiting a customer with the salesman that it becomes necessary to contradict what the salesman has said; perhaps because of a genuine mistake on the part of the salesman, or because of information he did not have, or because of special conditions relating to the customer or his order. The experienced sales manager will find a way of correcting the information in a way that does not reflect upon the salesman's credibility.

In his dealings with the sales force on a personal basis there will be times when he will have to say no, perhaps arising from a request for more money or some other change of circumstances. The sales manager will listen, explain the position and then, if necessary, decline the request without alienating the person.

A sales manager will devote as much time as he can to the special accounts, but he will endeavour to allocate his time among the smaller accounts in such a way that they too will feel special attention has been given them. Such an ability will come only with experience.

SALES MANAGEMENT'S TASKS

26. Sales meetings. It is usual for companies to organise regular sales meetings, which will vary in their nature from a yearly, or twice-yearly, sales conference, to periodical sales meetings.

27. Sales conferences. Sales conferences are occasions of intensive activity and usually extend from nine in the morning until seven in the evening. Their purpose is to bring together all the personnel of the sales function, including the sales manager, area managers, group leaders, salesmen, and executives related to the selling function.

There will also be the sales office manager, the buyer(s), the warehouse/despatch manager, the production manager, the designer, the managing director and the chairman.

The conference will probably be timed either at a period of low sales activity or just before the major sales period. It will extend for about two days, depending on how much work is to be accomplished. The main objective of the conference will be to bring together the two essential parts of the selling function, administration and sales. It will allow the salesmen to meet and talk over problems with executives whom they might otherwise only contact by telephone or letter. It will also provide an occasion for any new products to be introduced and explained by all concerned: designer, quality control, production, etc. Existing products may be subject to scrutiny and excessive complaints about any feature, or delivery, etc., dealt with. Salesmen's and the sales function performance will be reviewed and usually the managing director and sales manager will meet each salesman in turn and discuss his performance.

28. Periodic sales meetings. These might be held on a monthly, three-monthly or even six-monthly basis, depending on the needs they have to fulfil. Generally the speciality-selling organisations tend to have more meetings, but this is not always the case.

The meetings may be at some central point, e.g. head office, or they may be on a regional basis under an area manager or group leader and will be to discuss matters arising during the intervening period, or any special problems or products. They are generally less formal than the sales conference.

It is important that these meetings should have an objective, and if they occur too frequently it is not always possible to find one. As an example of sheer desperation the group leader who talked for three hours on the intricacies of shot-blasting would be hard to beat. He managed to send two salesmen to sleep and the rest to near hysterics!

Regular sales meetings are an excellent and worthwhile concept provided they do not take men away from selling without any specific purpose. They are occasions when salesmen can discuss common problems, offer advice and exchange ideas. Used in this way they can be a real motivation to salesmen.

29. Improved sales techniques. A sales manager has a responsibility to see that his sales force use the best possible selling techniques and also that their samples are in good condition. The essence of good selling is to develop a technique which will convey to the buyer an immediate message of what the product is about.

If possible, techniques should be capable of demonstration within the buyer's office or at an adjacent site or workshop. The sales manager can profitably spend time experimenting with products to find better, more convincing ways of showing them.

30. Sales office. The sales manager has a responsibility for the management of the routine of the sales office, although he will usually delegate the work to a sales office manager. While the routine work can be left to the sales office manager, it is important for the sales manager to ensure that the work of the department is related to the needs of the sales force and the customer, and does not become an end in itself.

The sales office will receive incoming orders, check them for accuracy of price, detail and delivery, record them on customer record cards or any other statistical system in operation, translate them on to standard forms and pass them on to the production department, usually through the production control department, or direct to the warehouse for despatch from stock. The methods employed will vary considerably from company to company. Items which are not available from stock, or require special attention, will be advised to the customers and arrangements made to make or buy in, according to the nature of the operation.

PROGRESS TEST 12

1. What are the elements of management? **(1)**

2. How does co-ordination assist the sales manager in managing the team? **(4)**

3. Define the fundamental responsibilities of management. **(8)**

4. What is the hierarchy of needs? **(11)**

5. Decision-making is a responsibility of management—what is the decision-making process? **(16)**

6. Define the different types of leaders. **(18)**

7. "The sales manager must be a good salesman." In which two areas do his selling tasks lie? **(20)**

CHAPTER XIII

Sales Records

INFORMATION NEEDS

1. Purpose of sales records. Sales records are written statements of a salesman's activities during a specific period of time in a particular area, and are used by sales management as a means of controlling the activity and expenses of the sales force. They are also used as a means of collecting information about the market, present activity and anticipated activity. They therefore fall into two categories, which are:

    (*a*) control of the sales force; and
    (*b*) an aid to market research and planning.

2. Effective selling. A man who has natural abilities, some experience and the correct degree of training should prove a good "salesman", but he will not, by these virtues alone, become an effective salesman. Effective selling is made possible by a sensible routine, an understanding of the territory, a predetermined presentation and most important, clear objectives and a personal goal. A salesman who leaves home in the morning, wets his finger to see which way the wind blows, and follows it, will not be effective! Elements which will determine effectiveness are:

    (*a*) efficient coverage of the territory;
    (*b*) sensible use of selling time;
    (*c*) effective journey planning;
    (*d*) ability to combine regular calls on established customers with creation of new customers;
    (*e*) ability to determine customers' needs;
    (*f*) correct use of territory customer records; and
    (*g*) ability to vary selling techniques according to the situation.

The salesman alone cannot be responsible for his ability to use all the elements making for efficiency. Sales management must see by continuous supervision and training that he understands his goals, his products and is acquainted with the methods known to be best in reaching them. Management of the sales

force will not be effective without the element of control, which it
will use:

(a) to determine where faults lie which prevent salesmen
reaching their goals; and

(b) to show how activities may be used more efficiently.

3. Controlling the selling effort. Sales management is ultimately
responsible for any weaknesses in the sales force, or in individuals.
The sales force cannot display periodic or sudden bouts of
efficiency but must be trained, equipped and motivated to run
continuously at maximum efficiency. Specially trained group
leaders, supervisors and managers will be responsible for assessing
the individual salesman's performance by:

(a) determining suitable goals;

(b) ensuring sensible control systems; and

(c) appraising subsequent performance.

Here we are concerned with the second factor, ensuring
sensible controls. These will be guide-lines to goal achievement
and, following the assignation of the salesman's goal, the next
step will be to devise a quantitative method of comparing
achievement against the set standard.

A salesman's ability to achieve his sales figures against goals is
a tool for sales managers to use in determining the over-all
efficiency of the sales force as well as of the individual salesman.
While it is effective as a means of discovering the less efficient
salesman (the idler will not have lasted long enough to need a
control system to discover him), its more important purpose is a
positive one—to motivate the sales force through a spirit of
competition and challenge, with a bonus to those who attain the
largest increase in their sales over their goals.

Control begins with the allocation of sales territories to
salesmen. This provides a sales area which will allow for adjustment, if necessary, without the loss, or otherwise negating of
existing sales records or customer records.

4. Territory organisation. The organisation of the sales force is
usually on a basis of allocating specific territories to each representative. This enables a salesman to specialise in one territory,
with its customers and conditions, and leads to a development of
the customer/salesman relationship. The territory is also the
usual basis for planning and budgeting of the sales force and
allocating quotas.

The sales records and statistics derived from them will enable the sales manager to exercise control over the sales force by making use of the figures which will be immediately available should he require them. These figures will also be kept in terms of the areas or groups into which the sales force is organised, and will be a check on the efficiency of the managers responsible.

It is important that a continuity of records is maintained, and it becomes necessary to distinguish between the results of the salesman on his territory and the territory itself as a facet of the organisation structure. This need necessitates separate information being compiled which is capable of independent analysis. This separation is important as discontinuity may arise from:

(*a*) changes in territorial organisation;

(*b*) increasing the number of salesmen; and

(*c*) changes in salesmen, due to dismissal, promotion, retirement or illness.

Each of these factors will cause decisions to be taken on the continuity of the sales records.

5. Territory planning. For the sales manager to plan for the development of the sales force and the entire selling function, it is essential that comprehensive sales statistics are available. These will enable an in-depth study of the facts and discernible trends to be accomplished.

Very often the sales manager will take decisions on the size and parameters of territory on the basis of his own experience, or that of his superiors or predecessors. This does not always ensure that industrial, urban and social changes can be recognised and accounted for in the system. It is equally important for these changes to be noted whether the company is selling products to consumers, via stores, industrial users or agricultural buyers; the relative size of towns, populations, etc., will be important.

6. Changing territorial conditions. The size of the territory will normally be calculated from a prediction of the amount of business it should produce.

EXAMPLE: A company selling electric cable to users, local authorities, industrial users, etc., had always had one salesman covering the South Wales territory; this practice had existed for some ten years, ever since the company had commenced selling in the area. The salesman had a quota set in terms of the sales turnover, extrapolated on a yearly basis. A consultant examined the territory as a part of a general survey and found that since the territory had been established there had been a massive increase in the number of industrial users, particularly in the western half of the territory, foremost among these four major oil refineries and a terminus. As a result of a new prediction of turnover it was concluded that the existing salesman could not adequately cover the territory and business was not being maximised; the failure to make an impact on the new industries was allowing competitors to establish themselves; the potential turnover was much larger than the current. The territory was therefore split and a new sales territory established.

7. Basis of assessment. In assessing the territory, the sales manager will consider different factors which would influence sales. These will naturally differ according to the type of operation. For predicting results in a consumer trade, e.g. grocery, the following would be guides.

(*a*) *Consumer supplier* will require information about the:
(*i*) general levels of income in the area;
(*ii*) distribution of customers and potential customers; among large and small buyers; and
(*iii*) consumer trends for the type of product.
(*b*) *The industrial supplier* will require information about the:
(*i*) general level of business activity;
(*ii*) nature of the business, i.e. heavy industry, light industry, chemical processing, and the relative percentages of each; and
(*iii*) the number of firms with local authority to buy, or with buying department in other areas; many companies, especially in development areas, are only manufacturing units, all administration being at head offices, in the Midlands, London, etc.

8. General level of activity. From these assessments it is possible to make estimates of the general level of business activity and the likely turnover; this will then have to be subjected to periodical review as a result of sales and sales-recorded information.

EXAMPLE: A company was established to sell a range of imported cosmetics on a direct selling basis. The area to be covered was in the south-west of England and contained few really large conurbations. From figures supplied by the main importer on the level of sales in other parts of the country it was possible to predict the likely level of sales in the new area; this figure was weighted to allow for a certain bias against cosmetics in the region and for a disproportionately aged population. It was

estimated that to obtain a satisfactory income, a salesman would have to have a minimum of 3,000 population. The area was then examined geographically and the population of the main towns determined. From this the number of salesmen per town or other area was predicted and the calling frequency. This figure then determined the need for group leaders, area managers, etc., on the basis of a logical span of control.

9. Journey cycles. A journey cycle is the period it takes a salesman to make a complete round of his territory in a particular route assumed to be the best way. A recorded system of journey cycles will:

(*a*) ensure the logical and complete working of the territory;

(*b*) enable prior planning of the journey;

(*c*) provide customers with a known frequency of calls, on particular days; and

(*d*) aid a new man to take over with the minimum of disruption.

All the aspects listed above aid the salesman in efficient working of his territory. In consumer selling the regular calling frequency is most important if the customer is going to develop a loyalty to products or brands. He must know when the salesman will call. A planned schedule of calls will ensure that the salesman has a clear understanding of who he is going to see, enable firm appointments to be made, and ensure he has the right samples and any additional information he will need.

10. Planning the journey cycle. Planning the journey cycle will depend essentially upon the ordering frequency of the customer. If the customer buys every week, month, or season then that basically will be the period of the cycle. It must be obvious that the buying period, by determining the frequency of the call, also affects the size of territories. If a salesman selling groceries has to call upon shops every week he must have a territory that can be covered in a week.

The industrial salesman may also have a regular calling frequency which is dictated by customer buying habits. Electric lamps are a product sold to industrial users on a regular re-order basis. But there are industrial products where the need arises from a problem and here the cycle can be longer.

There are many ways of planning the cycle. Figure 47 shows a cycle for a manufacturer of menswear. The territory is large but the main towns are concentrated in the south. The trade tends to buy at two seasons a year—for the pre-Christmas trade and for the spring/summer trade. The cycle has to ensure the salesman sees all his customers at least twice in a year to book their major orders, and the rest of the cycle will be for filling in. Those in the remoter areas will make use of direct ordering with the sales office. On a smaller scale the continuous cycle would be typical of most consumer sales, only the frequency would be greater.

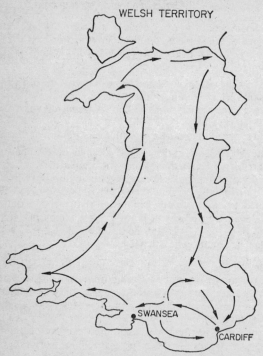

WELSH TERRITORY

SWANSEA

CARDIFF

FIG. 47. *Continuous journey cycle.*

Figure 48 shows a system where there is no set ordering time and the salesman has to ensure coverage in an orderly way but can always reach customers for the unexpected problem, or the urgent need. It requires the territory to be divided in four quadrants corresponding to north, west, south and east. Each is in turn divided into four again and numbered one to four. These correspond to the first four days of the working week. The salesman will begin the cycle by calling in the areas numbered "one";

i.e. north one, west one, and so on; to cover all four number "one" divisions will take until Thursday and the Friday is left free for any special calls, non-selling calls, e.g. architects who will specify for some future business, etc. Thus the whole territory

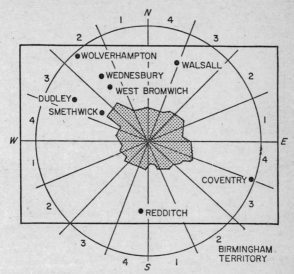

FIG. 48. *Quadrant journey cycle.*

can be covered in four weeks. It also means the salesman is never very far from any part of the territory as he is in each of the quadrants each week and in the event of an urgent need to see a customer, this can be done without upsetting the whole cycle.

COMMUNICATION NEEDS

11. Report writing. The sales manager, area managers, group leaders and the salesmen will all have a certain amount of report writing to do. The amount will tend to increase further up the organisation structure and will be necessary if each element is to work effectively. While this should form a relatively small part of the total work, particularly at the lower level, it is nevertheless important. It is essential to stress that the main responsibility of the salesman is to sell and he should not be overburdened with an excessive amount of report writing.

The sales organisation depends a great deal upon sources of information, both about the customers and the products. Salesmen have a useful task in providing information to aid sales management in planning and controlling.

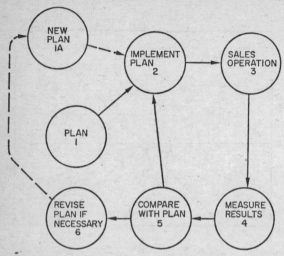

FIG. 49. *Management information circuit.*

The use of information is illustrated in Fig. 49, a schematic management information circuit showing how the plan is devised, implemented, measured, compared with predicted effect and subject to revision. The reports from the sales force, along with sales achieved, are a source of information for revision of the plan.

Reports should be clear, concise and conclusive. Where facts can be used they must be, but where opinion has to suffice it should be made clear that it is only opinion. Reports need not be long and should not take the writer more than a quarter of an hour at the most. Ideally they should be written as soon after the interview as possible, but where this cannot be done, at least the essential detail should be noted in rough form. Many firms issue report pads, or memorandum pads, and the salesman should be prepared to make use of them.

12. Who needs information? All the elements in the sales organisation need information. It comes in two flows, which are:

(*a*) *upwards* from sales force to management; and

(*b*) *downwards* from management to the sales force.

Figure 50 shows the main flows in an organisation structure and the nature of the information.

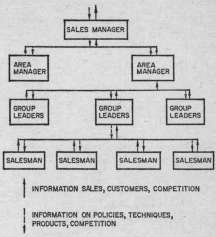

FIG. 50. *Flow of information.*

13. Levels of management. The different levels of management have particular needs for records. At the top level it will be a broad analysis of results as an aid to strategic planning. Lower management will want much more specific information as a means of operational control. It is possible to summarise the details of the needs as shown in Fig. 51.

(*a*) *Sales/marketing director* requires a summary of analysed results of performance against planned performance. This involves:

    (*i*) sales figures;

    (*ii*) selling and related costs;

    (*iii*) market trends;

    (*iv*) activity of competitors;

    (*v*) anticipated business for next period; and

    (*vi*) variation from plan.

(*b*) *Sales manager* requires details of over-all sales organisation's performance, including:

    (*i*) areas;

(*ii*) product;
(*iii*) customer categories;
(*iv*) new accounts;
(*v*) lost accounts; and
(*vi*) selling costs.

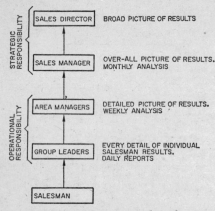

FIG. 51. *Differing record needs.*

(*c*) *Area managers* require detailed analysis of area results on a weekly basis:

(*i*) by territory;
(*ii*) number of calls per day;
(*iii*) how many new contacts; and
(*iv*) breakdown of sales by product range.

(*d*) *Group leaders* require comprehensive information on the performance of the salesmen under their direct control on a daily basis:

(*i*) number of calls per day;
(*ii*) percentage of new contacts;
(*iii*) number of interviews;
(*iv*) number of presentations;
(*v*) number of sales;
(*vi*) size of orders;
(*vii*) future anticipated business;
(*viii*) name and status of contact;
(*ix*) if salesman is working to plan; and
(*x*) if salesman is making effective use of training in presentation, technique, and samples.

14. Summarising information. The salesman is the source of the information needed by management to determine whether its sales policies are being applied successfully. It is necessary for the salesman in completing his records and reports to give explanations for any variation in his work from the prescribed plan. Similarly any results which indicate that sales are down on the planned level should also be explained.

Reports must give sales management the necessary information and, where it is needed, an interpretation of the facts. Management will need this interpretation if the trends are to be correctly translated. Only if management has all the information can it take the correct decisions.

15. Reporting by exception. Management by exception can be summed up in the phrase: "If everything is all right, don't tell me".

If management is to be free from unnecessary clutter so that it can concentrate on the really essential details, it must increasingly delegate the routine matters. Reporting by exception is an adaptation of this concept to the sales force. Essentially it leaves the day to day operations to the man on the spot so long as it can be sure that it will be informed of any problem that is either beyond the salesman's authority or jurisdiction.

16. Records and motivation. The two-way system of communication is an aid to motivating the sales organisation. At the top level, the sales manager will want assurances from the board that it is satisfied with the way its policies are being interpreted into positive results. The area manager will want assurances that his area's results are in line with quotas and other areas' performances. The salesman will want to know how he stands in relation to the other salesmen in the group, area or nationally. This will affect his security, income and prospects. It will assure him that his own interests are being cared for in terms of assistance, and that he is appreciated by the company.

17. Types of records. Salesmen will complete a number of forms or records in the period of a month. Some will be daily, others weekly and usually an aggregated monthly summary of activity will be produced.

(*a*) *Daily report.* This is usually completed in the course of the day's work and sent to the group leader each evening. It will provide the information needed to enable the group leader to keep up with daily progress.

(b) *Customer record card.* A filing system which each salesman will be required to keep and which will be returned to the company in the event of his leaving. It will record the names and addresses of customers, or potential customers, the person to see, the nature of the business, a record of orders placed or likely to place, and details of previous calls. The salesman should consult this before each journey as an aid to planning, as a reminder of any outstanding matters, and as a refresher before visiting a customer. It must be kept up to date and should be inspected by the group leader periodically.

(c) *Weekly activity summary.* Usually combined with a vehicle report (where a company vehicle is supplied) it will summarise the week's events, orders, new customers, special events, distance travelled, etc.

(d) *Monthly report.* This will aggregate the weekly records and also will predict likely business for the coming month and possible business for the following month(s). It is a guide to sales management in determining production requirements and longer-term trends.

(e) *Expenses form.* A salesman will be expected to keep a record of any expenses incurred and submit them on a regular basis. Sometimes a firm will give a fixed amount which is calculated to be sufficient for the salesman's needs.

PROGRESS TEST 13

1. What is the purpose of sales records? **(1)**

2. Can you explain the essential requirements that make the difference between a "salesman" and an "effective salesman"? **(2)**

3. Explain the purpose of a journey cycle. **(9)**

4. Report writing is essential to all engaged in sales. List the essential points of good report writing. **(11)**

5. What are the flows of information in the sales organisation? **(12)**

6. What is "reporting by exception"? **(15)**

CHAPTER XIV

Increasing Sales

MEASURING PROFIT

1. The business purpose. The success of a company is ultimately judged by its ability to make a profit. Profit is the objective and the criterion by which the measure of success is determined. It is also the means by which the company, in the long term, exists. It follows, therefore, that to expand, the company has to make *more profit*.

2. The business objective. For a company to realise a profit it is necessary to make a sale; this necessitates the creation of a customer—further than this it is important to create satisfied customers. The objective of business is profit—and its purpose is the creation of satisfied customers.

It is a management myth to define the business objective as being to maximise profit, in reality the prime business objective is long-term resilience through customer service. Profit as a term can mean different things, such as:

(*a*) an increase in the over-all profit of a company over a period of one year; or

(*b*) an increase in the amount of profit earned on a particular product.

In (*a*) the company is endeavouring to sell more, possibly by creating a wider range of customers. In (*b*) we are concerned with increasing profit, i.e. getting more out of each transaction.

3. Different concepts of profit. Different companies may put differing interpretations on what is meant by profit. A company may define profit to be:

(*a*) *the total expenditure over a period of a year* deducted from the total income over the same period;

(*b*) *a percentage deducted from all expenditure*, which would include depreciation, from the total income in the same period; or they may

(*c*) *aggregate all expenditure on obtaining business over a period of a year*, ignoring expenditure on advertising aimed at gaining business in the next yearly period, and deduct this sum from the total income of the period plus all outstanding money from sales effected during the year.

From the foregoing it is clear that profit is not an absolute concept, but is what individual management defines it to be.

4. Achieving the business objective. We have seen that the business objective is profit and the realisation of this objective is the criterion by which success is measured.

The formulation of commercial policy within the company is the basic concern of sales management in the strategy of increasing sales.

Management's prime elements of planning, organising, motivating and controlling are all directly applicable to the work of sales management. To set realistic objectives and individual goals, sales management needs to be aware of the divergent aims of the company in meeting its ultimate responsibility of achieving the required profitability. Unless sales management is aware of the over-all commercial policy, its strategy will not be congruent with the over-all corporate strategy. Conversely, top management, if it is out of step with a sales management that is customer-oriented, will aim for the greatest possible profit return from the business, and if that is pursued to extremes it can bring about the demise of the business. To maximise profit the company may:

(*a*) employ low-grade personnel at low wages;
(*b*) purchase cheap materials;
(*c*) maintain obsolescent equipment;
(*d*) cut-back on research and development;
(*e*) cut-back on advertising;
(*f*) maintain minimum product innovation; or
(*g*) impose a policy of variety reduction.

By a policy of low investment in labour, capital and resources, profits may be increased in the short term, but in the longer term the company will be overtaken by its competitors, and lose its markets.

The business should have as its objective not the maximisation of profit, but the least profit that it must earn to meet its costs.

5. Commercial considerations. The problem of defining and measuring profit is a difficult one. Accountants, businessmen and economists disagree on a suitable definitive solution. Two commercial considerations are:

(*a*) increased-net-worth theory;
(*b*) cost and revenue theory.

In the increased-net-worth theory, the profit a business has accrued over a set period of time is the difference between the net worth of the business at the commencement of the period and at its termination.

It is necessary to make adjustments for the withdrawal of capital and for the introduction of any additional capital. Among the many problems associated with this theory is the decision on which assets and liabilities are to be included. It also has a particular drawback from the viewpoint of the sales manager, in that the theory confuses "windfall" and "planned" profits. Windfall profits arise purely from chance whilst planned profits are the result of management planning and decision. Clearly if profit is to be a criterion by which sales management is to be judged, it is necessary to have a means of distinguishing between windfall and planned profit.

The cost and revenue theory reasons that the profit accrued during a period is the difference between the revenue earned and the cost incurred. It is difficult, however, to measure revenue exactly, and what exactly constitutes costs can also be a problem.

If the item purchased is totally consumed within the accounting period, the difficulties are not so great, but where the item is consumed only in part the problem becomes complicated.

EXAMPLE: A builders' merchant buys twenty tonnes of assorted timber. At the end of the particular accounting period the merchant has sold eleven tonnes of timber, part of which has been paid for. Approximately nine tonnes remain in stock. To distinguish between "capital" (stock remaining), "revenue" (stock sold and paid for), and liabilities (stock sold but not paid for, and maybe stock remaining unsold if this has not been paid for to the supplier) is a complex problem. It becomes further complicated when the concept of depreciation is introduced.

In spite of problems the cost and revenue theory has merits. The difficulties of distinguishing between windfall and planned profits are lessened.

6. Profit. If we are to judge the company's success by the amount of profit earned, it will follow that the higher the profit, the greater the success, but by itself the concept of profit does not provide a satisfactory measure. Too many companies in setting profit objectives fail to do so realistically.

(a) It is as serious to set the sales targets and profit goals too low, in the short term, as it is to set goals too high.

(b) Top management, by imposing objectives and exerting pressure on subordinates to achieve goals, frequently leads middle management to underestimate its profit targets.

(c) Managers must be motivated to determine realistic goals which will encourage their self-fulfilment needs.

(d) By a realistic use of management by objectives, short-term planning by managers must be made more consistent with top management's long-term strategy.

A company's resources have a value and the profits earned during a given period of time have to be related to this value.

7. The profit returned on capital employed method. If a company accepts this concept of profit it may restate its objectives: "The maximisation of the profit return on the resources invested in it."

To the sales manager the concept is important as it determines that the resources of a company are limited and should be put to their most profitable use.

ACHIEVING PROFIT

8. Selling up: selling more. To the sales manager, these terms may both be applied to the problem of getting a better return to the investment in stock or selling techniques. The choice of technique will depend upon:

(a) the nature of the product; and

(b) the nature of the market.

If the price of the product is raised in order to obtain a higher margin over the costs it follows that a better return will result.

EXAMPLE:
Product "X" cost £1·00: Margin 25%.   Profit £0·25.
Sales of 1000 of Product "X" . . . .   Profit £250·00
Product "X" cost £1·00: Margin 30%.   Profit £0·30.
Sales of 1000 of Product "X" . . . .   Profit £300·00

The example appears to make increasing profits a simple matter of increasing prices, but unfortunately economic principles determine the results of such an operation.

CONCEPTS OF DEMAND

9. Demand contracts as prices rise. This is shown in Fig. 52. From this economic fact of life, it follows, therefore, that if we increase prices in order to maximise profit, we face the prospect of selling less produce. The amount by which demand falls will depend on the "elasticity" of demand, which shows the responsiveness of consumers' demand to an increase in price.

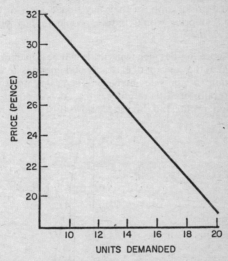

FIG. 52. *Relation between price and demand.*

10. Elasticity of demand. If things are elastic they stretch; the more they stretch the greater is their elasticity. If a small change in the price of a product leads to large changes in the quantity of the product demanded it is said to be subject to elastic demand. Conversely if a change in price leads to little change in demand it is said to be inelastic in demand.

If demand is elastic, an increase in price will produce a fall in demand. If demand is inelastic, a rise in price will not result in an immediate fall in demand—although in the long term consumers may seek alternative supplies or buy substitutes:

(*a*) In the event of salt increasing in price by 10 per cent, demand would remain constant; everyone needs salt, there is no substitute and in any case the level of demand is low and steady. *Demand is inelastic.*

(*b*) Should bread increase in price by 10 per cent, demand would possibly fall in the short term; consumers might try baking their own, but because it is an essential product and it is messy to make, the demand would soon rise again. *Demand is inelastic in the medium to long term.*

(*c*) If the price of beef increased by 10 per cent, the demand would fall immediately. People can do without beef, they may buy other meats, pork, lamb, or may buy tinned meat or even fish. Only a fall in price would induce people to buy beef again. *Demand is elastic.*

11. Importance to sales management. It will be apparent from the foregoing that the concept of elasticity of demand is an important consideration for the sales manager. Increasing price in an endeavour to raise profit is rarely feasible. As prices rise, demand, and therefore profits, fall. Figure 53 shows this.

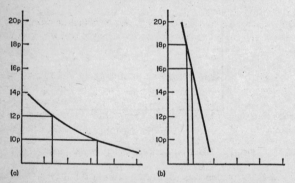

FIG. 53. (*a*) *elastic demand curve*; (*b*) *inelastic demand curve.*

The concept of elasticity can also be applied to price cutting. If a sales manager attempts to increase the quantity of products sold by cutting price he will need to know the elasticity of demand for the product. To give two examples, a cut in the price of pepper or of drilling equipment is unlikely to increase demand to any extent. Pepper is only needed in very limited amounts, and the demand for drilling equipment is in any case a derived demand.

12. Increasing profits. To increase profits the sales manager has two alternatives.

(a) *Lower costs* The lowering of costs may be achieved in various ways depending upon the nature of the product or service.

(i) increased utilisation of machinery or equipment;

(ii) by an application of product variety reduction, e.g. fewer colours in a range of paints;

(iii) rationalisation of staff, i.e. fewer representatives, office workers, etc; and

(iv) by use of capital equipment to replace higher labour costs.

(b) *Sell more effectively.* Sales management has a constant need to ensure that a higher proportion of sales is achieved per interview. More effective selling is a marketing problem and involves all the tools of marketing used in conjunction. For the sales manager it is an especially important task. He has to:

(i) think out the strategy;

(ii) evaluate alternative plans;

(iii) make decisions on solutions;

(iv) ensure policies are put into practice; and

(v) monitor results.

The creative aspect of the sales manager's task is essential and in performing his job he should be dynamic in creating new sales opportunities.

13. Creativity. A company manufacturing liquid metallisation treatments for maintenance work found its sales decreasing due to a general contraction of the market. The sales manager in exploring new sales outlets decided to exploit the growing market for liquid zinc coatings as an alternative to hot-dip galvanising. By examining the needs of manufacturers of building components, brackets, hinges. plates, etc., it was found that they frequently sent their work out to galvanisers for treatment. As a result of research it was shown how the manufacturer could make considerable savings by the use of liquid treatments. An entirely new market was created which soon equalled the former maintenance market.

It is especially important for new sales managers to realise that they have a special need to recognise and implement this fundamental element of the job.

Marketing implies a serious study of market trends in an attempt to obviate as many problems as possible, and to enable more positive predictions of sales to be made. If through the use of market, economic, and consumer research, it becomes possible to aim the product directly at a customer, it becomes possible to lower selling costs. In this process various sales aids may be employed:

- (a) sales promotion;
- (b) advertising; and
- (c) public relations.

14. Increase sales. To sell more often simply requires more effort; more attention to the needs of the customer, more thought in the selling process and perhaps longer hours and more effort with the customer. By widening the customer product mix it will ensure that more sales can be achieved. Clearly any such exercise must be closely monitored to ensure that the extra costs do not exceed the additional sales, or the results will be negated.

PROGRESS TEST 14

1. "Profit as a term can mean different things." Show two ideas of profit. **(2)**

2. What is the "increased-net-worth theory"? **(5)**

3. What factors will influence the choice of technique in terms of "selling-up"? **(8)**

4. How does the concept of elasticity of demand affect sales management? **(11)**

5. "Sales management needs constantly to ensure that a higher proportion of sales is achieved per interview." How does the sales manager accomplish this task? **(12)**

6. What sales aids may help to lower selling costs? **(13)**

CHAPTER XV

Appraisal of Performance

THE NEEDS FOR APPRAISAL

A sales force, whether it is "travelling" or sedentary in a retail store, has to be subjected to a periodic appraisal of its performance. The need for this arises out of:

(a) personality changes in the salesman, arising from over-confidence or general complacency;

(b) changing market conditions;

(c) product evolution; and

(d) new or improved selling techniques.

The purpose of the appraisal will be to satisfy management of the effectiveness of the over-all sales force as well as an appraisal of the individual's performance. For the consideration of possible promotion, bonus or salary increases, appraisals have to be regular and rational.

1. Major considerations. A sales manager will want more specific information in certain areas of the operation. He will want to assess the abilities of his salesmen in particular aspects which have a major effect upon the efficiency of the selling function. Major considerations will be upon the following points.

(a) Is the salesman obtaining *a satisfactory volume of orders*?

(b) Is the salesman providing *a satisfactory level of service* to maintain good customer relations?

(c) *If there are faults*, is the salesman to blame or is management lacking?

(d) *What effective action can be taken* to help?

The answers to these questions will determine the manner in which management at all levels will perform in the aspects of leadership, motivation and control.

2. Aims of appraisal. Formal appraisals of performance are not intended to enable management to make categoric decisions but to create conditions of confidence between management and sales force that will allow maximum co-operation between the policy-making and the operational bodies.

Formal appraisals were developed originally to assess the performance of workers in factories. Supervisors were asked to evaluate the abilities of their subordinates on a form. This system, known as "merit rating", was concerned with:

(a) quality and volume of work; and
(b) attitudes towards the firm and work-mates.

Following the use of "merit rating" it was found necessary to advise supervisors against inclinations to give what was known as a "halo-effect". This is seen in the way a supervisor faced with a number of values to determine about a man's performance will tend to believe that a man who is good or bad at one aspect will be equally good or bad at the others. This tendency has frequently been seen in appraisals of salesmen.

The appreciation of this human tendency to be biased is generally countered by varying the categories down the form so making the assessor deliberate on each answer.

3. Appraisal of performance. Having made allowances for the "halo-effect" the form will request information on the way the salesman carries out his duties. Normally the manager will accompany the salesman and make his appraisal from observation but other methods may be used. A number of reports will be made during the course of the year, the exact number depending upon the company's policy. The salesman can be assessed in the following ways.

(a) The manager will accompany the salesman on his day's work.

(b) The manager may make independent calls upon customers with the purpose of checking the salesman's effort when he is alone.

(c) Random checks may be made on the salesman's daily report to determine its accuracy.

4. Personal appraisal. When a sales manager or other supervisor accompanies a salesman on his day's work he will be watching his performance in several respects:

(a) his appearance and manner;
(b) attitude;
(c) experience; and
(d) administration.

None of these factors is as intangible as it may appear. The sales records will reveal a great deal about the salesman's attitude, experience and administrative abilities and the sales manager will bear this in mind in his personal observation. At first a salesman may display nervousness when dealing with customers under his manager's scrutiny, but with experience he will soon overcome this. A good manager will allow for this initially and try to put the salesman at ease. This will also show the manager's leadership qualities. It has been mentioned elsewhere (*see* XII, **23**) that there is a tendency for buyers to ignore the salesman and talk to the manager on these occasions. The manager will try to discourage this but a good salesman will also be aware of the problem and will overcome it by his experience and personality. It is a valuable aid to a good assessment, and it will show his ability to handle the interview and the customer.

5. Two-way reports. The appraisal of a salesman is not merely commenting upon the subordinate by the manager. It is a part of the manager's duties to co-ordinate and control those under him. Senior sales management, in assessing the manager's appraisals, will have this in mind and will want to see just how much work the manager or supervisor did with the salesman and how well he is motivating those under him. Most appraisal forms have a section dealing with "manager's comments and recommendations" and senior management will want to know:

(*a*) what the manager thinks of his sales force; and
(*b*) what action he is taking.

6. Statistical appraisal. In the modern business environment, statistics are the life-blood of market research and planning. They will be wanted by many departments for their own uses. Many of these statistics emanate directly from the sales force's results. They have to be collated and put in an easily understood form for use by management.

The salesman can, with a little practice and experience, keep records of his own performance and details of his territory in this easily assimilated form and make his own self-appraisals.

7. Moving annual totals. A target set for a salesman will usually cover a period of twelve months. If it commences on a particular date and finishes at the end of twelve months it is not always easy to determine current over-all performance at any point other than the final figure. With increasing needs for immediate and up-to-date information the method is not exact enough. The moving annual total, or M.A.T., shows at any point how the salesman's results compare with the previous twelve months. The example below illustrates a simple chart.

M.A.T. of Export Sales to Australia.
"P.A. INTERNATIONAL"

Year	Month	Actual Sales £	M.A.T. £
1969	January	1,500	—
	February	1,600	—
	March	1,450	—
	April	1,350	—
	May	1,800	—
	June	1,900	—
	July	2,150	—
	August	2,300	—
	September	2,450	—
	October	2,500	—
	November	2,200	—
	December	1,800	23,000
1970	January	1,450	22,950
	February	1,500	22,850
	March	1,600	23,000
	April	1,450	23,100
	May	1,800	23,100
	June	2,300	23,500
	July	2,800	24,150
	August	2,950	24,800
	September	3,050	25,400
	October	3,150	26,050
	November	2,800	26,650
	December	1,900	26,750

There can of course be no M.A.T. for the first twelve months' operations. At the end of twelve months a figure is available, in this example £23,000. Each successive month the new M.A.T. is calculated by deducting the corresponding figure for the previous twelve months and adding on the new monthly figure. For the M.A.T. at June 1970, the sales for June 1969 are deducted, i.e. £1,900, and to the remaining figure the sales for June 1970 are added, i.e. £2,300 making an M.A.T. of £23,500. This method continued over a period enables an appraisal of current performance at a glance. Thus the final figure for 1970 of £26,750 is an increase over the previous year of £3,750.

8. Moving average figures. The moving average is simply a refinement of the previous method which is obtained by dividing the total figure by the number of months it represents. Thus the moving average for June 1969 in the example above would be the total of January to June

$$= \frac{£9,600}{6} \text{ (number of months)}$$

giving a moving average of £1,600. This continued over a period will enable a salesman to see whether his sales are falling or rising in relation to the previous year.

9. Use of graphs. A salesman or a sales manager can make use of graphs to visualise a great deal of information simply. Two types of graph are most commonly used, although many specialist forms may be used. They are Lorenz curves and Z charts.

10. Lorenz curves. Lorenz curves may be used to illustrate the disparity arising from a disproportionate spread of sales over a number of customers. Examination of a salesman's results often show that the largest volume of business comes from a small number of customers. It is important for a salesman to know this. A simple example will illustrate the point:

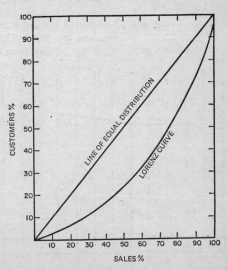

FIG. 54. *Lorenz curve.*

EXAMPLE: A salesman specialised in selling metallisation treatments to metal finishers, although in the rest of the sales force this type of business represented a small volume of total sales. This salesman worked in the Midlands where there were large numbers of metal finishers and he developed the business until more than 75 per cent of his sales came from three large firms. All three were completing contracts for admiralty and similar work which eventually they finished. When this happened they had no immediate use for the salesman's products and he, having spent so much time with them, had few substantial customers left.

A Lorenz curve will not identify the customers but it will make it clear where sales are coming from and enable further investigation and correction. Figure 54 shows that 70 per cent of sales comes from only 40 per cent of accounts, not a very satisfactory situation.

11. Z charts. A Z chart extends over a single year and incorporates three types of information.

(*a*) Individual monthly sales.
(*b*) Cumulative sales for the year.
(*c*) Moving annual total.

It is usual for a double scale to be used since the cumulative figure will be twelve times larger than the average and would result in the latter being too insignificant on the same scale. The

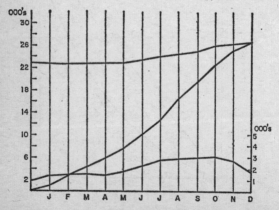

FIG. 55. *Z chart showing monthly sales and cumulative M.A.T.*

Z chart (*see* Fig. 55) is useful to the salesman for a continual check on his performance against the previous year.

12. Motivation by appraisal. People like to see how well they are doing. Stimulation to self-analysis and self-appraisal will lead to well-motivated salesmen and staff It will encourage a spirit of self-competition and lead to analysis of other factors by which sales and performance can be further improved.

PROGRESS TEST 15

1. In appraising the sales force, what are the major considerations?   **(1)**

2. What was "merit rating" and what was its major fault?   **(2)**

3. A sales manager accompanying a salesman will be watching his performance in several ways. What are they?   **(4)**

4. Appraisal forms put a responsibility on the manager. In which two directions will senior management want information?   **(5)**

5. What are moving annual totals?   **(7)**

6. What types of graph are most commonly used in presenting information?   **(9)**

CHAPTER XVI

Customer Creation

IDENTIFYING THE CUSTOMER

1. Who is the customer? A salesman, or his sales manager, frequently finds it difficult to identify his customer.

In many cases the real customer may be hidden behind a fog of distributors, wholesalers, factors or retailers. Even in industry, where the firm is known and the actual number of customers far smaller, it may be difficult to determine the real customer. If a salesman is told to sell lamps to an industrial user, does he visit the buyer or the electrician? If he has specialist equipment he may find that the buyer has no brief to buy and that the product needs explaining to a more technical man. This person may not actually buy the product, but will eventually be responsible for installing or using the product and may recommend the product to his buyer.

The sales manager of a menswear manufacturer believes his customers to be the buyers of department stores, menswear shops and mail order catalogues, but may not readily identify his customer as the woman in the family who buys for her husband and sons, or influences their choice.

In a similar manner the company making electric motors regards its customers as being the firms who buy motors to power electric drills or washing machines. It may not occur to the firm that its real customers are the carpenters, or garages that buy electric drills, or the housewife who buys a washing machine. In determining sales potential it has to study the needs of its ultimate consumers and not solely the requirements of a certain manufacturer who is an intermediary. It may be that faced with a choice of developing sales to company "A", making drills, or company "B", making washing machines, an eye to the economic outlook for consumer markets and construction or automobile equipment might be a better guide.

The decision as to who is the true customer is a significant one. The manufacturer who identifies the ultimate consumer at the end of a complex distribution chain will have an advantage over his competitors. The manufacturer of industrial chemicals who gives his salesman a brief introduction to the product, a collection of leaflets and a bag and then sends him out to sell, sell, sell, is not doing himself, the salesman or the customer much good. The salesman will waste his time in endless cold-canvass calls on the basis that "if you make ten calls a day someone will buy"; he will be incurring opportunity costs in terms of wastage of resources, not to mention waste of salary and expenses to the manufacturer, and also, by calling on the wrong firms, he may possibly antagonise potential future clients. This salesman's lack of success may be compared with the self-motivated salesman who sees the real buyer of industrial goods as the man with the problem; foreman, engineer, painter, etc., and endeavours to inform him of the product's abilities. Having sought and won approval of the man with the problem, he will have an introduction and talking point with the buyer.

REACHING THE CUSTOMER

2. Relating products to customers. It can safely be stated that once the manufacturer has succeeded in identifying the real customer he is able to match product opportunities to customer expectations.

> EXAMPLE: The author was once a consultant for a firm manufacturing chemical-resistant flooring materials. By far the largest volume of orders was specified by the Ministry of Public Buildings and Works (Department of the Environment), architects and consulting engineers. But after analysing sales and contracts it was realised that the real customers were military establishments, food manufacturers and water boards. When this had been determined and we has a clear understanding of the problems of these organisations, it was possible to satisfy their needs. The result was that numerous existing problems were solved and many more future problems foreseen and avoided by having our materials written into specifications.

There exist at any point in time many thousands of products. The whole marketing process begins with conglomerate raw materials; timber, wool, chemicals, iron ore, and the process extends to collections of finished goods in the hands of consumers; furniture, clothing, plastic macs, cutlery. For commercial, household or industrial uses, each has its relevant group of customers.

We can make simple deductions about the type of customers for general ranges of products. The customers for tights and lipsticks are mostly women, whereas smokers' pipes and shaving cream are mostly used by men. In an industrial context, the buyers of paint may be found in local authorities, ship building, contracting, baking and a thousand other industries and commercial undertakings.

3. The role of the manufacturer. After discovering how products are related to customers, the manufacturer must recognise that the needs and expectations of a particular group of customers must be fulfilled, and that he has a role to play in this process. If he undertakes his role successfully and identifies the needs of his customers clearly, he is then in a position to define precise objectives for marketing his product.

The salesman is now armed with the knowledge of:

(*a*) who his customers are;
(*b*) where they are to be found; and
(*c*) the nature of their needs.

Now the salesman can attempt to answer these questions.

(*a*) What can be sold?
(*b*) What quantities can be sold?
(*c*) At what price can they be sold?
(*d*) Where can they be sold?
(*e*) How can they be sold?
(*f*) When can they be sold?

The manufacturer must always keep in mind the needs of his customers, as social conditions and fashions are constantly changing. Many industries find themselves between two stools; too big to appeal to the purely local population out of loyalty, and too small to have a national repute.

EXAMPLE: A brewery found itself very much in the above situation. Its advertising campaigns were not showing much evidence of success and the sales from its off-licences were slumping badly. On analysis it was found that the brewery maintained a "traditional" type of off-licence while market research showed that more than 80 per cent of purchases of alcoholic drinks were made by women, who bought on impulse from the licensed supermarkets. These women were found to dislike going into an off-licence that looked like a pub. The recommendations were that the off-licences should be given a facelift to make them more appealing to women, a new shop layout to encourage circulation of customers on a self-service basis, and that a delicatessen should be established to widen appeal.

4. Profitable advertising. Chapter II, **21–31** showed how advertising attempts to reach the individual customer, both existing and potential. In addition, it must endeavour to select him from the large numbers of people who are actual or potential customers for other manufacturers. We must try to motivate him so that he will relate his needs to our particular product and so develop a loyalty to our brand. This may be based on seemingly trivial considerations, but such loyalty can be extremely powerful.

EXAMPLE: Tests have shown that loyalty to a particular brand of cigarette is largely a matter of belief in some quite trivial determinate. In one test 300 confirmed smokers, all loyal to one of three brands, were asked to identify cigarettes. All the samples were masked so that the brand was hidden. Of the 300 people tested, only 2 per cent could positively identify their particular favourite brand.

That advertising can be successful is manifest in the example just given and the continuing growth of advertising expenditure indicates the faith that manufacturers place in advertising. In many cases, however, success may be marginal. The cost of advertising must cover the total circulation, while from the total readership our customers may form only a small percentage.

EXAMPLE: We may advertise a specialist industrial floor cleaner and degreaser and will select a medium that will reach most of our class of customers. We can use the weekly trade journal *Cleaning and Maintenance*. This will reach the great majority of firms and individuals who are concerned with cleaning and maintenance generally, both in industry and commerce. A floor cleanser and degreaser, however, is not going to be required by all of these readers even. This means a part of the total circulation, even among a selected class of readers, may be wasted.

5. Wasteful advertising. Precise identification of the customers is essential to avoid wasteful advertising. The high cost of this is a growing problem and to avoid such wasted expenditure the questions of "who" and "where" are the customers must be answered accurately.

EXAMPLE: A successful European company decided to market its range of cigarette rolling papers in Australia. The company made no efforts to discover what kind of people rolled their own cigarettes, but on the assumption that it was sporting men the company decided to advertise in the sports papers published at weekends.

Initially the advertising was ineffective and retail sales were negligible. Their decision was to increase the size of the advertisement in the belief it would make greater impact, but once again the results were negligible. Ultimately full-page advertisements were arranged, but when no results were obtained the entire campaign was abandoned. It was never doubted that Australians roll their own cigarettes, but by making assumptions about customers without any consumer research the company failed to reach its real customers.

6. Deciding what appeals to customers. Different types of customer may require entirely different forms of information about the same products. The paint manufacturer may be required to sell his products to several types of customer:

(a) users of the product, e.g. industrial buyers for maintenance;

(b) re-sellers of the products, e.g. distributors, retailers or contractors; and

(c) ultimate consumers, e.g. the general public.

The successful salesman will recognise differences in the needs of his customers and by a process of product analysis, define two basic sets of information.

(a) What do customers want from my product?

(b) What can my products do for customers?

He might consider selling a twenty-litre drum of paint used for treating external rendering to three types of customer; industrial users, distributors or contractors and consumers, e.g. householders.

7. The distributor or contractor. The needs of the distributor and contractor are fundamentally different to the user and consumer, who are interested in benefits relating to their jobs, lives, property or comfort.

The distributor wants to know: "What will I get out of it?" The basic answer must be: "increased profit".

The increased profits may come from a higher profit per unit sold, or from an increased turnover. In addition the contractor may also benefit from an enhanced reputation if the product is new and successful. The distributor may also want assurances about levels of advertising and promotion.

8. The consumer. The ultimate consumer, or householder, is more likely to be motivated by his wife than by any desire to risk his neck painting the house! Our salesman may have to decide on a set of facts that will appeal to the woman of the house rather than the man. She will probably be interested in:

(a) good range of colours;
(b) clean, bright and new appearance;
(c) non-flaking or "chalking";
(d) non-toxity;
(e) a good brand name; and
(f) the social value of a freshly painted house.

Price will be of importance in that it must accord with consumer expectation, and ability to pay, and must also represent quality within a price range.

9. The industrial user. The salesman must understand the needs of the industrial user and think about the advantages of his product that will persuade him to buy. He could make a list of benefits for this drum of paint. It:

(a) seals and waterproofs surfaces;
(b) needs only a single coat application—low labour cost;
(c) is resistant to atmospheric pollution or weathering;
(d) has durability—low recurring maintenance costs; and
(e) is non-toxic—safety factor.

No mention is made of price per litre or drum, although he might relate price to the work involved; this will show the customer that he is saving money in the long term. The industrial user is concerned with solving a problem that threatens, or is actually damaging the business operation. Cost is considered as an opportunity cost—the cost of *not* applying a protective coating is the possible damage that could occur by neglecting to carry out the work.

The industrial buyer is always seeking some benefit which he is not getting at present. These may be:

(a) economy of time and money;
(b) savings in labour costs;
(c) increased productivity;
(d) simplified operations;

(e) improved safety;

(f) improved value of his products;

(g) enhanced selling power of his products;

(h) better performance of his products;

(i) increased reliability of his products;

(j) lower maintenance and service requirements; and

(k) ways to enhance his reputation as a buyer.

10. Effects of importance to the industrial buyer. Having aroused the buyer's interest in the product and enabled him to assess its worth to his organisation, the salesman will consider other effects that the buyer may realise are important:

(a) the effects of the purchase on his company; and

(b) the effects on other organisations whose fortunes are entwined with his company, such as:

(i) banks;

(ii) financial institutions;

(iii) insurance companies; and

(iv) other suppliers.

The buyer will want to be given sound reasons to justify his purchasing action. These reasons must be given by the salesman and will become the buyer's protection against criticism.

11. Commercial and retail buyers. Commercial and retail buyers may be men or women, but they will be motivated by many of the considerations of industrial buyers, such as:

(a) certainty of benefits;

(b) enhancement of their reputations;

(c) to avoid criticism for failure; and

(d) evidence of success elsewhere.

They will be doubtful of unsupported claims and promises and will need specific details of performance. The realisation of customers' and buyers' expectations and behaviour patterns has enabled manufacturers to adopt techniques of promotion that are oblique as they are not immediately concerned with the supplier's products. By concentrating on the buyer's difficulties with in-store promotions, training and staffing problems, cash flows and economies, suppliers can, through the efficiency of their sales force, have important and far-reaching effects on their sales.

EXAMPLE: Sears Roebuck have developed the method almost in reverse. In this example the buyer, Sears Roebuck, having deduced the needs of its customers and taken a decision to introduce a range of goods, will assist the supplier to finance, research and produce the goods.

12. Providing evidence. It is important for the salesman to prepare truthful, accurate and reliable evidence of the soundness of his selling information. This may be:

(*a*) *photographs* of other installations or work carried out (with the approval of the authority concerned);

(*b*) *testimonials or reports* from recognised customers or testing institutions, e.g. universities or government testing stations; or

(*c*) *comprehensive reports* on the nature of the buyer's problem and the salesman's suggestions for solving it.

The last method can also be used as a means of selecting customers from the mass of the potential but anonymous population.

13. The oblique approach.

EXAMPLE: A manufacturer of chemical resistant coatings discovered customers by offering a survey of corrosion problems. The campaign had a high response and salesmen were given the addresses of firms interested in the survey. They carried out a detailed survey of problems and made sound, practical recommendations. The response to the scheme was high and 15 per cent of reports produced immediate business. A further 12 per cent produced business within six months.

This scheme was successful in several ways. It (1) introduced the supplier to many buyers; (2) enhanced the reputation of the supplier for technical efficiency; (3) substantially reduced selling costs; and (4) firmly established the supplier on the market.

The surveys and reports were sent to buyers, engineers or works managers. They received all the facts and information enabling them to support their recommendation to purchase the coatings. The salesman provided the buyer with a defence against unfair criticism from his superiors.

This method of contacting customers is known as the oblique approach.

EXAMPLE: A company was an agency for a specialist surface coating manufacturer. The firm made high-quality coatings for a variety of specialist industrial problems associated with chemicals and corrosion, and also made external treatments for housing. The manufacturer did not advertise and was unknown in the area when the agency was appointed.

It was recognised that a major potential existed in the steelworks and chemical plants in the area, but as all work was placed through appointed site contractors who had agreed prices, it was "impossible" to sell to them. The price structure did not allow for any kind of discount which might have helped persuade the contractors to influence the buyers in choosing a product. After a fruitless period trying to sell to the large works and the contractors, a consultancy service was established.

The agency/consultancy undertook survey work for a painting contractor or a site contractor. In the beginning the work was invariably of a hazardous nature that was unsuitable for normal coatings. The contractor was interested because it enabled him to obtain work outside his normal range of jobs—he expanded his business. By a *joint approach* to the works, contracts were won, in which the contractor was able to charge a premium for special work and the agency won large contracts. *Both traded on the reputation and skill of the other*.

This was later extended to local authorities and hundreds of houses were treated, with the contractor acting as a subcontractor to the consultancy who actually undertook the work.

By this unorthodox oblique approach, which recognised that the prime needs of the works were to cure a problem with the minimum of risk to the *buyer*, many sales were achieved resulting in thousands of pounds' worth of business.

A PRACTICAL PROBLEM

14. Introduction. A firm of industrial paint manufacturers decides to sell a range of coatings suitable for metal work. It is decided to exploit the opportunities offered by motorway development and sell the coatings for bridge balustrading.

To the question: "who is the customer?" there is a bewildering array of possible answers. It could be:

(a) the painting contractor;
(b) the metal fabricators;
(c) the main contractor;
(d) the sub-contractor responsible for erection;
(e) the local authority;
(f) the consulting engineer;
(g) the consulting architect; or
(h) the Department of the Environment.

15. Areas of decisions. When deciding to whom we should try to sell our protective coatings we must consider the related questions:

(*a*) Who is responsible for the buying decision or specification?
(*b*) Who will actually purchase the paint?
(*c*) Who will finally apply the paint?

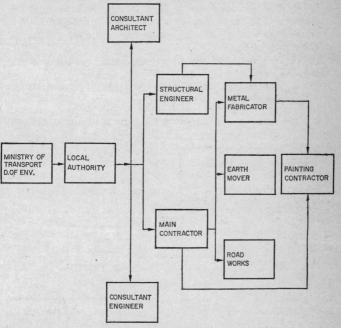

FIG. 56. *Authority structure.*

Although all the possible customers are involved in the use of the paint, only one will actually make the final decision to buy. It would therefore be a waste of time for the salesman to visit each of the possible customers; instead we must determine the responsibilities of each and so locate the key person who will decide on our paint. Figure 56 is a model authority structure of the situation.

16. Order of approaches by the salesman. By understanding the authority structure the salesman can make decisions concerning the way to tackle the organisations. These may be:

(*a*) *the painting contractor* who will apply finish coats and be interested in application costs;

(*b*) *the metal fabricator* who will make the balustrading and apply primers and possibly one finished coat;

(*c*) *the contractors* who will have submitted fixed price tenders for completed work;

(*d*) *the local authority* who, as agent for the Department of the Environment, will have over-all responsibility for the contract;

(*e*) *the consulting engineer* who wishes to ensure the structure is adequately protected;

(*f*) *the consultant architect* who is responsible for visual effects and over-all design; and

(*g*) *the Department of the Environment* which is responsible for determining specification.

A second model can be drawn to illustrate the order of calls to

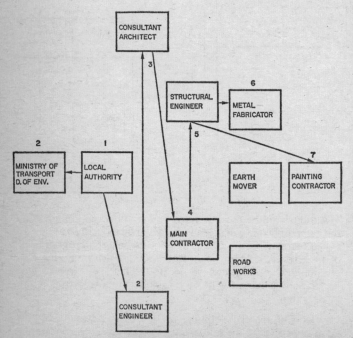

FIG. 57. *Flow diagram to show order of calls.*

convince all the authorities that our product is suitable and should be written into the specification, *see* Fig. 57.

It becomes apparent that these operations are a task for one salesman. If the salesman has initiated the customer creation process, he will now seek the aid of his sales manager and his total organisation. The sales manager will delegate parts of the task to other salesmen; in this way a co-ordinated approach is possible. If the job has originated at management level, the task will have been delegated from the beginning.

In this way the individual and distinctive needs of each of the authorities can be calculated. A co-ordinated logical sales approach with specially prepared sample materials, technical information and advice can follow.

PROGRESS TEST 16

1. Discuss the role of the manufacturer, showing why a recognition of his role must precede the definition of precise objectives for marketing the product.   **(3)**

2. How may advertising help in seeking out the customer?   **(4)**

3. How do the needs of industrial users, distributors and consumers differ?   **(7–10)**

4. Commercial and retail buyers will be motivated by many considerations. What will these be?   **(11)**

5. What is the oblique approach?   **(13)**

6. How may the use of models help in understanding customers?   **(15, 16)**

CHAPTER XVII

Marketing Strategy

PROBLEMS OF STRATEGY

1. The firm in its environment. Successful adaptation in a company must be measured not only in the magnitude of current profits but also by longer-term resilience. A company is like a living organic being; it exists in time and within a particular environment at any one point in time. An organism, to survive, has to be capable of adaptation—a process of change by which it modifies itself to a form better suited to the evolving environment. The organism itself will have a better chance of survival if it can also alter, or at least modify, its environment. Thus the organism, or the company, and its environment may be said to react with each other.

2. The company. The company experiences its environment in several ways.

(*a*) By flows of information:
  (*i*) in terms of letters;
  (*ii*) press comments;
  (*iii*) reaction to advertising; or
  (*iv*) competitors' activity.
(*b*) By flows of money from:
  (*i*) payments for goods or services;
  (*ii*) rising or falling sales; or
  (*iii*) reaction of share prices, etc.

3. The environment. Conversely the environment, that is, the world in which the company operates, experiences the company in different ways.

(*a*) By flows of information through:
  (*i*) press releases by the company;
  (*ii*) advertising;
  (*iii*) other publicity; or
  (*iv*) financial statements.
(*b*) By reaction to the firm's projected image:

(*i*) by purchase of its goods and services; and

(*ii*) by contributing to its share prices.

These flows are illustrated in Fig. 58.

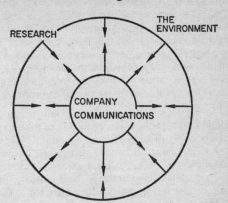

FIG. 58. *The relationship between company communications and the environment.*

4. Relationship between company and customer. On a more selective basis we can determine definite flows between company and customer (potential or actual), as in Fig. 59.

Clearly a firm and its customers share an environment, but they also share it with thousands of other customers and suppliers, known and unknown. It is said that "any law, anywhere in the

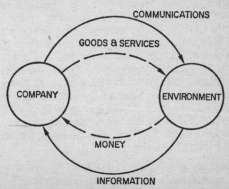

FIG. 59. *Relations between company and customer.*

world, affects the liberty of the individual by some small degree",
so also any activity by either company or customer can affect the
individual firm's future prosperity.

The manufacturer of refrigerators who sees no threat in the
long-term plans of the tour operator offering package holidays
abroad is not aware of the true nature of his competition. People
with limited resources of money will have to decide: "This year,
will we buy a new refrigerator, or have a holiday abroad?"

Similarly the industrial processor who does not pay heed to the
public's growing concern with pollution is failing to appreciate
the long-term ramifications of his particular environment.

5. Strategy for an uncertain future. Evolution is the modification
or adaptation of an organism. The evolution of the company may
be brought about by discreet changes in policy. Whether these
changes are more than random or fortuitous, or are to be a
creative adaptation of policy, is a fundamental question underlying long-term marketing strategy. Undoubtedly firms have
made fortuitous changes in policy which have led to success, but
the path is littered with good ideas which occurred at the wrong
point in time, or which failed to appreciate the wider implications
to the environment, whether physical or psychological. Thus it
may be that in the final analysis of success for supersonic trans-
ports, the criteria will not be economy, safety or speed, but the
public's feelings towards atmospheric pollution, noise or living
space; whether these feelings are founded on truth or not is
hardly important.

The depth analysis of motivational research has found ample
evidence that people's reactions to propositions are rarely
rational, but far more likely to be of an emotive nature.

In 1953 the Chrysler Corporation assumed that their customers,
being rational people, would be influenced in their choice of a
car by parking difficulties, fuel consumption and the many practical aspects of modern living. They interpreted these assumptions
into model planning and produced the logical answer to just those
considerations. The result, however, was a fall in their share of the
American car market from 26 per cent in 1953 to around 13 per
cent in 1954. The ill-fated Ford Edsel car project, also conceived
on sound logic and backed by market research, foundered upon
the buying public's irrationality.

6. Decision-making. This lies at the heart of strategic planning.
Since all management decisions are based upon information,
clearly there is a problem in predicting the future. One may, on the

evidence available, question the extent to which long-term planning is possible in a world in which uncertainty prevails and the only certain aspect is the continued disorder.

Management faced with responsibilities to shareholders, employees and customers has the dilemma of satisfying all three. A large dividend this year may well satisfy the shareholders, but if it is followed by liquidation the next year it has failed in all three responsibilities. Thus the company faces conflicting demands on whether:

(a) to optimise its current activities; or

(b) to ensure adequate provision for the future.

The company can achieve such conditions only by maintaining current production while exploring potential products and markets for the future. To accomplish this, the company must ensure that there is sufficient emphasis on forward planning.

This brings us back to the concept of evolution, but here as a continuous process of decision-making based on a systematic examination of a firm's assets, capabilities, and resources in relation to the changing environment.

7. Uncertain conditions. An economist has summed up the problem of forecasting by saying: "forecasting is very difficult, especially about the future."

A method is required that will enable the firm to examine itself critically and systematically, and provide a basis for comparison with competitors' capabilities and the market's likely future needs.

8. Progression of projects. Decision-making in such a situation is further complicated by the progression of projects that present themselves for screening, evaluation and decision. So many times management is faced with the possibility of rejection of an idea in the belief that something better is about to emerge. This type of decision can be reduced to a binomial state in which one poses only one question at a time.

(a) Is it good?—if no, reject; if yes, pass on.

(b) Can we make it?—if no, reject; if yes, pass on.

Each question allows one of two answers, one of which will automatically reject the proposition, the other which will pose a subsequent question until all possibilities are eliminated. This process, which forms the basis of computerised decision-making, may well speed up the entire process, but if computerised management decision-making speeds up the sorting of futile ideas, we simply process nonsense quicker than ever before: "rubbish in—rubbish out!"

Perhaps the worst aspect of binomial decision-making is that it is non-adaptable. It asks a question to which there can be only two possible answers, "Yes" or "No". It rejects that which is not appropriate to the moment and, in doing so, fails to project an idea into a situation which may exist in ten or fifteen years' time, which is the degree of forward planning that is needed if strategy is to maintain a rational development in a highly technological age.

PLANNING FOR THE FUTURE

9. Systematic study. If the search and sorting process is concentrated on areas or products that the company can study systematically, it can reduce the reject percentage to an acceptable, and a controllable, level. This in turn, however, may lead to shortcomings in long-term plans and allow opportunities to be missed. The company should pursue a policy of planned product replacement based on a detailed knowledge of the following.

(*a*) *Market:* what market does the company believe it operates in; what are the wider implications of the market and the competition; what market should the company aim to be in, in ten or fifteen years' time?

(*b*) *Production capability:* what are the skills and abilities of the plant, equipment and staff; what uses can the buildings, land and equipment be put to?

(*c*) *Consumer or user trends:* what will our customers need, or be persuaded to demand in the future; what economic, technical, educational and social changes will take place to influence customers?

10. Capital investment analysis. The success of a company's long-term plans for the future depends on effective capital investment analysis. This starts with the recognition and quantification of fixed assets and capital proposals. For each new project proposed, revenue and costs cash flows are predicted over the lifetime of the project. That these flows should be marginal is necessary to provide proper comparison with the other flows within the firm; only additional revenues and costs generated over the lifetime of the project must be considered. If it turns out that the lifetime of the project exceeds the budget under consideration, the period is extended for the purpose of analysis. In traditional capital investment theory it is necessary that all projects which may become available during the forthcoming budget period be anticipated before a decision is made. Then with the projects enumerated and the flows calculated, the worth of each project is evaluated with respect to both its net return to the firm and the entailed risks. In this way capital investment analysis ensures that all projects which the company proposes to introduce are properly costed out before they are launched.

There are three common methods for ascertaining the profitability of each project.

(a) Pay-back method.
(b) Return on investment method.
(c) Present-value return on investment method.

These methods of making capital equipment decisions can be also applied to decisions about what markets to enter or what products to develop. Capital investment theory has been extended to the entire spectrum of business investment decisions, but product-market investment differs from capital investment, and adaptations of the theory are necessary for a practical approach to strategic decisions.

Capital investment theory is seen, therefore, to be concerned with evaluation and selection. Recognition of the need for decision and formulation of alternatives are assumed to have taken place before and external to the area of analysis, as often happens with so many management science models.

11. Strategic decision-making. In strategic decision-making it can be determined that the process involves four steps. These are:

(a) *recognition* of the need to make a decision;
(b) *formulation* of alternatives;
(c) *evaluation* of alternatives; and
(d) *selection* of alternatives for decision.

This process is shown in Fig. 60.

Since capital investment theory is concerned only with the last two steps, evaluation and selection, it is incomplete for our purpose in strategic decision-making It may be used as a "tool" of strategic decision-making once the areas for evaluation have been ascertained by other processes.

12. Charting the future. Capital investment theory, while efficient

for capital decisions, cannot go beyond "today". Our product
search process requires that we should go beyond "today" and
into the uncharted areas of the future. Unfortunately all the
charts and statistics of performance will be no more than a guide

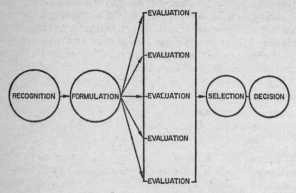

FIG. 60. *Strategic decision-making.*

to the immediate future. They cannot show changes that might
come in:

    (*a*) public opinion;
    (*b*) consumer trends;
    (*c*) government decisions;
    (*d*) economic effects; or
    (*e*) technical innovations.

The highly profitable and successful firm may well be encouraging technological breakthroughs by rivals by trying to cut
the ground away from beneath them; rather like a ferry which by
its success proves the need for a bridge, which eventually puts the
ferry out of business.

13. Continuing product succession. With growing emphasis on the
economic utilisation of available facilities and the high rate of
technical change, industrial companies, like consumer companies,
are thinking in terms of continuing product succession and review.
That this can lead to its own difficulties was evidenced by the
growth of polyethylene plants at a time when existing producers
were asking the government to limit imports in an attempt to
reduce over-production. In an industry like petrochemicals, where
product development and plant construction can take years, the

long-term trend is of vital importance and has to be perceived at the outset.

In these circumstances it becomes important to devise a method whereby a company's plant, experience and human resources can be related to developing market needs, or adapted to meet changing conditions. The need is also evident in retail store development, where trends in consumer buying, home freezers, discount stores, out-of-town shopping and pedestrian precincts have all exerted considerable influence in recent years. Such a method of determining strategy should enable a company to:

(*a*) plan its development on a *continuous basis*;

(*b*) determine its future *systematically*;

(*c*) *recognise the environment*; and correctly interpret changes in it;

(*d*) be aware of *market requirements*; and

(*e*) be capable of *exploiting opportunities* as they arise.

ROLE AND STRATEGY

14. Planning by role. In order to be able to plan by role, a company must be aware of its true nature and recognise where its experience and resources enable it to play the optimum role. A method has to be devised which will enable a company to plan its development according to a definite role. Planning by role will undoubtedly prove a better long-term strategy than planning by objectives, as it provides for in-built adaptability which enables a company to evolve within the marketing environment in response to technological, environmental, economic and social changes.

Before being able to plan its strategy a company must have a clear concept of its role and, most important, of its identity. Only when identity and role have been determined can planning by objectives become relevant. The corporate identity so determined must be of a dynamic nature capable of evolution and adaptation to market pressures. It must be recognised that since the company accepts the value of adaptation, then it must also be prepared for its identity to evolve over a period.

15. Evolving corporate identity. The determination of corporate identity may be by different methods, but the use of models provides a positive approach that involves all the management skills within a company. Such a model of corporate identity would relate a company to its market, and reveal the true nature of the company's resources and skills. It will also confirm the nature of the competition that faces the company, and by so doing reveal the exact extent of the environment in which the firm operates.

The type of model will vary greatly according to the business of the company, but its adaptability and certainty of application to each individual firm makes it a particularly effective tool. Models will necessarily vary according to the company and also, in particular, according to whether the company is consumer-oriented or user (industrial) oriented.

FIG. 61. *Consumer market model.*

16. Consumer companies. Consumers have limited resources in terms of money, time and wants. At any time their decisions to buy goods and services will vary according to the degree of satisfaction they believe will derive from purchasing certain goods or services. A man who buys cigarettes may cease to buy them and will then spend his money on which will give him greater satisfaction. However, his initial decision to stop buying cigarettes may well not have been the desire for other goods. It may have been due to:

(*a*) a shortage of money;
(*b*) more urgently required goods;
(*c*) reports on the harmful effects of smoking;
(*d*) particularly attractive advertisements for other goods.

The temptation to buy tobacco at all may be overcome by advertising for, or impulse buying of, other merchandise, e.g., sweets, potato crisps or chewing gum. Depth interviewers in motivational research have revealed that the acts of smoking cigarettes and sucking sweets (particularly chewing gum) are all outward expressions of oral satisfaction. A person faced with a decision to buy a brand of cigarettes, or a packet of chewing gum, is measuring his potential future satisfaction in ways other than the relevant costs.

17. Wider relationships to the market. Our company may well, by examination of the places where people buy their cigarettes, discover that they are closely related to the entertainment industry; people smoke, eat crisps or chew mints when they play bingo, go to the cinema, watch television or go to a football match. But this in turn is connected to other aspects of life such as

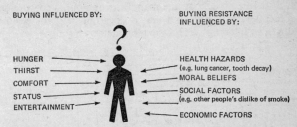

BUYING INFLUENCED BY:

BUYING RESISTANCE INFLUENCED BY:

HUNGER

THIRST

COMFORT

STATUS

ENTERTAINMENT

HEALTH HAZARDS (e.g. lung cancer, tooth decay)

MORAL BELIEFS

SOCIAL FACTORS (e.g. other people's dislike of smoke)

ECONOMIC FACTORS

FIG. 62. *Influences on consumer buying decisions.*

the public's reaction to evidence of lung cancer, tooth decay, football riots and all the manifest problems of society. The conflict between the various influences is shown in Fig. 62.

But once the company has recognised that its role is to provide a certain form of satisfaction in whatever terms people experience the product, it is at least in a position to play its full role and offer whatever products fit in with its capability, its resources, and its marketing experience. The move by cigarette manufacturers Imperial Tobacco into the potato crisp industry is an example of such related abilities being exploited to the full.

18. Industrial companies. When the industrial firm considers its role in the manner of the consumer company, it appears difficult to relate products or services in the same way. Apart from the consideration of product markets, the industrial company has also to consider the nature of its particular skills, and its resources in terms of capital investment. The aircraft manufacturer who turns to making automatic vending machines may well use his knowledge of precision engineering, but whether an aircraft assembly shed, towering twenty metres high, is ideally utilised for assembling a coffee dispenser two metres high is questionable; consider the cost of heating, for example. Similarly the tinplate works that seeks to defer closing down in the face of changing conditions and turns to making road signs and metal poles may be using metal working skills and plant suited to cutting, rolling and forming, but if it does not have the marketing knowledge for entering a highly competitive and limited market, it will not be successful.

19. Exploring the company's role. A firm in the complex and technical field of air compressors, seeking product diversification and a strategy for the future, may investigate what its particular skills fit it for, other than the manufacturing of air compressing equipment. It may well find that it does not have to seek new products for it has not yet fully exploited its own skills.

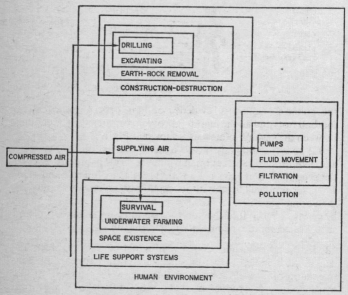

FIG. 63. *Discovering the company's role.*

The model in Fig. 63 has been constructed to examine the company and it concludes that its essential skill is in compressing air. From this realisation of identity, its role in the future can emerge. The model explores the role of compressed air equipment in three possible directions.

20. Future alternative decisions.

(a) By continuing its present production, it can optimise current skills in the field of drilling. But it can explore this environment further and determine that in this field its future is bound up with other activities. Drilling is connected with excavating, and this in turn is related to earth and rock removal, which in turn is related to the construction and destruction business. This in turn is clearly related to man's activities in adapting his larger environment; seeking new mineral wealth, road building, new towns, developing countries, harbour works, and so on.

(b) The second area of exploitation leads to *supplying* air, which is used basically for survival and can be adapted to such activities of the future as underwater farming; (a recent survey showed that some sixteen major firms in the U.K., including brickworks, engineering, aircraft, steel and agriculture are all active in this future industry). Space existence is a related area to underwater farming and both fall within the encompassing role of life-support systems. Again we are faced with industries yet in their infancy but, given expanding economies and, more important, expanding populations, they will grow in importance. Again we are concerned with the dynamics of population and the human environment.

(c) Our third area for consideration is the area of pumping fluids. A firm able to pump air has a knowledge of moving fluids, and with the growing threat of pollution and shortage of water supplies, the filtration, movement and storage of water, perhaps several times over, or even in perpetual use, becomes a reality. A firm able to see its role as manufacturers or, more important, technologists, in fluid movement is well placed to move into the field when opportunity is ripe. Once again we are in an area where the common denominator is the human environment and population growth.

21. Fulfilling its role.

Our company, then, after exploring several prospects, none of which goes outside its present technical expertise, finds itself related to three aspects of the human environment. It will alert itself to any changes, any government reports, whether in Britain, Europe or elsewhere, any warning reports, indeed any published or unpublished information that implies there is a need for skill in the pumping or storage of air or fluids.

The company, having identified its true nature and accepted its role, can take quicker decisions, because it is not moving out of its particular field of experience, skills and abilities.

22. Long-term strategy.

A company that has determined its identity and role is capable of decision-making with the minimum of delay; it will have recognised that a company asking itself "What business are you really in?" must proceed with caution until it has examined itself thoroughly.

Long-term strategy is at best a hazardous business, but at least the uncertainty can be minimised and more than offset by the company that is poised ready to accept whatever changes fit its general resources and assets. Our strategy then must consider the following questions. Does it:

(a) extend into the future?
(b) consider existing experience and capabilities?
(c) provide for continuing market review?
(d) simplify decision making?
(e) allow for planned opportunism?

Only if strategy fulfils at least most of these conditions can a firm hope to maintain its current profits and not dissipate its energies in a thousand and one product-market ventures, or lose its chances of survival in a very uncertain future.

PROGRESS TEST 17

1. How may the company experience its environment? (2)
2. What conflicting demands face a company in its decision-making? (6)
3. What are the three common methods for evaluating the worth of each project? (11)
4. In continuing product strategy what should be the aims of the company? (13)
5. How does the use of models assist in evolving corporate identity? (15)
6. What questions should long-term strategy aim to fulfil? (22)

CHAPTER XVIII

Managing Customers

UNDERSTANDING CUSTOMERS

1. Consumer research. The modern business environment has called into being many ways of determining information necessary to prediction, planning and a more exact understanding of conditions, present and future, including market research, product research, motivational research and research into employees. Consumer research exists to investigate consumer trends generally and to find out what consumers are doing, rather than to discover essential facts about customers, as personalities.

Such information as is available about consumers is, more often than not, rather precise but lifeless statistics, again recording what has happened, not an appreciation of what customers will do.

2. Results of research. Much of consumer research derives from the activities of advertising, which needs to know how people might react to advertising messages and promotional propositions. It succeeds in realising and accentuating the essential diversity of human nature. The general concepts deriving from advertising research of consumers' behaviour are that:

(*a*) human beings are self-motivating, and complex;

(*b*) they are reasoning and intelligent, but capable of making irrational decisions as often as rational;

(*c*) their motivations are largely a result of emotion, custom or prejudice;

(*d*) they differ in nature and personality;

(*e*) from the foregoing, they form widely different desires and buying behaviour; and

(*f*) their differences in buying behaviour will differ widely even within our particular society.

3. General trends. From the foregoing it is reasonable to assume that distinguishable relationships will exist between buying behaviour and changes that arise in society, and the psychological influences that affect individuals. It is possible to recognise general trends. For example:

(a) the way in which particular models of motor cars have varying success is largely derived from visual impression or styling and not from the mechanical ability. This is itself dependent upon consumers' attitudes to the modern world;

(b) package holidays rely upon the general feelings of holiday-makers towards certain countries and resorts and rarely to degrees of temperature, rainfall and the facilities in which they all compete.

4. Differentiating the product. A company can gain distinct advantages from recognising that consumers, and industrial users, react in different ways to propositions, and that these reactions are often less than purely rational. A product may be presented in such a way that in the minds of buyers it is differentiated. This may be derived from styling, colour, materials, packaging, delivery, distribution, or alternative uses.

EXAMPLE: A company made building chemicals, and among its products offered a tile adhesive. The product was essentially no different to many other adhesives; its price was in line with others and generally it was a product with low differentiation. In trying to create new customers it was impossible to offer a real advantage to customers. In line with competitors the product was one relying on loyalty for its share of the market. The company hit on the idea of packaging the adhesive in plastic buckets instead of the usual can. Immediately, customers grasped that the product was different, simply because when the adhesive was finished they had a supply of very useful buckets.

5. Significance of consumer trends. It is essential for a company to try to appreciate the underlying significance of apparently trivial consumer trends, such as the choice of bright colours in men's shirts, or trends in women's fashions which often gain a momentum of their own and defy the fashion houses' attempts to change them.

There has developed in recent years a need for self-expression, which, if related to the hierarchy of needs referred to in XII, **11**, may derive from a satisfying of lesser needs such as physiological, safety and security. This self-expression is manifest in new hobbies, homes, do-it-yourself holidays, sports and the wider range of leisure activities.

It becomes important not only to research basic reasons for patterns of consumer buying, but also to examine the wider implications of human behaviour patterns as a whole. Consumers are not simply persuaded by rational considerations of price, utility and presentation, but also by basic motivations deriving from expectations and behaviour determined by attitudes, experiences, social responsibilities and the way in which the person's particular group consider the object of his interest.

6. Individuality and communication. It is easy to regard consumers acting *en masse* as being something apart from the rest of humanity—a man in a shop buying an article is often considered to be different from a man at home, or work. It must be remembered that both the buyer and the seller are individual humans, equally prone to thoughts and opinions, even though research on consumer behaviour is usually reduced to rows of statistics. The needs of the customer will alter with changing social conditions, while consumer trends may alter with changing life styles.

Advertising does make attempts to relate its messages to its concept of the customer although even here it usually fails to present the customer as a variable human being. Thus it fails to make the most of its communicatory abilities. The success of an advertising message must depend upon more than the rational content, as much of the communication of meaning is conveyed in ways other than verbal.

7. Personal characteristics. Research into the factors relating to customers' buying decisions invariably reveals the critical element in buying or not buying to be distinctive personal characteristics. This has been revealed especially in areas where the population is formed from widely differing origins, race, religion, education, income, etc., and yet it has been shown that decisions about purchases of cars, clothing, even foodstuffs, derive from variances in personalities and not expressly from the other factors. If a man buys a bright red shirt, it is generally because he has an extrovert character, and not because of any particular background, similarly a man who insists on a formal striped tie is also displaying a particular behaviour pattern.

8. Confidence of consumers. It has been evident from recent studies of consumer behaviour in buying that confidence is a strong determinant of whether a purchase is made or not. It does not rely heavily upon how much money a person has, but rather on how he views the future. In this a consumer's behaviour reflects fundamental attitudes concerning his appreciation of the economic picture.

During the 1960s the general economic trend was downward, and the prospect of increased unemployment produced a general feeling of uncertainty; uncertainty of the value of money, of the prospects of employment and of investment. When in 1971 the government produced a budget that was intended to boost the economy by expanding consumer demand, it did not produce the predicted effect, largely because consumers were pessimistic about the future. People who have suffered unemployment, or had to pay high interest rates on loans, or seen their savings whittled away by inflation, will not readily respond to assurances that all is now well. Most important, because people regard prospects with pessimism, the result confirms their belief.

The general attitudes of consumers determine over-all business prospects because capital investment is only undertaken if the demand from consumers warrants it.

9. Systematic consumer knowledge. To correctly interpret consumer attitudes, particularly in relation to the needs of business, it is necessary to provide systematic knowledge about:

(*a*) the ways in which consumers form attitudes;
(*b*) methods to determine the fundamental attitudes;
(*c*) how negative attitudes can be changed; and
(*d*) the way in which particular attitudes are self-selecting for communications about products or services.

There are over-all behavioural attitudes such as consumer feeling about the state of the economy, but in addition there are specific attitudes which apply to consumers' individual reactions to product propositions. For each product, and for each brand name, there will be positive and negative reactions from consumers, but frequently the manufacturer will not detect these. Consumers presented with decisions as to whether or not they will buy a product will be significantly influenced by their fundamental attitudes. Attitudes to colour in clothing may derive from earlier experiences when "flashy" might have been the current description instead of "trendy".

A manufacturer desperately trying to promote a product with little success may not have fully understood the underlying attitudes of consumers to the product. The attitudes of consumers may have little basis in fact, but they are important to the ultimate buying decisions.

MOTIVATING THE CUSTOMER

10. Communicating the message. A tremendous amount of money is spent yearly by manufacturers on advertising or otherwise communicating messages about their products. If this is to succeed it has to have an impact upon the consumers or users that will motivate them to buy the product. Whether or not customers will be so motivated will depend upon three factors.

(*a*) How people *react* to the message.

(*b*) How frequently they are *exposed* to the message.

(*c*) How effectively they *recall* the message.

The ability to recall the message effectively is dependent upon memory.

11. Memory. Memory is connected with imagery inasmuch as it depends on the ability to call back images of something that has already occurred. An experience does not simply happen and get forgotten; a vestige of it will be retained in the mind. The vestiges that remain may be no more than ephemera, or they may have a lasting effect, and may be brought back to mind with great intensity. Exposure to an advertisement may pass almost without recognition and yet a person can see something in a shop which promotes recall and may lead to an impulse purchase.

12. Recognition and recall. Recognition is a much simpler process than recall. The sight of a product, or even a similar advertisement, may bring back memories of the original experience. Recall is a voluntary effort to remember an image; a consumer faced with a problem attempts to recall a product, or a brand that has been seen somewhere, but has not consciously registered deeply enough. It is important for management in promoting products to recognise two important factors which will influence consumers' ability to recall advertising messages. These are that:

(*a*) *repetition* of an experience enables it to be recalled more readily; and

(*b*) *the intensity of the original stimulus* will make recall easier.

Any promotional campaign must ensure that the message:

(*i*) conforms to consumer attitudes;

(*ii*) is repeated sufficiently to form strong images in consumers' memories; and

(*iii*) is intense enough to register positively, enabling certain recall.

13. Benefits to consumer. It has been put forward in Chapter IV that industrial goods constitute a "derived demand" whereas consumer goods are wanted for the satisfaction they themselves provide. Nevertheless even consumer goods are wanted for the benefits they bestow on the purchasers; television for relaxation or leisure, coffee for a stimulating drink, etc. Before individuals become customers for particular products they must have a need which they want to satisfy, e.g. the need for entertainment, or refreshment. This will create a "notion" for something.

When the person has conceived a notion for something, he is thinking in terms of how the product or service will benefit him. The following process will be formed.

(*a*) Anticipation of benefits.

(*b*) Desire for the product service.

(*c*) Desire grows into a positive need.

(*d*) The person is stimulated to seek information.

(*e*) The person becomes a potential customer for a particular product/service.

14. Conclusion. It is necessary for manufacturers to recognise that whatever form of production they are engaged upon, industrial, consumer, or service, consumers are motivated by their conception of what the product will do for them. The management of customers makes it essential for this aspect of derived demand to be thoroughly understood and implemented through an understanding of what customers believe they want, and then so directing communications that they fulfil these personality needs, no matter how trivial they may appear to the manufacturer.

PROGRESS TEST 18

1. What are the general concepts derived from advertising research of consumers' behaviour? (2)

2. How does the hierarchy of needs influence consumer trends? (5)

3. How do personal characteristics affect buying decisions? (7)

4. "To correctly interpret consumer attitudes, particularly in relation to the needs of business, it is necessary to provide systematic knowledge." What questions should we seek to answer? (9)

5. Whether or not consumers will be motivated by communications will depend upon three facts. What are they? (10)

CHAPTER XIX

Communication in Marketing

THE TOTAL COMMUNICATION NEED

1. Communication needs. The purpose of marketing communications is to provide information about the product in a favourable way, to motivate customers to want the product, and to inform them where it may be obtained. Communications, however, to be effective, must go further than simply explaining the company's products. They must also distribute favourable information about the company, its policies and activities. Marketing communications include all those activites which dispense information, such as:

(a) advertising;

(b) sales promotion;

(c) public relations;

(d) the sales force;

(e) stationery, including letter headings, invoices, business cards, etc.; and

(f) vehicle signs.

All of these systems of communication will be directed towards:

(a) creating an environment in which the *company's products will receive favourable reaction* from consumers or users; and

(b) *encouraging sales of the company's products by stimulating demand* and so achieve a satisfactory return on investment.

2. Communication and the marketing objective. The marketing objective will be the result of corporate strategy and long-term planning translated into departmental objectives, it will have been determined by market, economic and social research. Once the objective has been determined the role of communications in the marketing-mix will be decided.

There is a range of activities which marketing management can employ to realise its objectives and together they will make up the marketing-mix; they will be combined to give the most satisfactory combination to reach the actual or potential customers. *See* Fig. 64.

The actual way in which the marketing-mix will be composed will depend, among other things, upon the strategy of the company and the manner in which it regards its role in satisfying customers. All marketing-oriented companies will use these various activities in different ways, which will reflect the type of product, the market, competition and distribution costs.

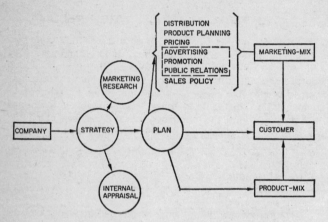

FIG. 64. *Communications in the marketing-mix.*

(*a*) A company dominating the market for a particular range of goods may rely upon its *reputation and public relations* for communication and competitive pricing to maintain its share of the market.

(*b*) A company selling products with little differentiation in a highly competitive market will be forced to *advertise heavily and promote extensively* to ensure its position in the market is maintained.

(*c*) industrial suppliers may place *less emphasis upon competitive pricing if their product is specialised*, and their communication may be limited to advertising in restricted-circulation magazines. Their communications will be largely by the sales force and public relations.

3. Changing needs for communication. The needs for communication will change as market conditions change and a company at the launch of a new product will feel it necessary to adopt different communications to those employed when the product is established.

(*a*) Initially the company will communicate by advertisement and sales promotion to ensure that as many potential customers as possible learn about the product in a favourable way.

(*b*) Later when a strong market position has been established the company will need to maintain a certain level of advertising.

(*c*) When competitors begin to affect the company's share of the market it will have to adopt a different communications strategy. It will now see the need to develop sales promotions as a means of lowering the price to customers without changing the listed price and setting off a price-cutting "war". This effective use of sales promotion is a communications technique.

(*d*) At some time competitors will possibly develop a rival product with undoubted improvements and for a time the company may not be able to offer its own improved version or new product. At this point the communications will again change with an advertised decrease in listed price and a concerted promotional campaign.

BEHAVIOURAL ASPECTS OF COMMUNICATION

4. Market segmentation. Market segmentation exists when a product relates strongly to certain consumers within a market population. One purpose of marketing is to identify these groups. This will frequently reveal opportunities existing in an unsatisfied, or *discrepant*, market. This can lead to product innovation or to the promotion of existing products by highlighting a unique feature which will make them clearly recognisable to the target segment. Examples of this practice can be seen in the way many very general products, such as washing powders, aspirin, and toothpastes, become specific to certain segments by strongly relating one, perhaps trivial, feature to a group of people who believe it to be important.

In today's competitive conditions segmentation is inevitable because of the ways in which products at different stages of their development interact with the market. Management's choice is not if it should segment, but rather how to maximise the results of segmentation. Strongly competitive markets which are often dominated by a few giants make it vital for a company to differentiate its products from those of its competitors. The soft drinks market is typical of one dominated by a few big firms, but many smaller companies still survive. This may be by:

(a) concentrating on local markets;

(b) by producing products appealing to small segments of the market which would be unprofitable for the big company to tackle;

(c) by product innovation.

An example of the latter was the introduction of the wide-mouth, small bottle, but inevitably this was rapidly copied by the market leader.

In the process of promotion and product innovation, the components of the total communication-mix are intimately related to consumers' behaviour in an area where personality is seen as the only factor common to all consumers.

5. Determining the significant product characteristics. To implement a communication policy based on segmentation it is not sufficient to know which products are acceptable to consumers. It is also necessary to determine the significant product characteristics which are preferred or rejected by consumers in relation to competitors' products. Thus marketing must develop a capability to create or change attitudes and not simply to respond to them. If marketing cannot do this, it cannot exert sufficient influence on over-all business strategy.

Marketing management has at best only a marginal control over its environment and claims of being able to manipulate it really only arise out of an intuitive conception of the environment's expectations. Max Gunther said "A hunch is a conclusion based on facts that your mind has accurately observed, stored and processed. But they are facts you don't consciously know because they are stored on some unconcious level of awareness." While marketing men have to rely on hunches and business experience, this should not preclude a more scientific approach.

6. The changing environment. In the conditions of an expanding affluent society, marketing largely rode on an optimistic, acquisitive behaviour pattern, rather than creating it. In the present conditions of high unemployment, generally high interest rates and credit restrictions, a manager who understands his firm's environment and is able to predict trends and modify his promotional tactics in response to it is better able to survive. However he would be even more successful if he was able to form favourable consumers' attitudes to his products.

A company's research into its consumers' behaviour must aim to understand the distribution of preferences for a range of characteristics. It must be able to:

(a) predict the size of the market segment for products having specific characteristics;

(b) evolve a meaningful promotional strategy from an understanding of consumers' attitudes;

(c) relate this information to the consumer through media and personal communications.

This is exemplified by dairies who have encountered resistance from housewives to their offers of regular early morning deliveries of bread, butter, potatoes, etc. Success can only stem from promotions that favourably reflect housewives' attitudes.

Once research has identified the distribution of consumers' preferences they can be matched with known demographic, social or behavioural characteristics of the target market. It is then possible to isolate particular groups which most closely accord to the perceived product advantages. It is to these groups, or segments, that communication can most profitably be directed.

7. The communications problem. Circumstances may arise when an identified set of preferences cannot be satisfactorily implemented into the product's characteristics. The political scene is an example of this. Each party tries to attract as many voters as possible, but is only able to encompass a certain range of appeals into its manifesto, otherwise it will simply shift along the spectrum from right to left or vice versa. It can, however, attempt to change attitudes.

Marketing, too, has to understand that people resist information which they perceive as challenging their attitudes and a product which does not accord to consumers' attitudes is likely to be rejected. This process of rejection may begin with a dislike of marketing methods, such as direct selling, even before the product is considered.

Door-to-door selling of cosmetics must initially depend for success on housewives' attitudes to this form of selling, which attracted much adverse publicity in recent years. In the same way the offer of credit or hire-purchase facilities is influenced by the individuals' attitudes to owing money.

8. Motivating the purchaser. The concept of motivating a purchase raises questions of "how far can a potential purchaser be motivated?" Psychology says that motivation is a state of tension created by a drive. Advertising endeavours to provide information related to the consumers' perceived need, that will act as a cue and provide the drive. Our needs generally fall into two broad categories, which are:

(a) biogenic; and
(b) psychogenic.

In our society it is possible for the biogenic needs, for food, shelter, etc., to be satisfied by the social services, thus leaving all the other needs broadly psychogenic. Thus we do not eat in a smart restaurant to satisfy only the biogenic need of hunger, but also the psychogenic needs for social status, ego, etc. A bedtime drink will best succeed in the market if the mother perceives herself in a situation in which she is satisfying her child's need for nourishment, goodness, sound sleep and any other desirable characteristics. Milk alone would do equally well, as much as sound brushing without toothpaste equally protects teeth, but this is avoided because in our society we feel the need to "belong" to a well-ordered, caring, malted-milk, toothpaste-protected class. It is akin perhaps to the carrying of lucky charms, which may not confer protection, but those who carry them would rather not risk the consequences of not carrying them. If a child's teeth decay, is it the fault of the mother who did not buy the "right" toothpaste; a powerful if negative force. We avoid rather than ignore these truths because, as we shall see, we avoid information which causes us to question entrenched beliefs.

9. Hygiene factors. To what degree an advertisement will prompt the anticipated reaction by the consumer will depend on *hygiene factors* (*see* XII, **12**). The concept is based on the belief that motivation is not something that can be done to people, but is something they do themselves. What can be done is to create circumstances in which consumers become self-motivated.

It may be safely assumed that there are factors in buying which do not encourage a positive buying decision but only reduce the reasons for not buying; it is these we may term hygiene factors. For example, a prospective buyer of a car may wish to buy it for its comfort, safety, status and elegance. The manufacturer helps him to obtain what he wants by providing hygiene factors such as guarantees of free service, replacements or provision of credit on reasonable terms. Therefore, the factors of service, replacements or credit can no longer be used either consciously or subconsciously, as reasons for not buying the car and although the customer is not primarily concerned with the buying of service, it does play a part in the decision-making process.

Product characteristics provide the bases for motivation while the environmental factors surrounding the product are hygiene factors. In the purchase of a domestic appliance the following might be included.

Hygiene	Motivation
credit terms	status symbol
reliability	simplicity
availability of service	labour saving
delivery	design
reputation	cleanliness
price, etc.	colour, etc.
how it compares with alternatives	what it does for you

In hygiene terms a buyer is frequently faced with a choice of alternative products and will try to identify the one with the least area of doubt attached to it. The more doubts that can be removed from the product when a consumer considers purchasing, the closer he will be to the neutral line between not buying and buying. Once over the neutral line the remaining factors will be motivators to a buying decision.

10. Consumer expectation. Expectation is the biggest motivational factor in selling. Consumers are more likely to experience disappointment, however, in their purchases when they have a high expectation. The big purchases which are given a greater degree of pre-purchase evaluation will, conversely, produce the greater post-purchase disappointment. Faced with a range of cars, washing machines, etc., each claiming special features, and each having areas of doubt about them, how can we be entirely confident of our eventual selection? In psychological terms, the consumer will experience *cognitive dissonance*.

People's experience of their environment can only be obtained through their senses by the perception processes. The ability to make sense of the information perceived is cognition. If the information received about a product is contrary to the consumer's beliefs, he or she will have either to change his beliefs or reject the information. If the incoming information is strongly contrary to the existing belief, the recipient is therefore likely to reject it as being biased or simply wrong, because acceptance would require a change in attitude which would be difficult to accept.

It is therefore difficult to change beliefs that are strongly held or felt to be important. Marketing management will try to avoid attempting to change attitudes in those segments where the probability of change is low since there will be a waste of resources. They will instead allocate resources to segments where the probability of change is high. The question is then, "Under which circumstances is attitude change most likely to occur?"

11. Strength of attitudes. Broadly speaking, the probability of change varies inversely with the strength of the attitude. The stronger the consumer's predisposition, the less likelihood is there of changing that attitude by persuasive communications. There are four reasons for attitude strength.

(*a*) If the existing state of knowledge is limited, attitudes will be more susceptible to change and there will be less commitment to a belief.

(*b*) Attitudes that are closely related to the person's self-concept, e.g. morals, are more resistant to change and are strong motivation values.

(*c*) Attitudes that are intimately connected with other attitudes are difficult to change, e.g. political or social attitudes.

(*d*) Personality will affect resistance to change to a strong degree. People with strong beliefs are less likely to change attitudes in response to new information than those who have no strong beliefs.

In the 1950s the American Sheep Producers' Council was concerned at the rapid decline in the consumption of lamb. It discovered, through research, that this was the result of housewives' attitude to lamb, which they still associated with wartime mutton. By a process of communication they sought to dispense information to counter these attitudes. They undertook an extensive programme involving media advertising backed by lectures to housewives, cooking demonstrations, radio recipes and informative advertising in women's journals.

12. Advertising and commitment. The strength of commitment is the most important element in a particular attitude and has therefore a strong connection with resistance to change. This factor is important in understanding attitudes to advertising and communications as a whole.

Consumers who are strongly committed to a preference in

products become dissonant when they feel that preference is being challenged. This has important effects in the introduction of new, or replacement products. Consumers who have developed a loyalty to a long established brand are likely to become dissonant and tend to avoid or denigrate the new information. Thus a large advertising effort is needed at the outset of a new product launch, and manufacturers will often retain successful brand names even when the product changes, e.g. Daz and New Daz, Cortina I, II, III and IV.

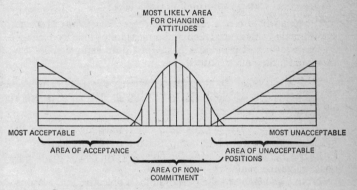

FIG. 65. *Possibilities for changing attitudes.*

Fig. 65 shows how attitudes may range along a spectrum, from a position that is most acceptable to a position that is most unacceptable. Between them is an area of non-commitment in which the possibility for changing attitudes is strongest.

PLANNED COMMUNICATIONS

13. Planning the communications campaign. The marketing operation must always be controlled in a way that allows flexibility owing to the fact that so many of the aspects involved are beyond the company's control.

Marketing management needs an analytical approach to problem solving that will obviate inspired guesses as a basis for action. Since all objectives are easier to understand and problems resolved more readily when set down, it is necessary to establish a plan for a communications campaign as much as it is for a selling operation.

14. The communications plan. Any campaign must be planned in order to avoid misunderstanding among the personnel involved in its operations. It will also serve to co-ordinate the various activities that will be concerned in its successful implementation: advertising, sales promotion, public relations, sales management, finance, production and distribution. The communications plan must ensure that all are working towards the same goals. The essential requirements of the plan are that:

(*a*) it can be understood quickly and simply; and

(*b*) all the necessary information is available.

The plan will also be a record in retrospect of the way in which the campaign was undertaken and a measure of its effectiveness. In this way it will provide a basis for future campaigns and a measure for their effectiveness.

15. Communications plan structure. All the separate plans involved in the over-all campaign will have a similar basic structure of objective, method, and explanation.

(*a*) *The objective* will have been determined by the over-all marketing strategy of which communications will be a part.

(*b*) *The method* of achieving the objective will be set down in a concise, factual manner.

(*c*) *An explanation* of the purpose of the objective and reasons for the proposed methods of achieving it will be given.

16. Communications copy proposal. The purpose of the communications copy proposal is to ensure that the advertising agents or department create ideas that will correspond closely with the over-all communications plan. A company proposing to launch a product aimed at exclusive shops would not want advertising of a ribald, humorous type. Industrial products have to be advertised or otherwise subject to communication in ways that will appeal to the needs of industrial users. The advertising department must ensure that staff responsible for creating ideas are familiar with the essential points of the product, its purpose, any special points of merit, special achievements, etc. In this way time will not be wasted on producing copy out of step with the over-all plan. It will detail the proposals in the same three ways.

(*a*) *Objective.* This will outline the creative objectives in terms of the method of appeal, underlying psychological reasoning, types of customer, and the way the product fits in with the company's policy.

(b) *Methods*. How it is proposed to communicate the creative ideas to the market.

(c) *Explanation*. The underlying company policy, essential product knowledge and points of superiority.

17. Media proposals. The media to be selected for communication of the marketing plan will be the responsibility of a special planning section. They, like the creative section, will have to operate within the parameters of the company policy and objectives.

(a) *Objective*. Details of the customers, who they are, industrial or consumers, home or abroad, high or low income; how they may be reached and the frequency needed.

(b) *Method*. The proposals will include details of how the plan will be achieved within limits of the budget; the media selected and costs.

(c) *Explanation*. Details of why the plan has been so designed.

18. Selected strategies. Communications can include advertising, sales promotion, public relations or the use of the sales force. Each method will require a similar set of statements to ensure co-ordinated effort.

19. Ancillary information. The plan will require the collection of a wide variety of information on the market, product, consumers, distribution, media, and market and economic research. This will be compiled in the form of a report that will be circulated to all the departments or sections responsible for the accomplishment of the plan. Again these data will enable continuity to be established with future plans and will be added to or modified as the market evolves.

20. The total communications concept. The communication of information is central to any marketing campaign, whether it is conducted on an international, national, or purely local basis. It creates the need for information by the requirements of understanding the product's market position. It then disseminates information in answer to consumer information needs and to create a favourable attitude in the market towards the company and its products.

EXAMPLE: A company was endeavouring to expand its sales operation in South Wales. It marketed a range of cosmetics but found difficulty in recruiting suitable personnel for direct selling and also in creating customers. The results of a marketing consultant's enquiry revealed there was (1) lack of definite market information, (2) lack of positive identity in the market by consumers, (3) a general consumer suspicion of direct selling methods, (4) not enough emphasis on the local nature of the company, (5) reluctance on the part of potential sales personnel to sell a little known product, and (6) lack of information on market opportunities.

From the foregoing it was evident that what was required was not so much simply advertising, which had been tried without success, but an over-all communications campaign, involving public relations, sales promotion, training and advertising. By a combination of all these elements of communication in response to marketing research a successful campaign was carried out which answered all of the original problems, and established the company's sales operation on a sound footing.

PROGRESS TEST 19

1. What activities would you include in marketing communications? (1)
2. How will the marketing-mix depend upon company strategy? (2)
3. What are the changing needs for communication? (3)
4. Explain the relationship between hygiene factors and motivation in a buying situation. (9, 10)
5. What is the basic structure of a communications plan? (14)
6. What is the total communications concept? (20)

Appendixes

Examination Technique

1. Marketing examinations. Marketing is not a subject to which a candidate can apply precise, quantitative answers. It is largely derived from two studies, economics and the behavioural sciences, neither of which is very precise, since essentially they concern human behaviour. The candidate should appreciate therefore the necessity of thinking of marketing questions in applied terms. Most people have marketing experience even if it only derives from being the customer. Those candidates already possessing business experience should apply the questions to their own experience as it will help in formulating answers.

2. Need for knowledge. The nature of marketing problems presents difficulties both to candidates and the examiners who have to assess the candidate's knowledge from a fairly concise answer. It is advisable, if the candidate is to impress the examiner with his depth of knowledge, for him to obtain the widest range of information. This can be obtained from reading as widely as possible, but for the best results this should be undertaken critically, examining each work in the light of the total subject and relating it to practical experience. Read as many books as possible as they will all invariably put emphasis upon different aspects. It is also very helpful to read current literature; *Financial Times*; *Sunday Times*; *Business News*; *The Economist*; also trade journals, government publications and technical publications.

3. Preparing for the examination. Some candidates work themselves into a state of near-exhaustion in preparation, leaving little energy and imagination for the examination. Candidates should learn to relax and gain confidence from experience. It is not necessary to obtain 100 per cent marks; the actual pass mark will vary but is generally around 50 per cent. It is useful if candidates can develop an examination technique of their own. Wherever possible the candidates should prepare by answering questions under the conditions they will face at the actual examination. It is generally possible to obtain past examination papers, and these can be a guide to the form of question.

4. The examination. Examinations will last a precise time. Candidates should get themselves as ready as possible before the start, pencils sharpened, pens filled, watch wound and placed where it can be seen easily. Some examinations allow the candidate a set time to read the questions before work commences, but in any case the candidate should read all the questions carefully and make a preliminary selection; he should include an appreciation of the amount of time the question will take to be answered, and how much time can be allocated. It is a useful aid to develop an ability to present information in graphs, annotated diagrams, flow diagrams and other forms of visual communication. Often a diagram can present a great deal of information in easily explained form and allow time for those aspects needing script.

5. Standard required. Examinations vary considerably in the degree of knowledge needed to pass them. Candidates should try to discover the standard required and aim at that; certainly no lower.

6. Problem questions. It has already been pointed out that marketing generally has imprecise answers. Nevertheless, some questions will have answers which will be fairly predictable. Try to avoid questions with discussive, disputatious answers, as valuable time can be spent in presenting a rationalised case.

7. Presentation. Assessors will have a large number of papers to mark and will not be prepared to spend their time in deciphering bad writing and awkward presentation. Good writing can take time but bad writing costs valuable marks. Between the two will be an optimum standard of legibility. Good presentation will frequently aid reading and a clearly set out examination paper will encourage the assessor to devote more time and look more favourably upon the candidate's efforts.

Examination Questions

1. To what extent is it necessary for a marketing-oriented company to have marketing executives in line-management positions? (Institute of Marketing)

2. How do marketing managers in capital goods industries determine priorities as between the requirements of the market and technical research and development? Do present practices meet all needs? If not, where would you suggest improvement is needed? (Institute of Marketing)

3. What criteria should the marketing manager apply in evaluating alternative channels of distribution? (Institute of Marketing)

4. Describe how you would set up performance standards for the purpose of evaluating the effectiveness of the individuals engaged in a sales force and draw up a simple specimen of an appraisal form. (Institute of Marketing)

5. Enumerate the chief responsibilities of management towards the individual salesman and discuss, in detail, how these should be discharged. (Institute of Marketing)

6. What would you say are the tools of the marketing man's trade? (Institute of Marketing)

7. Are there any essential differences between a company's corporate plan and its marketing plan? (Institute of Marketing)

8. What are the important stages in training sales people? What actions are required by management at each stage? (Institute of Marketing)

9. Evaluate the role of marketing management in sales forecasting, as opposed to the role of the professional forecaster. (Institute of Marketing)

10. Distinguish among an external salesman, a merchandiser, and a technical representative, in terms of the employee's duties, personal characteristics, training and general management. (Institute of Marketing)

11. What are the responsibilities of a salesman towards his customers and his employers? Analyse especially the areas where

these responsibilities are likely to be in conflict. (Institute of Marketing)

12. You are requested to recommend to a company how much advertising money it should spend next year. List the main factors you will have to consider in determining the figure to recommend, and give reasons for including them. (Communications Advertising and Marketing Research Foundation)

13. Describe the ideal conditions for the use of a salesman's incentive scheme. Give examples of both long- and short-term schemes and consider the relative merits of individual and group incentives. State your views on the merits and dangers of incentives at all levels in the sales force. (Communications Advertising and Marketing Research Foundation)

14. What is the importance of job analysis in the management of the firm? Draw up a job specification for the particular post you occupy. (Communications Advertising and Marketing Research Foundation)

15. It is sometimes said that the sales force "pushes" and media advertising "pulls" sales. What does this mean? (Communications Advertising and Marketing Research Foundation)

16. You are the export manager of a company manufacturing earth-moving equipment. How would you apply forecasting techniques to the problem of predicting sales in West Africa? Describe the different time periods of the forecasts. (H.N.C. (Marketing), Cornwall Technical College)

17. A product life cycle describes the manner in which a particular product may be introduced, mature and finally decline. How would you relate the various communication aids and market research to the changing needs of the product? Illustrate the answer by means of a product with which you are familiar. (H.N.C. (Marketing), Cornwall Technical College)

18. Sales management of consumer goods will find shop distribution its most important consideration in arranging distribution of its products. Distribution will include "actual" distribution and "sterling" distribution. Distinguish between the two and give examples. (H.N.C. (Marketing), Cornwall Technical College)

19. Must any large firm inevitably have problems of effective communication? (G.C.E. "A" level Business Studies, Cambridge Examining Board)

20. Can management be conducted scientifically? (G.C.E. "A" level Business Studies, Cambridge Examining Board)

21. As the marketing manager of a manufacturing company

producing machine tools, you have been requested by the managing director to determine the potential sales of a new machine tool. What procedures would you follow and what sources of information woud you use to arrive at a decision? (Institute of Work Study Practitioners)

22. In company "A" the managing director has fifteen people reporting to him. In company "B" five people report to him. Both companies are engaged on similiar activities. State, with reasons, which organisation is likely to be the more effective. (Institute of Work Study Practitioners)

23. What is the purpose of market research and what different categories of information are obtained? (Institute of Work Study Practitioners)

24. What is meant by the term "span of control" and what are the factors involved in determining its span? (Institute of Work Study Practitioners)

25. What are the main pricing policies used in retailing? (Certificate in Supervisory Studies (Distribution), Falmouth Technical College)

26. What do you understand by the buying–selling cycle? (Certificate in Supervisory Studies (Distribution), Falmouth Technical College)

27. There is a general pattern which should be followed when conducting all types of interviews with staff. Describe the stages necessary to achieve a successful result. (Certificate in Supervisory Studies (Distribution), Falmouth Technical College)

28. What factors must be considered when determining customer motives and buying behaviour? (Certificate in Supervisory Studies (Distribution), Falmouth Technical College)

Bibliography

Aaker, A. A. & Myers, J. G., *Advertisement management*, Prentice-Hall, 1975.

Allen, P., *Marketing techniques for analysis and control*, Macdonald & Evans, 1977.

Boyd & Levy, *Promotion: a behavioural view*, Prentice-Hall, 1967.

Brech, E. F. L., *The principles and practices of management*, Longmans, 1975.

Brown, J. A. C., *The social psychology of industry*, Pelican, 1970.

Buskirk, R. H., *Principles of marketing*, Holt, Rinehart & Winston, 1975.

Dale, E., *Management: theory and practice*, McGraw-Hill, 1975.

Deverell, C. S., *Business administration and management*, Gee & Co. Ltd., 1974.

Drucker, P., *Managing for results*, Pan Books, 1967.

Drucker, P., *The practice of management*, Pan Books, 1968.

Engel, J. F., etc., *Consumer behaviour*, Holt, Rinehart & Winston, 1972.

McGregor, D., *Leadership and motivation*, M.I.T. Press, 1968.

McGregor, D., *The human side of enterprise*, McGraw-Hill, 1960.

Morgan, C. T. & King, R. A., *Introduction to psychology*, McGraw Hill, 1975.

Packard, V., *The hidden persuaders*, Penguin, 1970.

Roger, L. W., *Marketing in a competitive economy*, Associated Business Programmes, 1974.

Smallbone, D. W., *The practice of management*, Staples Press, 1967.

Staudt, T., *A managerial introduction to marketing*, Prentice-Hall, 1976.

Woodward, J., *Industrial organisation: theory and practice*, Oxford University Press, 1965.

Index

Index

Details of some other Macdonald & Evans
publications on related subjects can be found
on the following pages.

For a full list of titles and prices write for the
FREE Macdonald & Evans Business Studies
catalogue and/or complete M & E Handbook
list, available from Department BP1,
Macdonald & Evans Ltd., Estover Road,
Plymouth PL6 7PZ

Advertising
DAVID SHELLEY NICHOLL

Written to portray accurately the nature and scope of the advertising industry, this book covers topics such as: the need for, and organisation of, the industry; the anatomy of an agency; planning a campaign; the adman's arsenal; and a future in advertising. The latest edition, which will be suitable for BEC courses, makes particular reference to commercial radio, and takes account of changes in media, customs, conditions and statistics. "The most useful advertising textbook to be published in a long time." *Broadcast*
Illustrated

International Marketing
L. S. WALSH

This HANDBOOK is concerned with those aspects of marketing that are applicable only to the international field and those that require a special emphasis and a deeper knowledge than are necessary in the purely domestic environment. It is aimed at students of marketing and business studies in universities, polytechnics and colleges of technology, as well as students of professional bodies.

Marketing
G. B. GILES

A HANDBOOK which will prove invaluable to students and businessmen alike, whether they are seeking a basic grounding in marketing or are specialists in other fields who wish to see their

Details of some other Macdonald & Evans
publications on related subjects can be found
on the following pages.

For a full list of titles and prices write for the
FREE Macdonald & Evans Business Studies
catalogue and/or complete M & E Handbook
list, available from Department BP1,
Macdonald & Evans Ltd., Estover Road,
Plymouth PL6 7PZ

Advertising
DAVID SHELLEY NICHOLL
Written to portray accurately the nature and scope of the advertising industry, this book covers topics such as: the need for, and organisation of, the industry; the anatomy of an agency; planning a campaign; the adman's arsenal; and a future in advertising. The latest edition, which will be suitable for BEC courses, makes particular reference to commercial radio, and takes account of changes in media, customs, conditions and statistics. "The most useful advertising textbook to be published in a long time." *Broadcast*
Illustrated

International Marketing
L. S. WALSH
This HANDBOOK is concerned with those aspects of marketing that are applicable only to the international field and those that require a special emphasis and a deeper knowledge than are necessary in the purely domestic environment. It is aimed at students of marketing and business studies in universities, polytechnics and colleges of technology, as well as students of professional bodies.

Marketing
G. B. GILES
A HANDBOOK which will prove invaluable to students and businessmen alike, whether they are seeking a basic grounding in marketing or are specialists in other fields who wish to see their

own functions in a wider context. In the latest edition, the text has been revised to include references to legislation on consumer protection and to major current issues in the field of economics such as inflation and the energy crisis and their impact on marketing decisions. This book is suitable for relevant higher level BEC courses.

Marketing Research
TONY PROCTOR & MARILYN A. STONE

Industry's growing appreciation of the value of marketing research has created a demand for courses to provide students with a fundamental knowledge of what marketing research is, and its practical applications to business. This HAND-BOOK presents the subject in a simple and concise manner, using examples from the authors' own considerable industrial experience. It is aimed primarily at university students, but will also be most useful to D.M.S., Higher National Diploma (Business Studies), Institute of Marketing Diploma and M.R.S. Diploma students.
Illustrated

Marketing Techniques for Analysis and Control
P. ALLEN

This book relates new techniques of analysis and control to the marketing function and provides much of the knowledge required by students taking final examinations in the Higher National Diploma in Business Studies and the Diploma in

Management Studies as well as those studying for a wide range of other related management and business courses. "A book . . . to be read and used as a stimulus for creative thinking on selling and marketing." *Selling Today*
Illustrated

The Practice of Exporting
P. ALLEN

This HANDBOOK provides a lucid guide to the structure, purpose and personnel of the export market and makes a basic understanding of its complexities easy to obtain. Forecasting, promotion, and documentation of transactions are among the topics covered in detail, and anyone studying for the appropriate diplomas of the Institutes of Export and Marketing will find this an invaluable working text.
Illustrated

Retailing
ROGER COX

This HANDBOOK attempts to show in a simple and straightforward way many of the problems associated with retailing and how they may be solved. It deals in turn with the organisation of the industry, the theory and practice of retail location, merchandising, and the administrative aspects of running retail firms. "The text can be recommended to distribution students working for H.N.D., R.M.S. and C.R.S. examinations and to those who will take the new BEC level 3 tests." *Retail and Distribution Management*
Illustrated